LEGENDARY LOCALS

OF

WESTFORD

MASSACHUSETTS

THOMAS G. PAQUETTE

LEGENDARY LOCALS

ISBN 978-1-4671-0032-8

Legendary Locals is an imprint of Arcadia Publishing
Charleston, South Carolina

Printed in the United States of America

Library of Congress Control Number: 2012936282

For all general information, please contact Arcadia Publishing:
Telephone 843-853-2070
Fax 843-853-0044
E-mail sales@arcadiapublishing.com
For customer service and orders:
Toll-Free 1-888-313-2665

Visit us on the Internet at www.arcadiapublishing.com

Dedication

This book is dedicated to those individuals who give tirelessly of themselves for the good of the community of Westford, Massachusetts, and specifically to the Westford Historical Society and Museum, which has worked to preserve Westford's long and rich history.

On the Cover: From left to right:
(TOP ROW) Ada Day (Courtesy of Westford Museum, page 108); John Davis Long, Massachusetts governor and secretary of the Navy (Courtesy of Library of Congress, page 64); Cinder, fire dog (Courtesy of Westford Fire Department, page 74); James Payne, machine operator (Courtesy of Westford Museum, page 19); Catherine Abbot, teacher (Courtesy of Westford Museum, page 26).
(MIDDLE ROW) Sherman D. Fletcher, town treasurer (Courtesy of Westford Museum, page 24); Ellen Harde, author, mover and shaker (Courtesy of author, page 69); William Edwin Frost (Courtesy of Westford Museum, page 24); Mary Elizabeth Perrins, Apple Blossom queen (Courtesy of Westford Museum, page 22); John W.P. Abbot, entrepreneur and public servant (Courtesy of Westford Museum, page 78).
(BOTTOM ROW) Alice Hildreth, town clerk (Courtesy of Westford Museum, page 62); Andrew Kusmin, artist and preservationist (Courtesy of Kusmin Arts, page 56); Hildreths (Courtesy of Westford Museum, page 107); Robert Oliphant, author, genealogist, and historian (Courtesy of Robert Oliphant, page 54); Sarah Allen Sharp, visitor (Courtesy of Westford Museum, page 112).

CONTENTS

ACKNOWLEDGMENTS

I would like to give special thanks to the Westford Museum and Historical Society for its dedication to preserving the history of Westford and specifically for its support and assistance with the research on this project. Special thanks to Dr. Robert Oliphant for his contribution to the introduction. I would also like to thank all of the individuals, organizations, and businesses who gave of their time to ensure the success and accuracy of this book: Ellen Harde, Andrew Kusmin, Penny Lacroix, Robert Oliphant, Pam Fletcher, Nashoba Valley Ski Area, Kyle Allen, Nancy Russo, Beth Shaw, George Fletcher, Alan Fletcher, Peter Whitcomb, Mederick "Midge" Zaher, David McPhee, Alan Fletcher Jr., Kimball Farm, Geoffrey Hall, Alfred Garside, Virginia Burnham, Paul and Leah Lemieux, Paul J. Royte, Newell Tillman, Jonathan Damon, Brian Herzog, Erin Vosgien, David Brody, Michael Ashe, Bill and Beth Sweeney, Isabel Sweeney, Maryellen Sweeney, Andrew and Beverly Garside, Carl and Lillian Garside, Paul Garside, J.T. Smith, Alfred Garside, and Marilyn Day.

Unless otherwise noted, all images appear courtesy of the Westford Historical Society and Museum; specifically, the Charles L. Hildreth Collection, the Abbot Worsted/Frank Penney Collection, the Quincy Day Collection, and the 1896 Commemorative Pamphlet for the Dedication of the J.V. Fletcher Library.

INTRODUCTION

I was born and raised in and around Westford. Joining the US Army at the age of 20, I spent the next 20 years living all over the country, from Alabama to Alaska, only to return all these years later to where I started. Upon my return, I set out to find a project that would "re-introduce" me to the community I had lost touch with. I was honored to be chosen to author *Legendary Locals of Westford* and thought it would be a nice way to get back in touch with my roots. I could not have imagined the journey it would take me on, or the admiration I would come to find for the diverse collection of individuals that I have encountered along the way.

Growing up, I always felt that Westford was a unique community—warm and welcoming with a small-town feel but with easy access to the conveniences of the world around it. I considered the people of Westford unique as well, with their profound dedication to the community in which they live. Having moved away and lived in dozens of similarly sized towns across the country, I returned with a broader perspective on my home. I came to the conclusion that Westford is in fact unique, and that the people who call it home have a commitment to their town that I have seen nowhere else.

Although I always thought it to be so, and having solidified that belief in my travels to other places, I could never have imagined just how committed the residents of Westford are to their community. Every single person who I have had the pleasure of sitting down with gives back to their town in some way. From the people who give their Saturdays to pick up trash along the roads to those who teach at the community center, coach Little League, or dedicate countless hours to the preservation of Westford's proud history, everyone I met gives back in some way.

In conducting my research, I came to realize that this dedication to community and service is not unique to today's residents of Westford, but it has been the hallmark of citizens all the way back to the town's founding in 1729.

The area that we now know as Westford has an extremely rich history, which began long before the town's founding. With the region's wealth of waterways, including the Merrimack and Nashua Rivers, it is likely that Native Americans—more specifically the Pawtucket and Nashoba tribes—called this area home.

Westford, originally part of West Chelmsford, saw its first settlers in the 1650s to 1660s and grew very slowly until the early part of the 1700s. Early settlers relied on subsistence agriculture and grazing of cattle, but as the population grew, so did the demand for manufacturing and the industries that support it. The first sawmill was constructed in 1669, orchards began to sprout up in the 1700s, and tanning, brick-making, and other support industries followed suit.

Like many New England communities, Westford was rich in granite. The town saw its first granite quarry open in 1826–1827, and since then, has consistently provided granite and granite products to communities throughout New England and the rest of the country.

With the arrival of the railroad in 1848, connecting Westford to Chelmsford, Lowell, Groton, Ayer, Nashua, Acton, and Boston, and the consequential ability to transport goods in and out of town, Westford saw a dramatic increase in industrial development. With this new mode of transporting goods to surrounding New England communities, the granite quarries stepped up production, and new and exciting businesses began to emerge.

Manufacturing, and the industries required to support it, began to take hold in 1853, when Jonas Prescott and John W.P. Abbot began the Westford Forge Company. Soon after, in 1854, Charles G. Sargent and Francis A. Calvert started shops that manufactured machinery for cotton and woolen mills. Such machinery was in high demand as textile mills began cropping up all over New England around that time. C.G. Sargent & Sons is pictured on page 116. In 1855, Sargent joined with John W. and John W.P. Abbot to form the Abbot Company. The company, which produced worsted yarns, expanded several times and by the late 1870s had established worsted yarn production as the prominent industry in Westford.

From the founding of the town to the present day, the residents of Westford have done their part in service to our country. From the Revolutionary War to the recent conflicts around the world, the people of Westford have always stepped up to do their part in defense of our nation and its freedoms and principals. Westford saw 300 of its residents serve in the Civil War; 36 never returned home. Westford citizens served with honor in both World Wars, Korea, and Vietnam, and many are serving overseas today.

Westford's population has grown steadily since the 1870s. The growth of local industry, specifically the quarries and mills, saw immigrants from Canada and Europe flocking to the area to start new lives. To support the residents, schools, libraries, and other services were introduced to the town. Westford Academy was incorporated in 1792, with the first school being built two years later. It served as the schoolhouse until 1897, when a new building was opened. The original school building now serves as the Westford Museum. These first two buildings have been replaced by new, additional buildings, the latest having been built in 1973. The residents of Westford have had the foresight to preserve the history of the town, evident in the fact that all four buildings that have served as the Westford Academy are still functioning today. The Westford Social Library was started in 1797, and in 1896, with a generous donation from J. Varnum Fletcher, a new library building was constructed. It is still in use today. Nashoba Valley Technical High School opened in 1969, and many other elementary and middle schools have opened through the years to support the growing population.

Although the arrival of the automobile and the improvement of local roads in Westford saw a reduction in the use of the railroad, freight still travels daily over the historic Stony Brook Railroad, and the line came to serve as a major corridor for Pan Am Railways. Westford has continued to evolve; with the decline of the mill industry after World War I, other industries have sprouted up, continuing Westford's standing as a very desirable place to live. With a population in 2010 of 21,951, and a commonsense approach to balancing modern development with preservation of historic resources, there is no doubt that Westford will continue to be a popular place to live and a source of pride for all who live here.

This book only scratches the surface of the wealth of notable figures who live and have lived in this wonderful community. It is my hope that, if nothing else, it serves as a spark to cause people to dig deeper into the rich and interesting history of Westford, Massachusetts.

CHAPTER ONE

The History

The residents of Westford are very proud of their town. The events that shaped the town into what it is today date back to the 18th century. Through good times and bad, peace and war, depression and economic prosperity, the people of Westford have always done their part to improve the community in which they live. Traveling around town, one can not help but notice the legacy of Westford's predecessors and the indelible marks that they made on the past. Not only do the people of Westford have a rich history, but they also have deep appreciation for that history and an understanding of the importance of maintaining a connection to the people who came before. The early settlers of the area were dedicated to the nation they were struggling to create. They gave of their time, wealth, and lives to ensure that future generations would have a nation to call home and an education with which to build upon that new nation. They did not shy away from war, sending their family members into harm's way to secure their freedom: in the Colonial wars; in the Revolutionary War, in which they paved the way for the Declaration of Independence from Britain; and in the Civil War, where they gave their lives to preserve the Union and help a young United States find its way. Although sufficiently occupied with the business of creating a new nation, the residents of Westford wasted no time in establishing roots in their new home. They created places of worship, beginning with the First Parish Church United, which also served as the meeting place for town government until 1870. They ensured economic security with the establishment of industry, including businesses such as the Abbot Worsted Mill. These businesses recruited workers from Canada and as far away as eastern Europe, adding to the growing population and bringing with them the skills to build a new home and the drive to leave a legacy that future generations would be proud of. Having the foresight to realize the importance that quality education would play in the future of their new community, the residents also established the Westford Academy, one of the oldest public high schools in the nation.

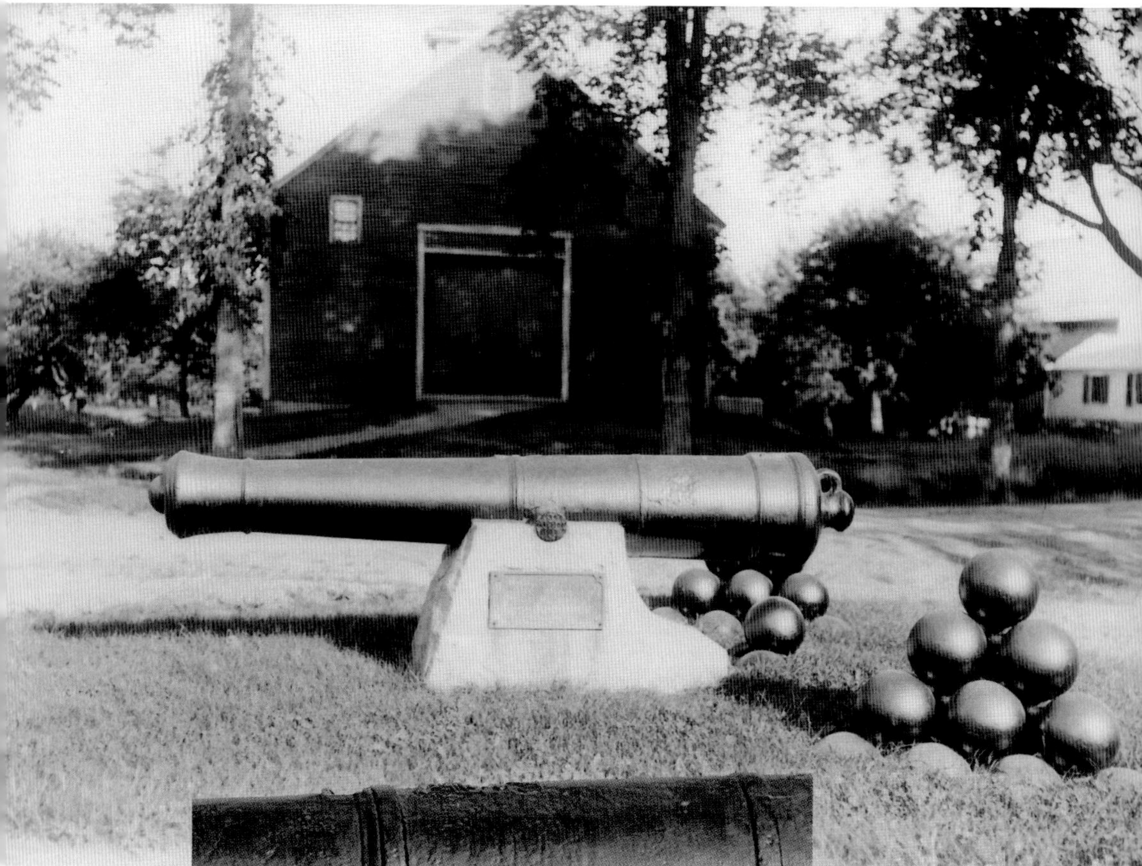

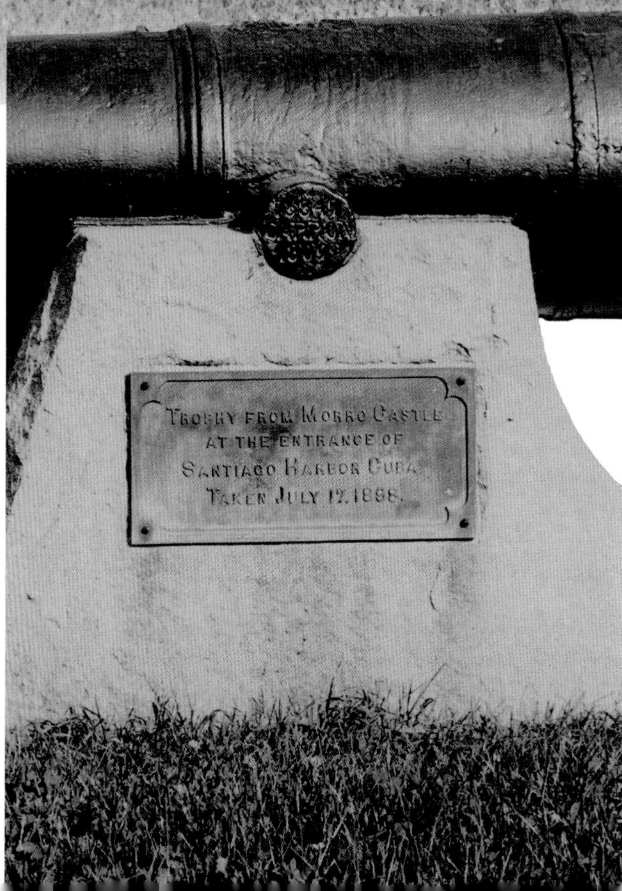

Cannon on the Common

This cannon (images taken on June 3, 1908) stands watch in a prominent position on the Westford Town Common. Plaques affixed to the granite base read, "Trophy from Morro Castle at the entrance of Santiago Harbor Cuba, Taken July 17, 1898." and "Loaned as an Object Lesson to the rising generation of the Valor of American Soldiers Dedicated June 23, 1899."

Grieg's Corner

This photograph from December 31, 1905, is part of the Charles Hildreth photograph collection at the Westford Museum. It provides a glimpse into the conditions of thoroughfares at the time. Note the trolley rails, and the lack of pavement. The telephone poles are not heavily laden with wires, as one would see today. This view is looking east on North Main Street, Graniteville, towards Greig's Corner.

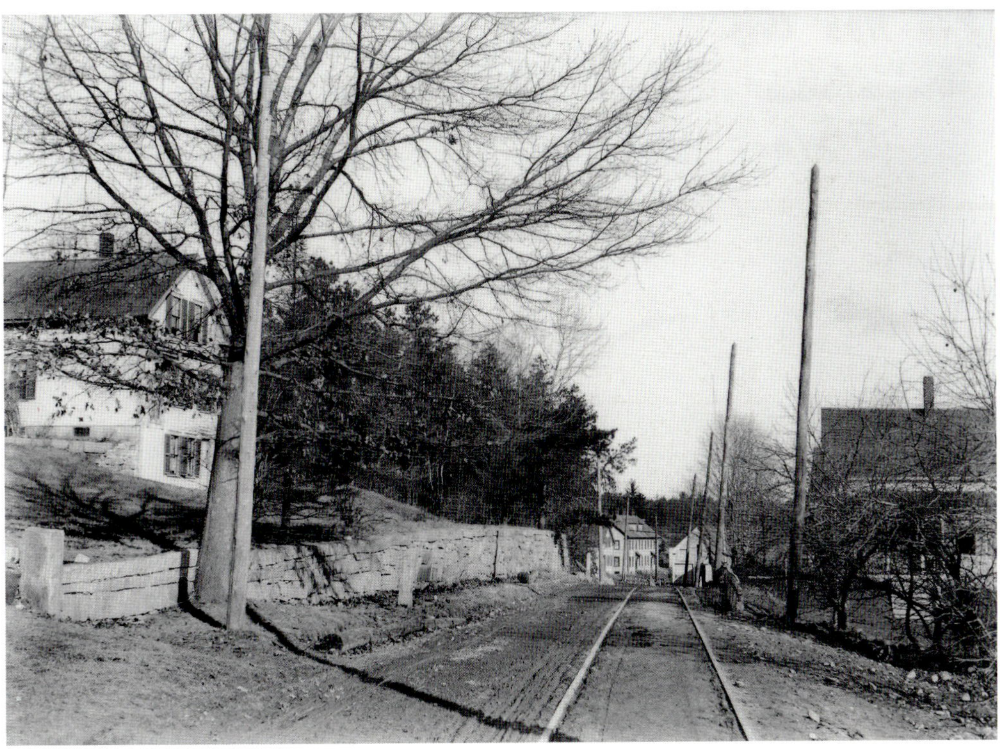

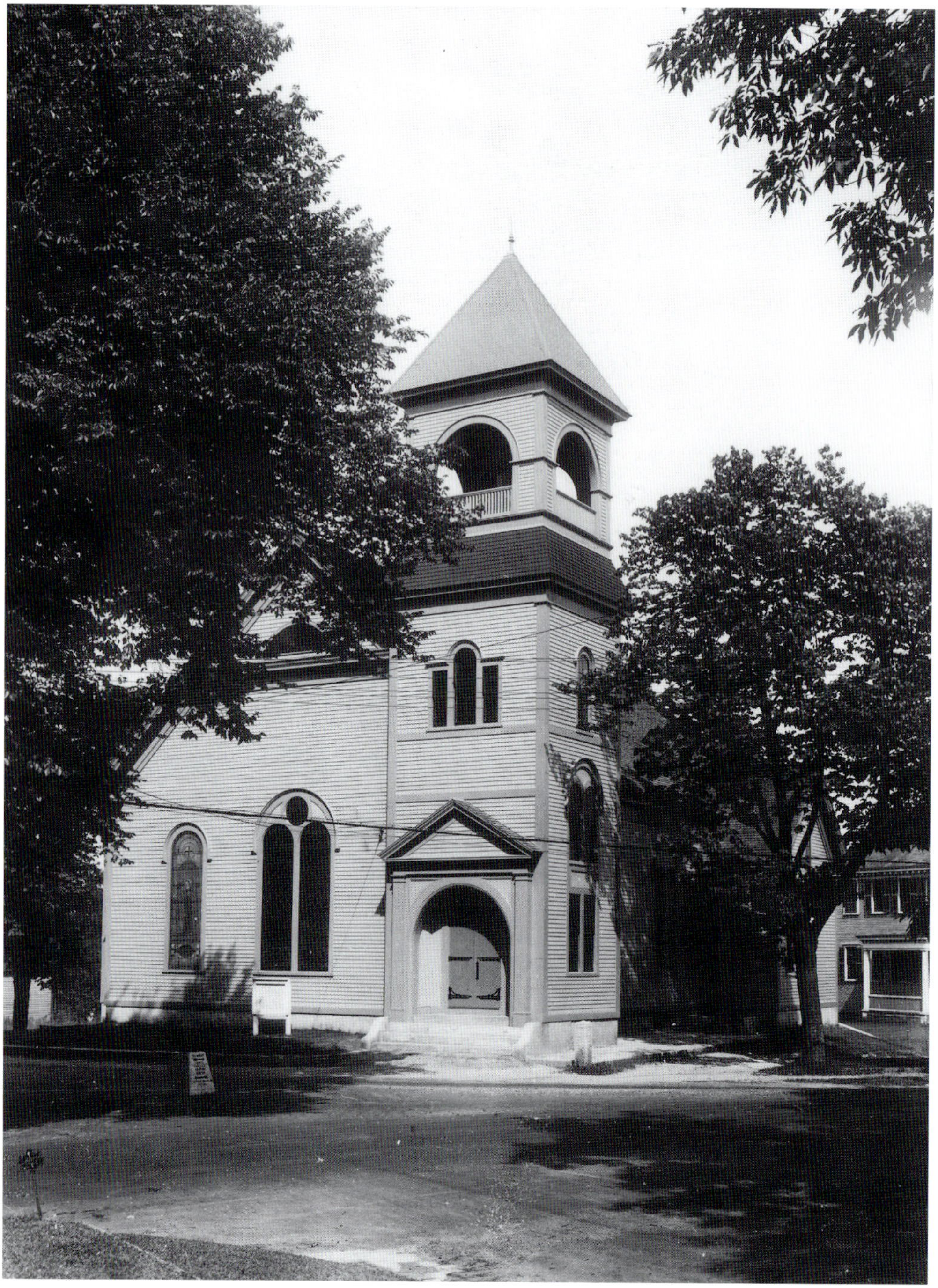

Congregational Church

Built in 1829, the Union Congregational Church is seen here in a 1928 photograph. The image was captured by Charles Hildreth and gives a glimpse into the original use of this building. Today, the building serves as the Parish Center for the Arts (PCA). The PCA was formed in 1999 through the efforts of local residents to preserve and showcase the arts in and around the Westford area.

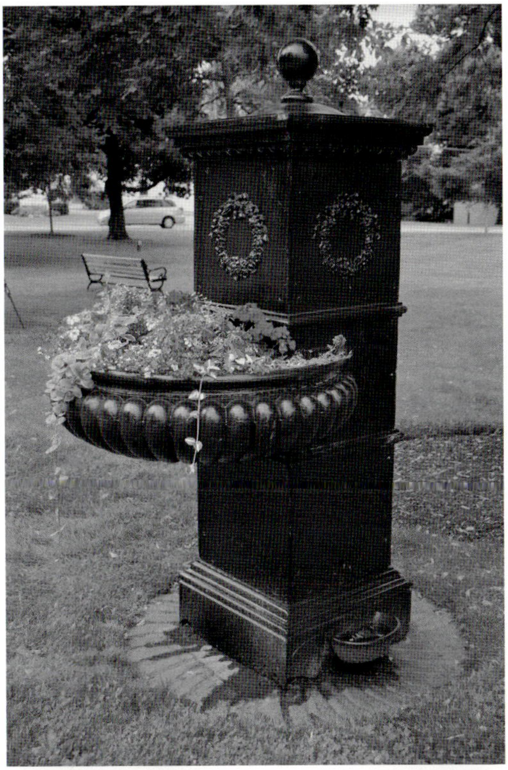

Iron Watering Trough

This ornate watering trough was presented to the town by the Westford Grange in 1913. The upper trough, now bearing flowers, was at the proper height for horses, while the lower troughs at the base provided water for other animals. The trough was moved north a few feet to its current location after widening of Boston Road left it sitting in a precarious spot. (Author's collection.)

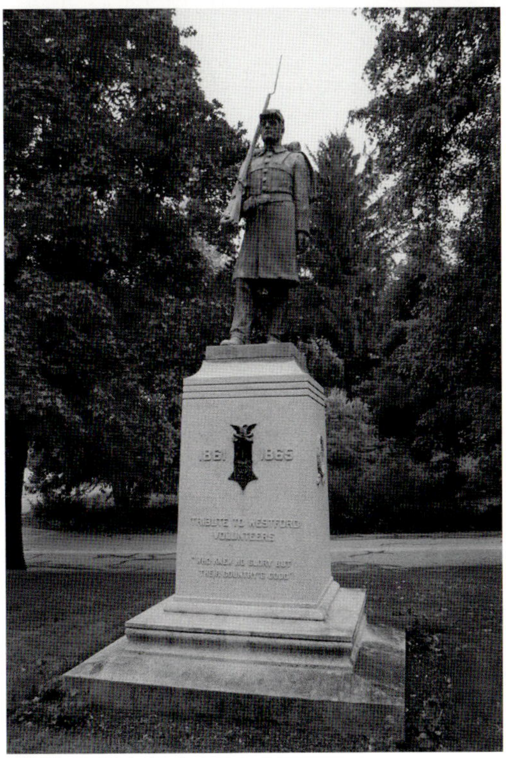

Civil War Monument

Dedicated in 1910 and located adjacent to the town common, Westford's Civil War Monument was erected to honor the soldiers from Westford who served in that conflict. The monument was a gift from Col. Edwin D. Metcalf of Auburn, New York, son of William Metcalf, who served as the only commissioned officer from Westford in the Civil War. The monument was dedicated on Memorial Day in 1910, during a gala ceremony with an address by former governor John Davis Long. (Author's collection.)

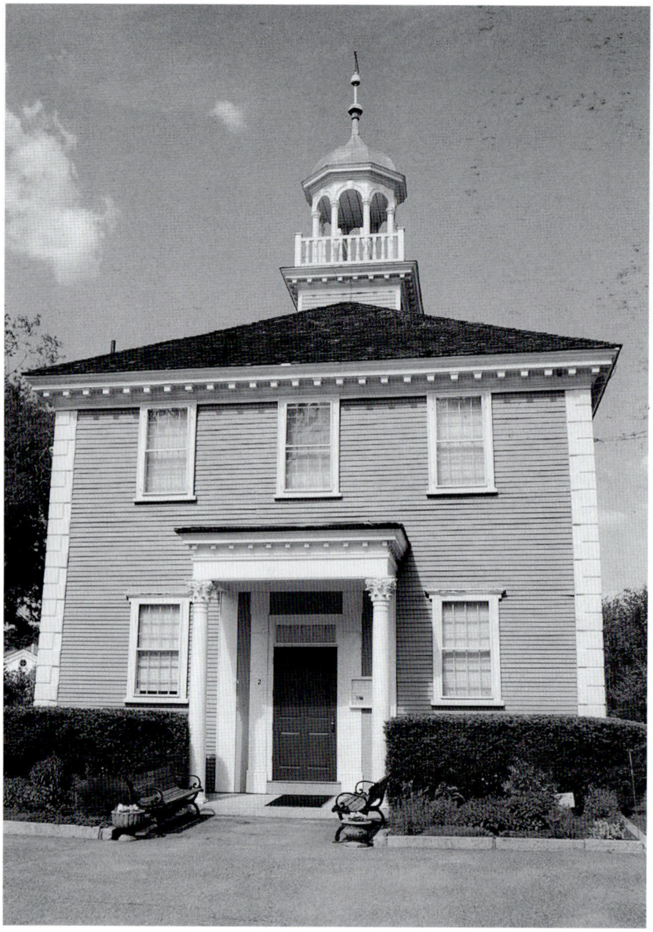

Westford Academy

Incorporated in 1792, Westford Academy has a long and proud history. The academy was formed "for the purpose of instructing the youth of both sexes in useful science and literature and in the principals of morality" and was initially incorporated as a private school. Prior to the construction of the original schoolhouse, classes were taught in the town meetinghouse. The original schoolhouse was built in 1794. The bell in the schoolhouse was cast by Paul Revere, and his son John attended classes at Westford Academy starting in 1799. A recasting of the original bell is displayed inside the Bell Lobby of the current Westford Academy building on Patten Road. The original building served the purposes of the town for 103 years, and in 1897, the town opened the second Westford Academy building, designed by H.M. Frances. The second school building was used for its original purpose until 1955. It now serves as the Roudenbush Community Center. In 1955, the third Westford Academy building opened its doors, on Depot Street, and served the town for just 18 years before the swelling school attendance required yet another structure to be built. In 1973, the current academy building on Patten Road was constructed. Westford Academy had an inaugural class of 32 students. In 1895, the town began to pay students' tuition to ensure that all residents could attend, due to a state law requiring towns with a population of more than 500 to provide public education. In 1928, the town bought it from the trustees, officially making it a public school, but it retained the name "Westford Academy" and allowed graduates continuing eligibility for scholarships offered by the Westford Academy trustees. In 2004, more than 1,400 students attended Westford Academy, with 85 percent moving on to four-year colleges or universities. The graduating class in 2012 was nearly 400 students. (Author's collection.)

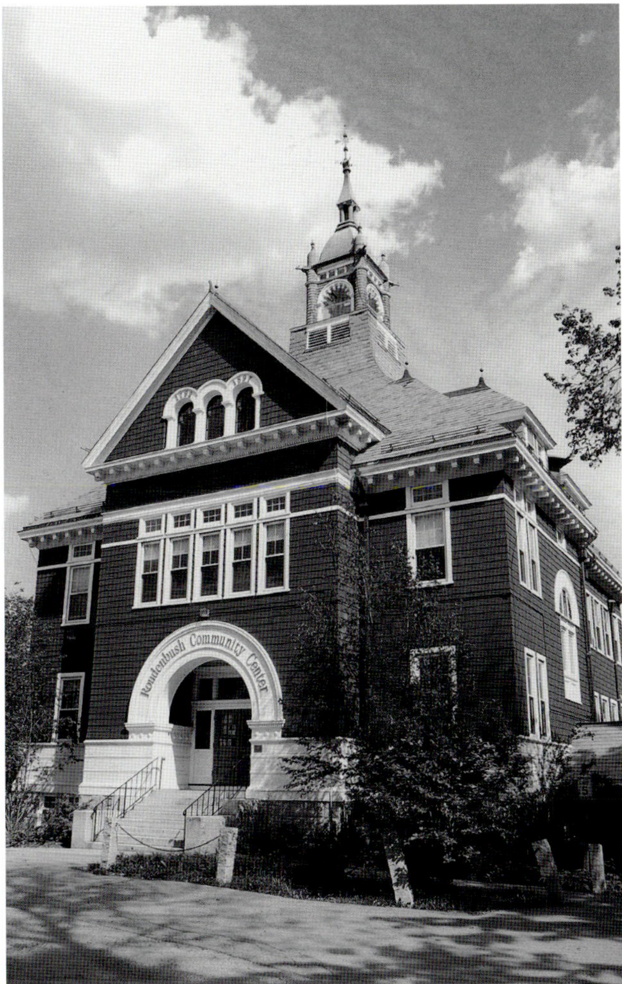

Second Westford Academy

Built in 1897, this structure served as the second Westford Academy. Upon the construction of a new building in 1955, this school building was repurposed by the school department for various uses. It currently serves as the home of the Roudenbush Community Center. (Author's collection.)

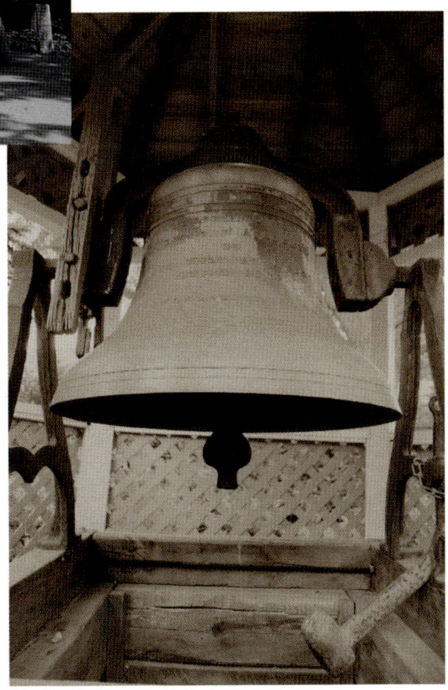

Second Westford Academy Bell

This bell, donated by John William Abbot on August 2, 1897, hung in the bell tower of the Second Westford Academy building (now the Roudenbush Community Center). The bell was removed from Roudenbush in 1977 when the tower housing it was found to be structurally unsound under the weight of the bell. It is currently displayed next to the original Westford Academy (now the Westford Museum) on Boston Road. (Author's collection.)

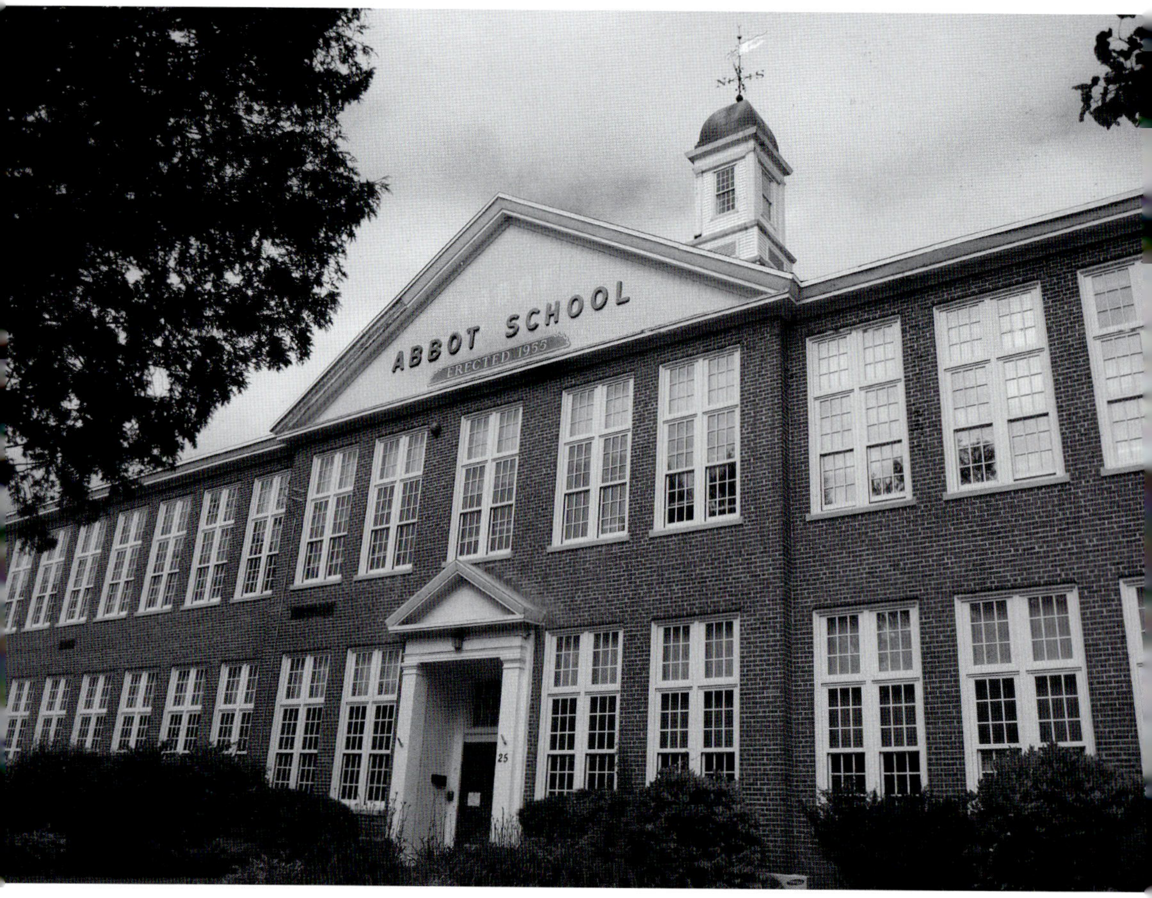

Third Westford Academy
Built in 1955, this structure served as the third Westford Academy. Upon the construction of the current Westford Academy building in 1973, this was repurposed as the Abbot School. The building currently serves grades three through six. (Author's collection.)

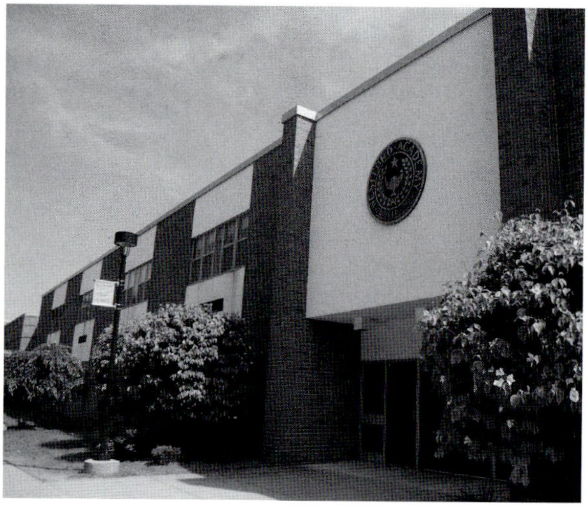

Fourth Westford Academy
This 1973 building serves as the current Westford Academy. Roughly 1,500 students now attend the school, which is recognized as a model of success around the country. The original 1792 school bell, cast by Paul Revere, is on display in the Bell Lobby of this building. Since its construction in 1973, the school has seen the addition of a performing arts center and a new gymnasium, as well as a new wing for classrooms, completed in 2000. (Author's collection.)

First Parish Church United of Westford

Established in 1711, predating the incorporation of the town, the First Parish Church has a long and proud history. The current meetinghouse, the third since the church began, was built in 1794 and also served as the town meetinghouse until 1868. (Author's collection.)

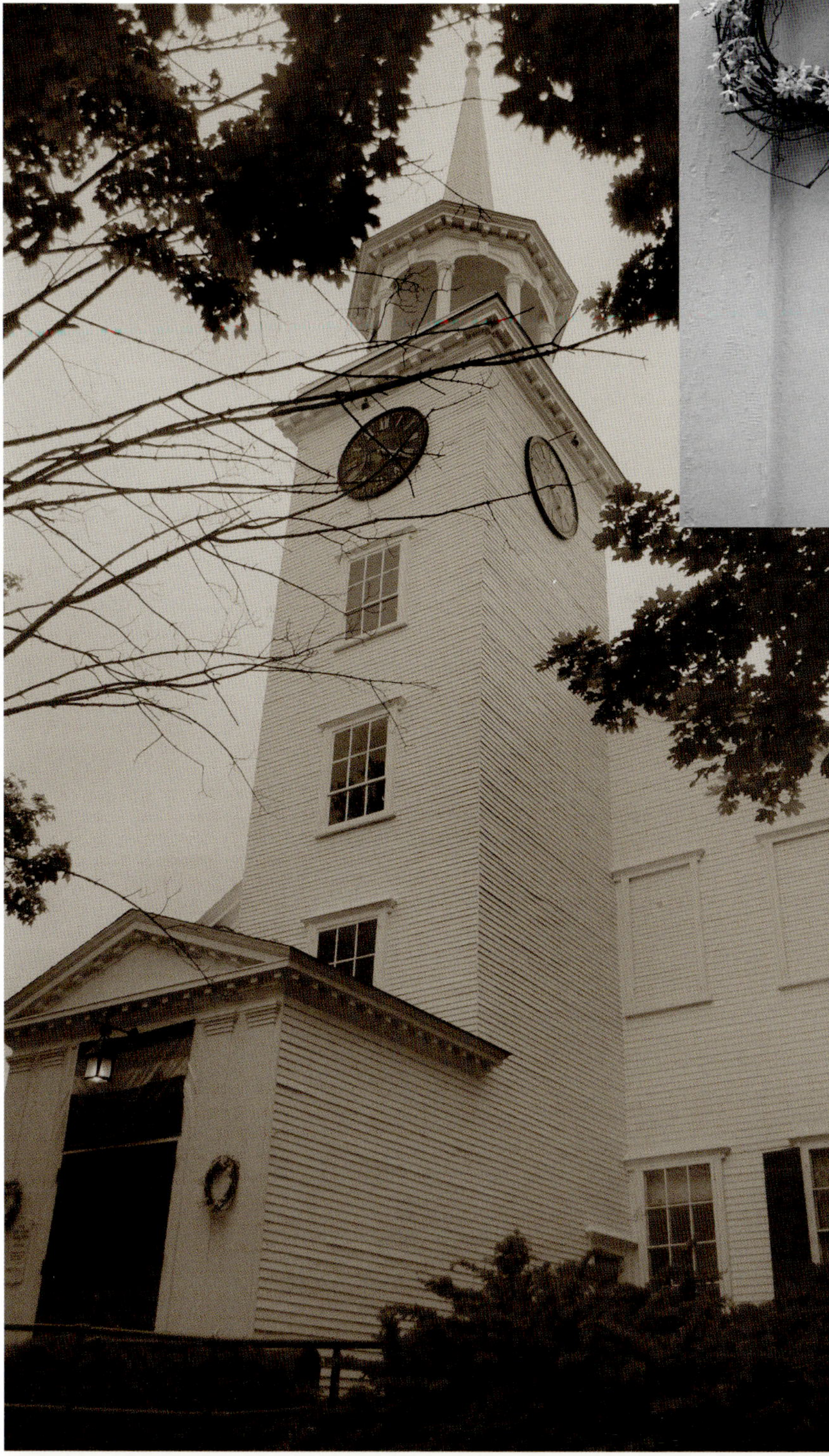

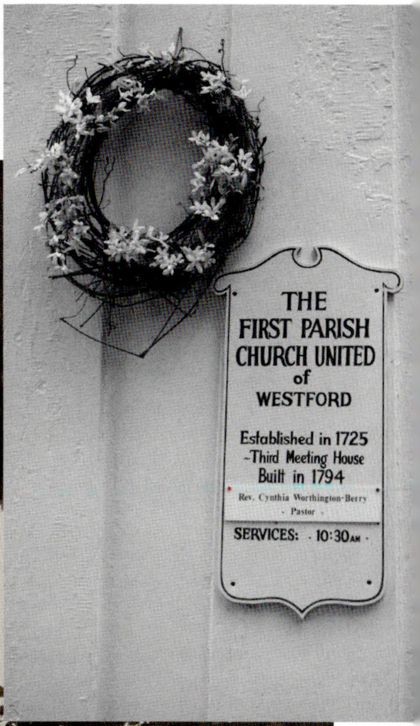

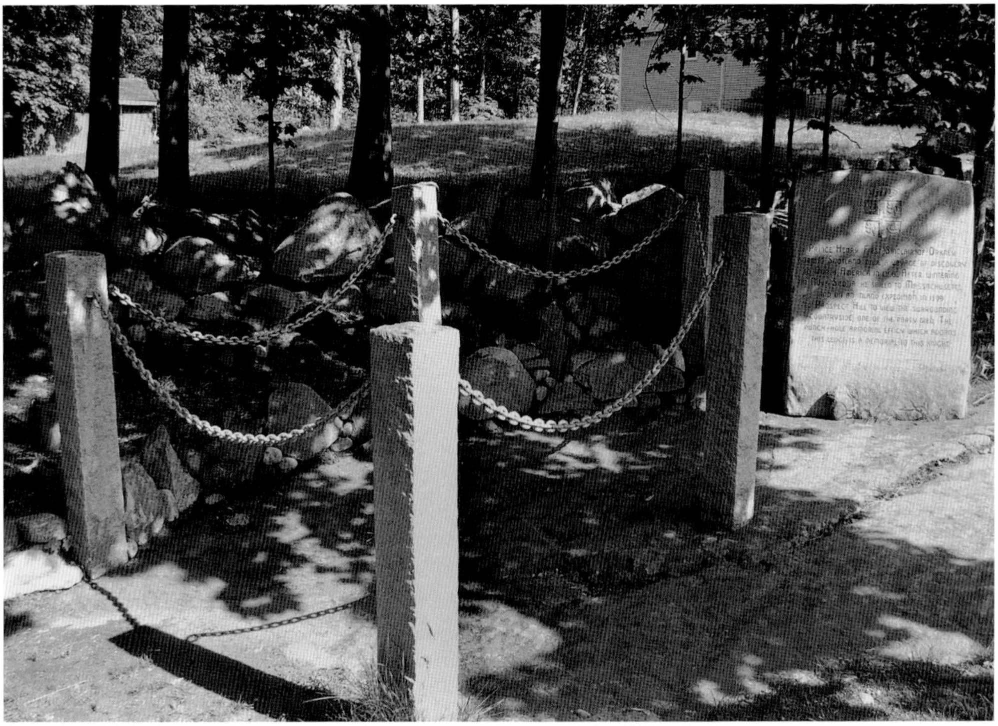

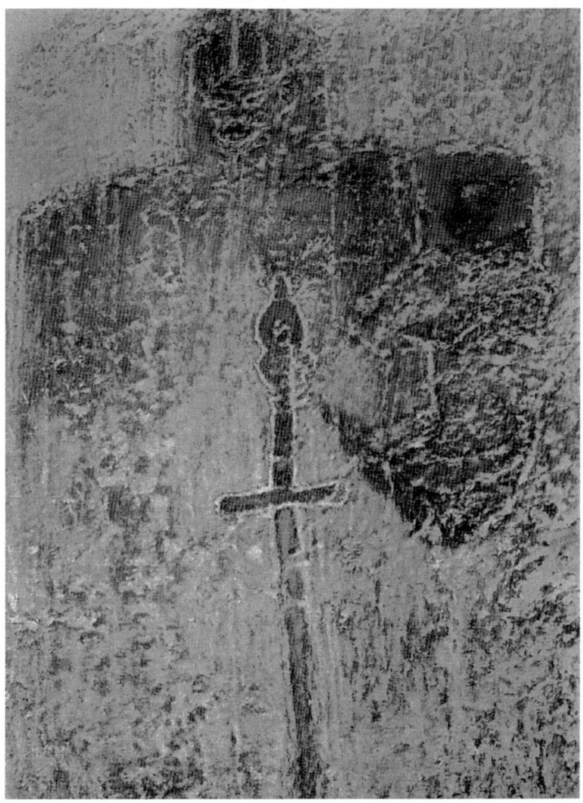

Westford Knight

The legend of the Westford Knight is woven into the rich history of Westford. A carving in ledge rock on the hill approaching Westford center shows what is purported to be a medieval sword and, some claim, the image of a knight of the 14th century. Although there are many opinions about the origin of the carving, the legend's place in Westford history is incontestable. Some claim the carving to be evidence of the explorations of Earl Henry Sinclair of Scotland in 1399, and some believe the image to be the effigy of Sir James Gunn, Sinclair's lifelong friend and travel companion. The site, a destination for tourists from around the world, is located on Depot Street and is identified with a granite marker. It has been the subject of many literary works, including the novel Cabal of the Westford Knight, by Westford novelist David Brody. (Courtesy of David Brody.)

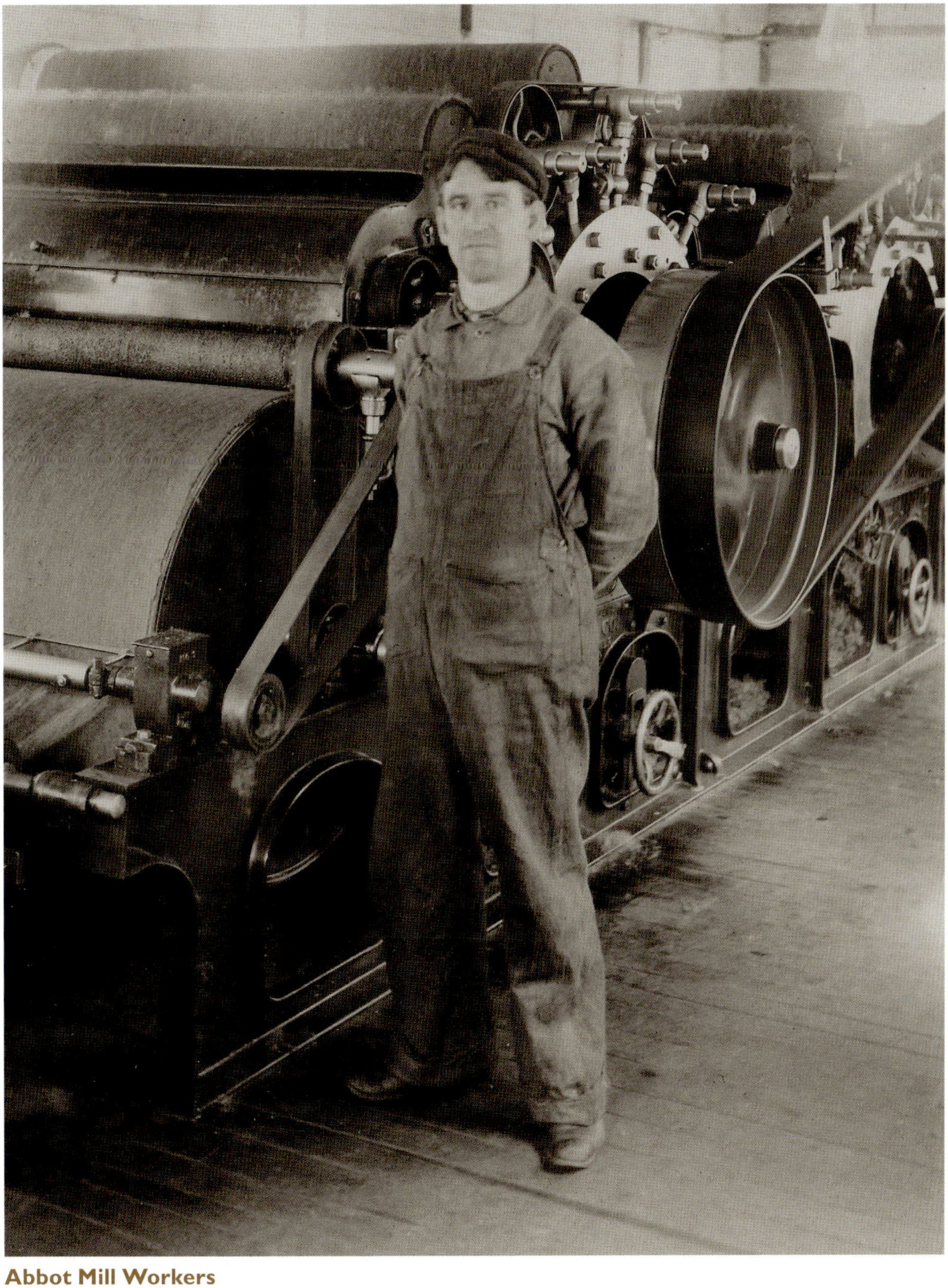

Abbot Mill Workers
James Payne, a machine operator, poses for a photograph depicting life at the Abbot Worsted Company around the turn of the 20th century. It is said that while many mills in the area recruited single people, the Abbots encouraged entire families to move to the area to work in the mill. By 1915, due to active recruitment by the Abbot Mill, a large portion of Westford's population was born outside of the United States. Many of the immigrants were French Canadians, but others came from Ireland, England, Scotland, and Russia.

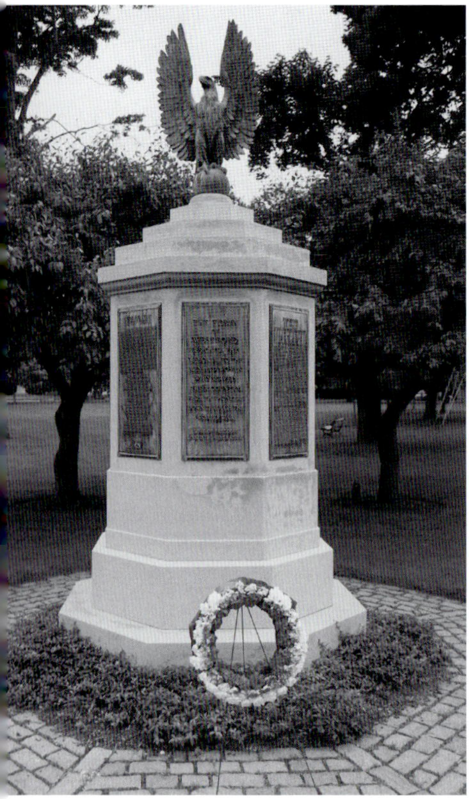

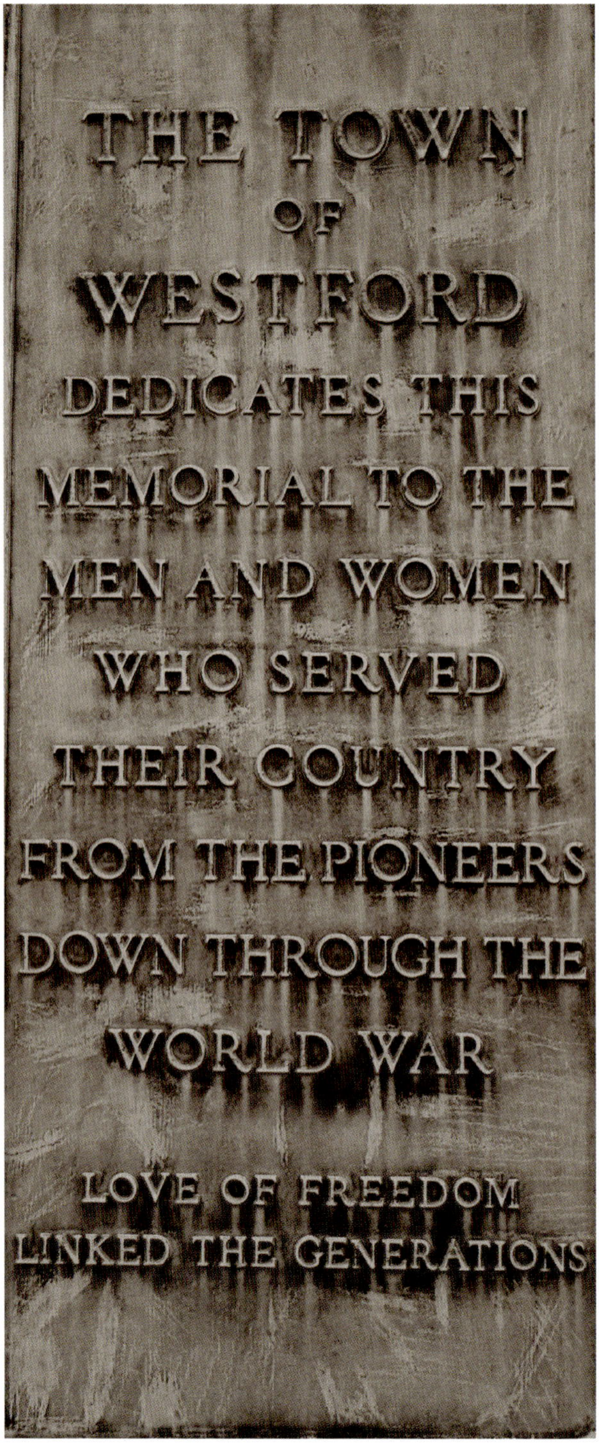

War Memorial

Located on the town common, the War Memorial (above), given by the Town of Westford, is dedicated "to the men and women who served their country from the pioneers down through the World War." The memorial was placed on the common in late November 1924. (Author's collection.)

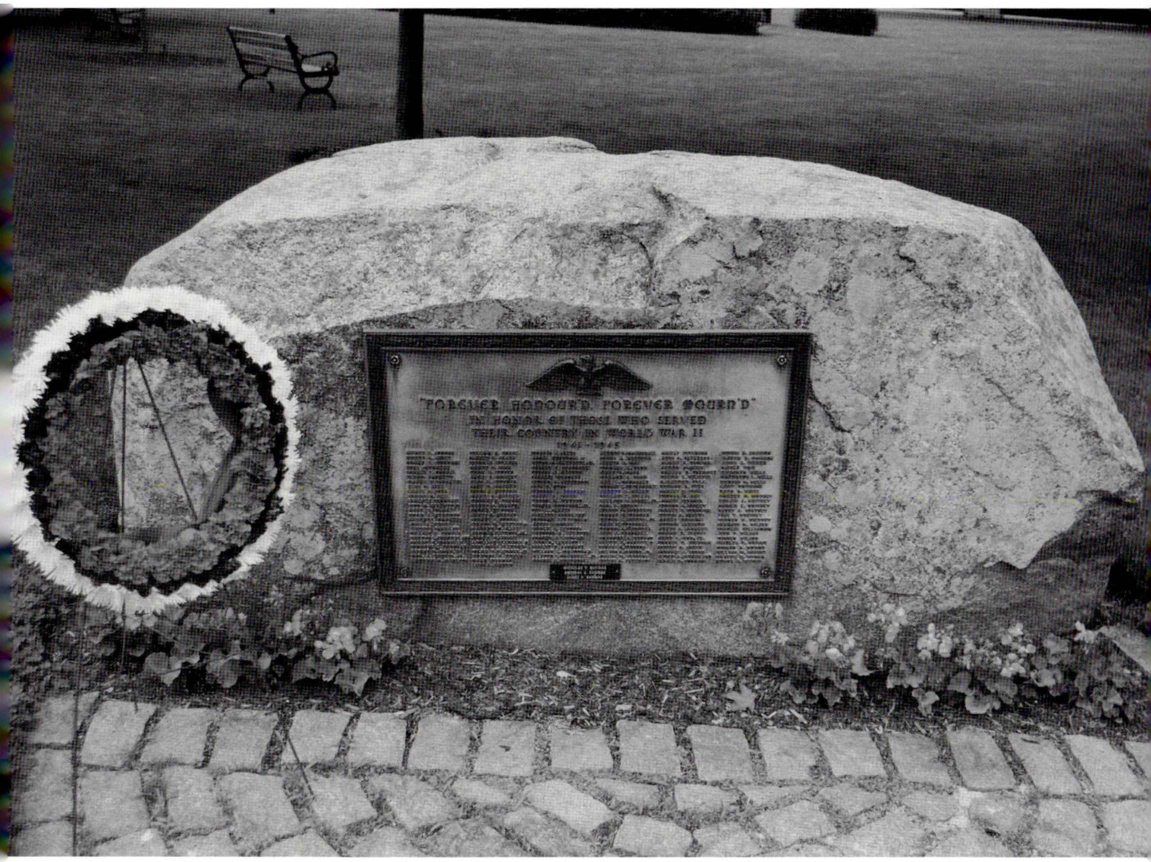

World War II Commemorative Plaque

This plaque, honoring the men and women who served in World War II, was dedicated in 1947 and is located on the town common across from the Parish Center for the Arts. The bronze plaque listing the names is affixed to a boulder from Blake's Hill. The boulder and plaque originally sat just west of the J.V. Fletcher Library and were moved to the common in November 1996. (Author's collection.)

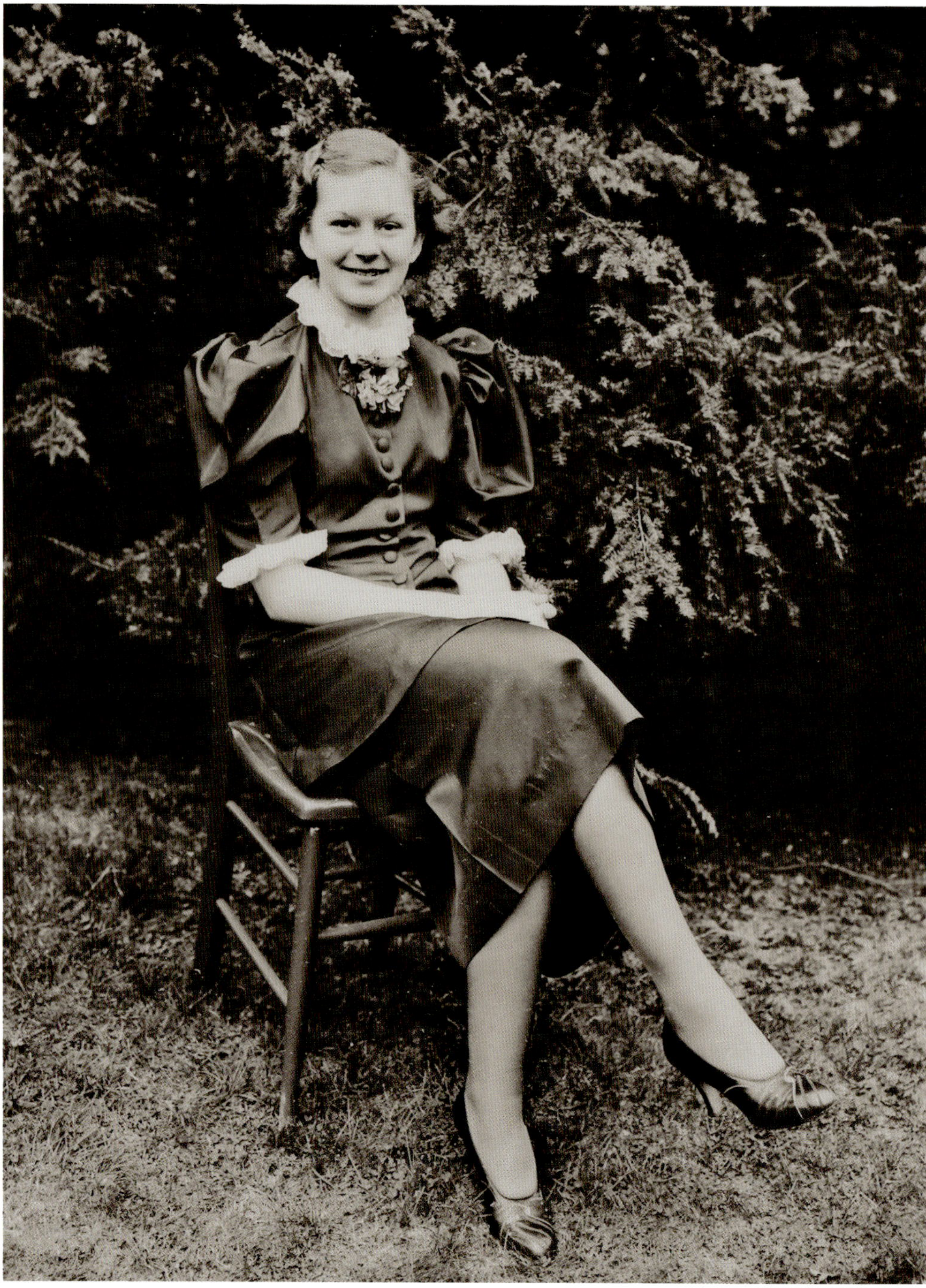

Apple Blossom Queen

Mary Elizabeth "Beth" Perrins, the second Apple Blossom queen, is seen here posing for a formal portrait on April 26, 1936. Massachusetts governor James M. Curley was present to crown Perrins. The Apple Blossom Festival is an annual tradition dating back to 1935, when a small group of local businessmen came together and launched the first event.

CHAPTER TWO

The Visionaries

In 1850, the population of Westford was 1,473. Despite this relatively small number of residents, the town was home to an incredibly large number of visionary people. These citizens understood the value of community and were motivated to make their environment a better place in which to raise their families. They saw the value of participating in the events that were shaping their new nation, understood the importance of developing their fledgling economy, and realized that providing a quality education to their children would ensure the long-term success of their town. The Honorable John Abbot, a lifelong resident of Westford, served in the state senate, worked with the administration of the Westford Academy, and laid the cornerstone for the Bunker Hill Monument in 1825. The Honorable Joseph Henry Read held several positions in the local and county government and served as director of the Stony Brook Railroad for 20 years. Abiel J. Abbot was an industrial leader and served both the Westford Academy and the Westford Public Library. These men, and many other men and women of Westford, understood the value of serving their community. They saw the need for being involved and did not shy away from ensuring a better tomorrow.

Sherman Dewey Fletcher

Fletcher (1810–1886) was born and educated in Westford. The son of Seth and Sally Fletcher, he married Emily Augusta Fletcher in 1839. He served as town treasurer from 1853 to 1886. He had two children, Cornelia Augusta and Sherman Heywood. He and his wife are buried in Fairview Cemetery. Fletcher operated the Wright & Fletcher general store on Main Street. An image of his residence can be seen on page 120.

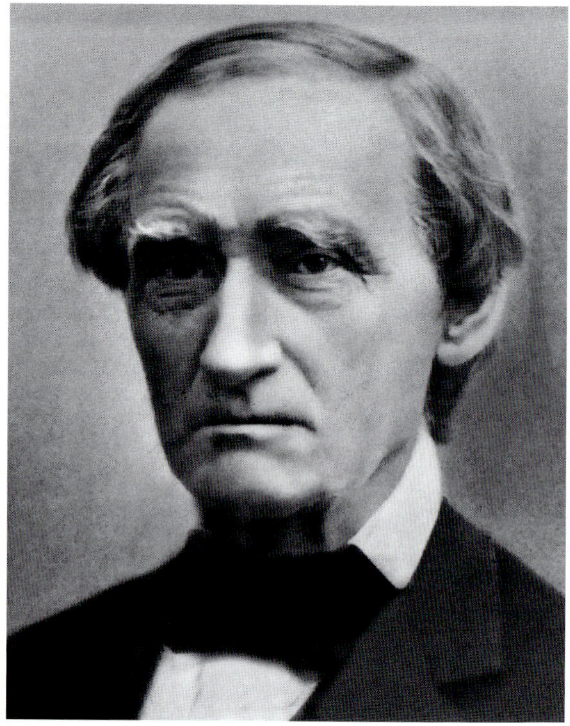

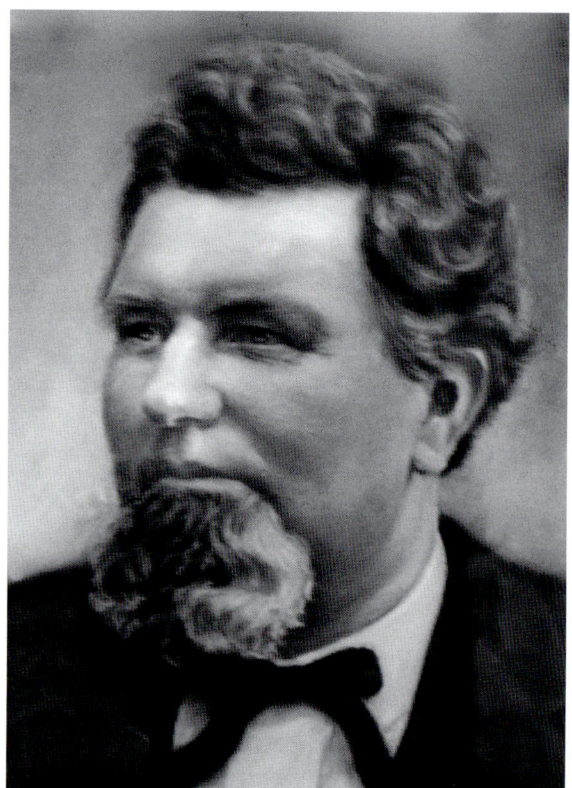

Charles Grandison Sargent

Sargent (1819–1878) was a prominent businessman whose mark on Westford can clearly be seen to this day. In 1854, Sargent came from Lowell to open the firm of Calvert & Sargent with Francis A. Calvert. The company's main business was the manufacture of machinery for the processing of wool products. In 1857, he partnered with John W.P. Abbot to form what became the Abbot Worsted Company. The partnership was short-lived, and Sargent sold his interest in the company to Allan Cameron. In 1862, he bought his partner's interest of Calvert & Sargent. The company was renamed Charles G. Sargent & Sons, and upon his death, his sons assumed control of operations.

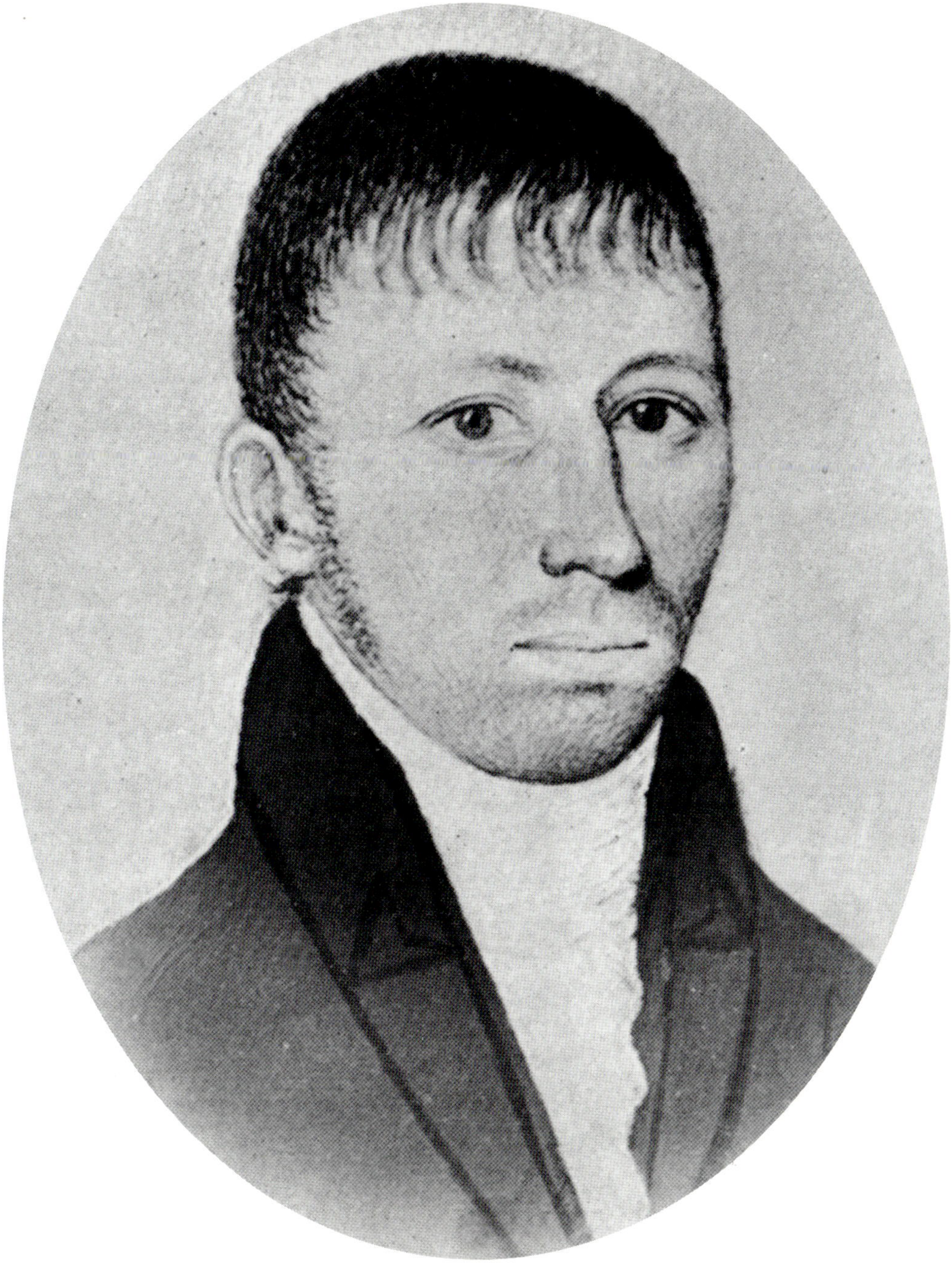

Hon. John Abbot

Abbot (1777–1854) was born, raised, and lived his life in Westford. Graduating from Harvard in 1798, he served as preceptor of Westford Academy for two years. After studying law, he opened a law office in Westford. In addition to serving as a trustee for the academy, he served as treasurer of the trustees for 50 years. He was a state senator for one term and served on the convention for revising the state constitution in 1820. As grand master of the Masons of Massachusetts, he laid the cornerstone for the Bunker Hill Monument in 1825 with Revolutionary War hero Marquis de Lafayette by his side.

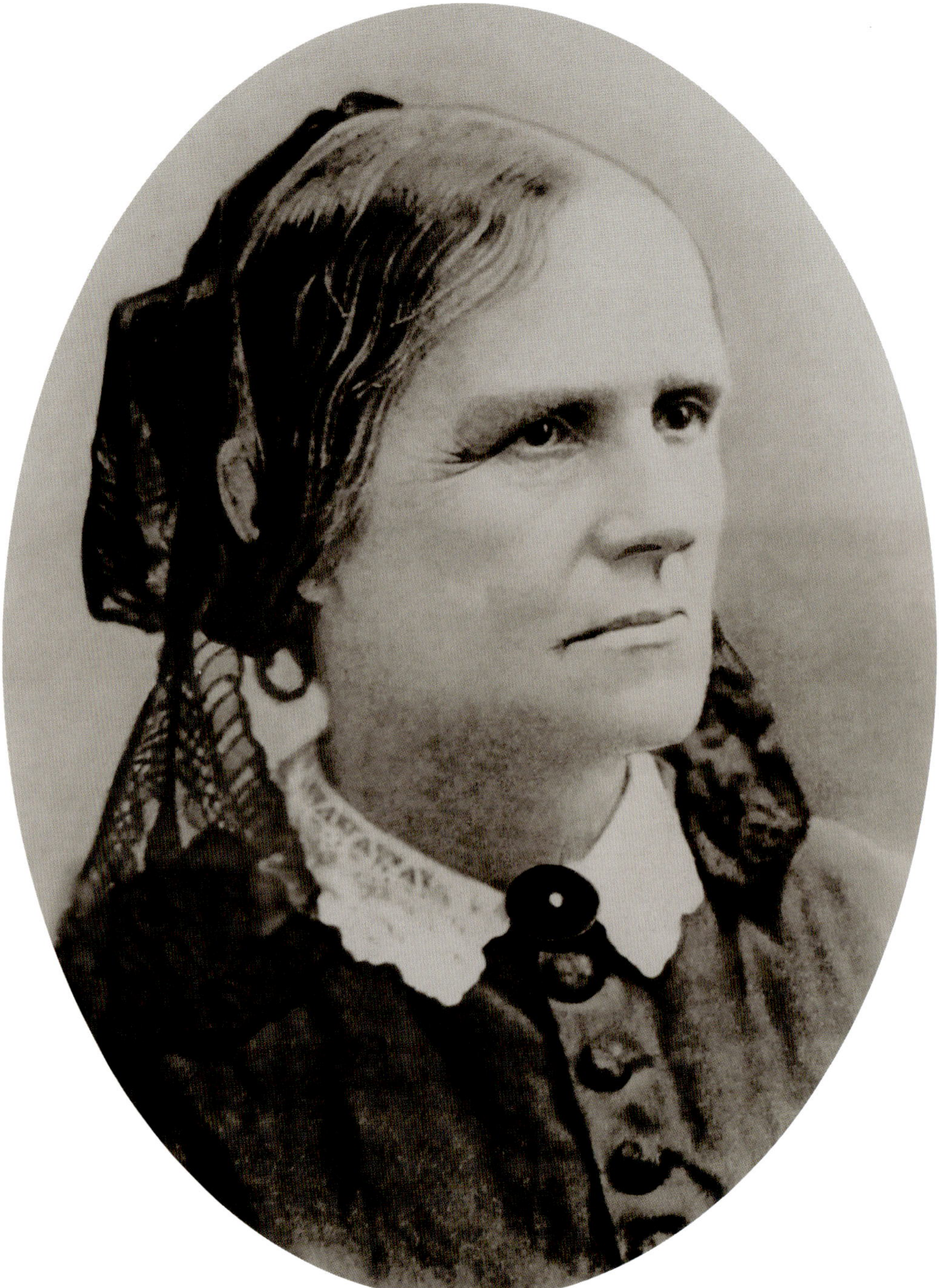

Catherine Abbot
Abbot (1808–1891), from Hampton Falls, New Hampshire, came to Westford in 1829, where she held the position of preceptress of Westford Academy for two years before vacating the position to marry John W.P. Abbot. She was known throughout the town for her kind and sympathetic demeanor, and was a significant benefactor of the Unitarian Church, the town library, and Westford Academy.

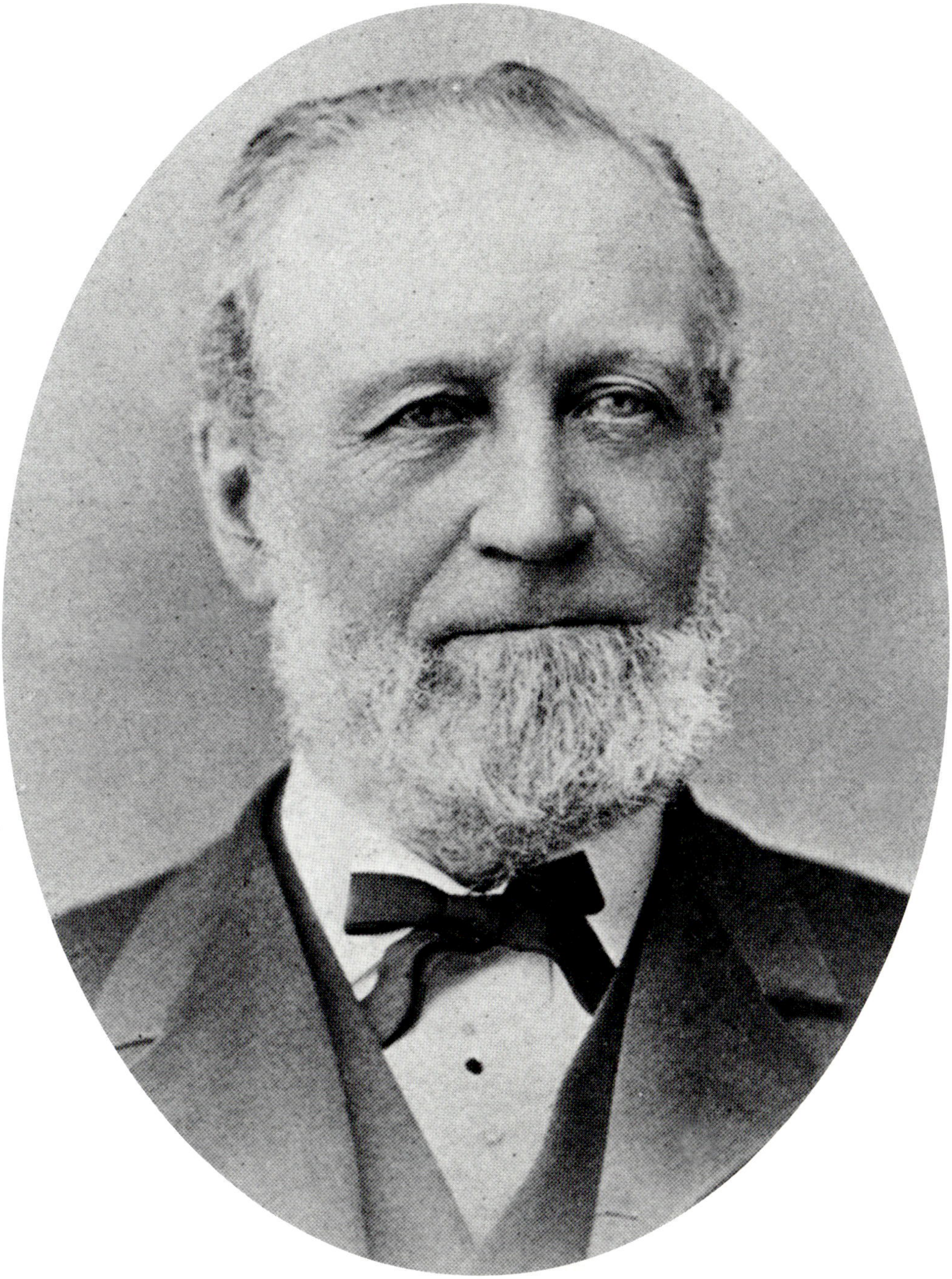

Allan Cameron

Born in Ross-Shire, Scotland, Cameron (1822–1900) received his education in Scotland before immigrating to the United States in 1843. In 1857, Cameron moved to Westford and became an active partner of the Abbot Worsted Company. He purchased Charles G. Sargent's interest in the company when Sargent left to focus on his other business interests. He served as a trustee of Westford Academy and as a school committeeman in 1872. To see an image of Allen Cameron's residence, please see page 115.

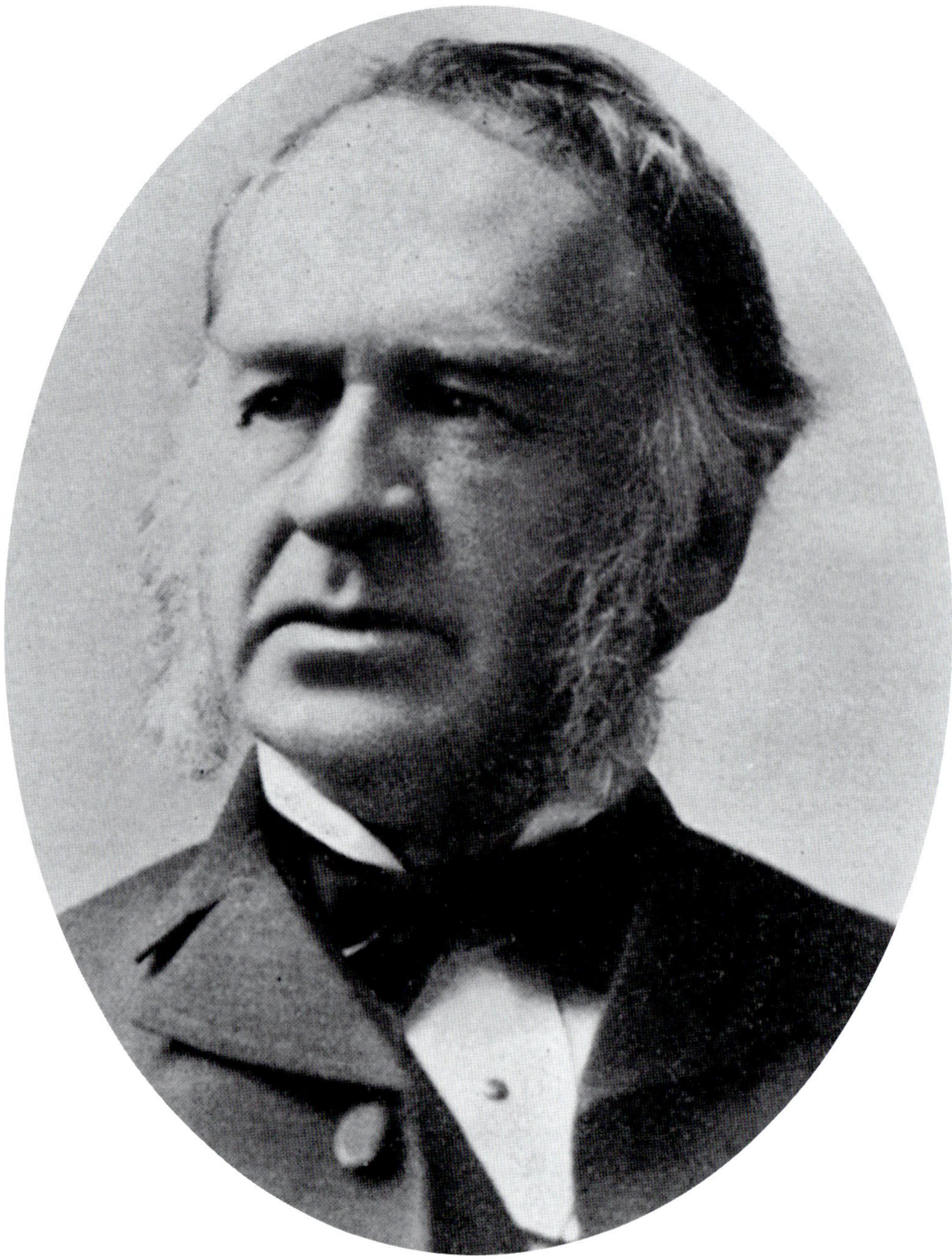

Charles Lewis Hildreth

Hildreth (1823–1909) was born in Concord, New Hampshire, and educated at the Academy in New Ipswich, New Hampshire. At 22, he moved to Lowell to begin work as an apprentice in the Lowell Machine Shop. After three years, he moved to Philadelphia to serve as foreman for Bement & Dougherty. Two years later, he returned to the machine shop to serve as foreman. He split his year between Lowell and Westford, where he maintained the Hildreth family farm.

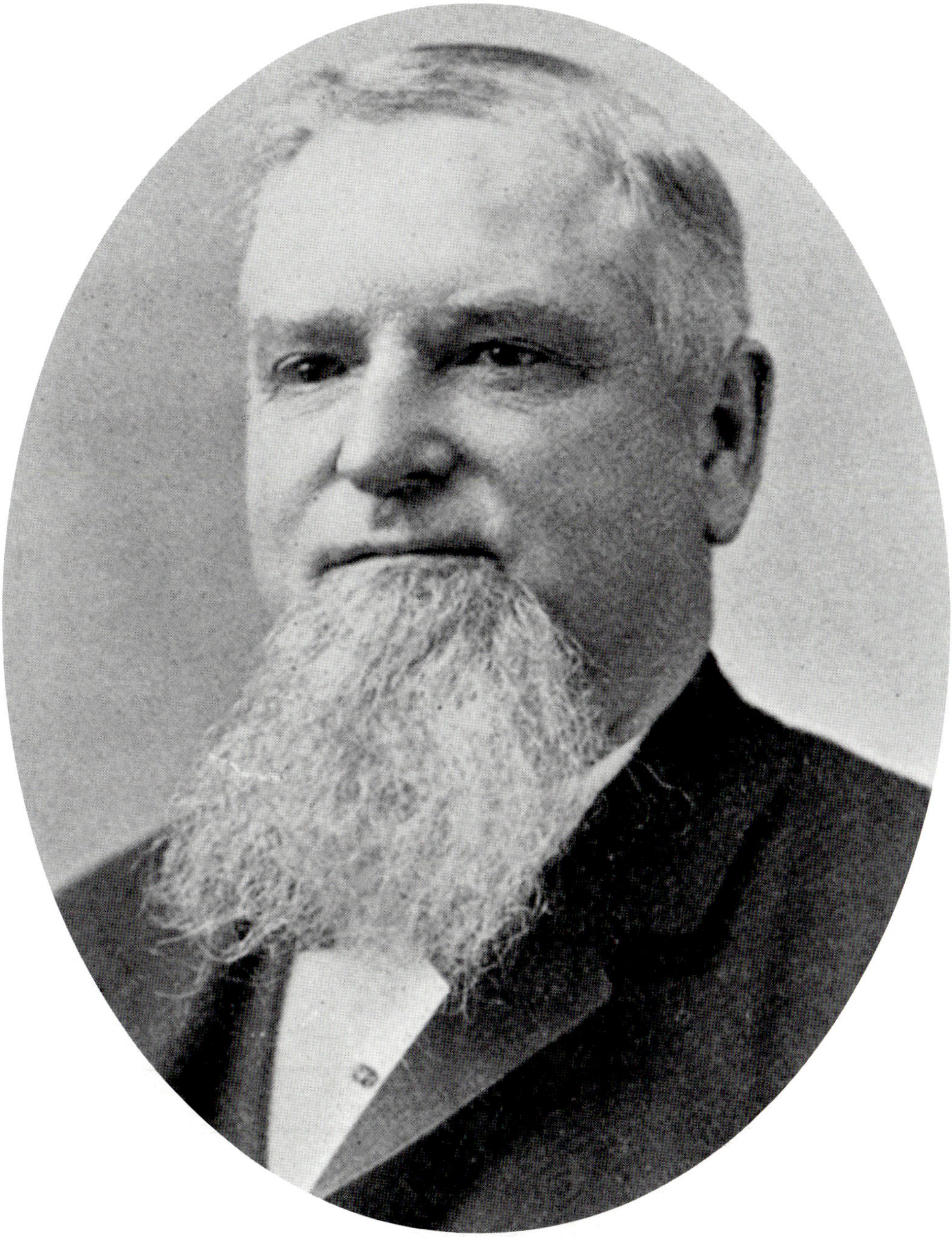

Hon. Joseph Henry Read
Born in Westford and educated at Westford Academy, Read (1835–1901) held many public positions, including selectman, school committeeman, auditor, and moderator. In 1872, he was chosen to serve in the General Court, and in 1876, he was elected county commissioner, a position he held until 1897. Throughout his public career, he maintained his family farm, which was known for the quality of its apples and cider. He also served as director of the Westford Mutual Fire Company and director of the Stony Brook Railroad for 25 years.

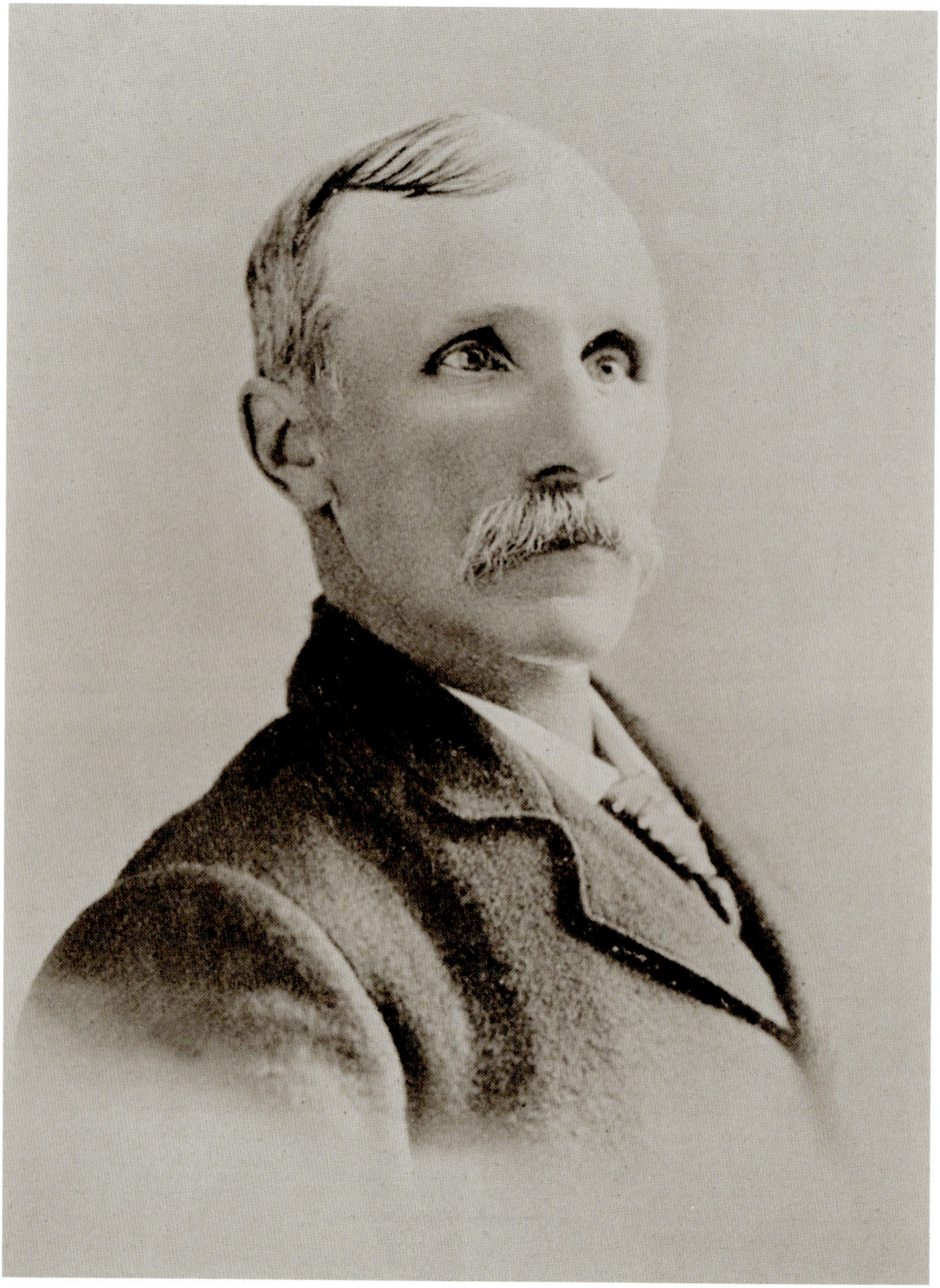

William Henry Harrison Burbeck
Burbeck (1840–1917) was born in Westford and attended school at Westford Academy. He held the distinction of being the first postmaster at the Coldspring Post Office, which was located at the Westford Station on the Stony Brook Railroad. He was one of the principal owners of Heywood & Burbeck, grain dealers, and served on the Westford Board of Assessors.

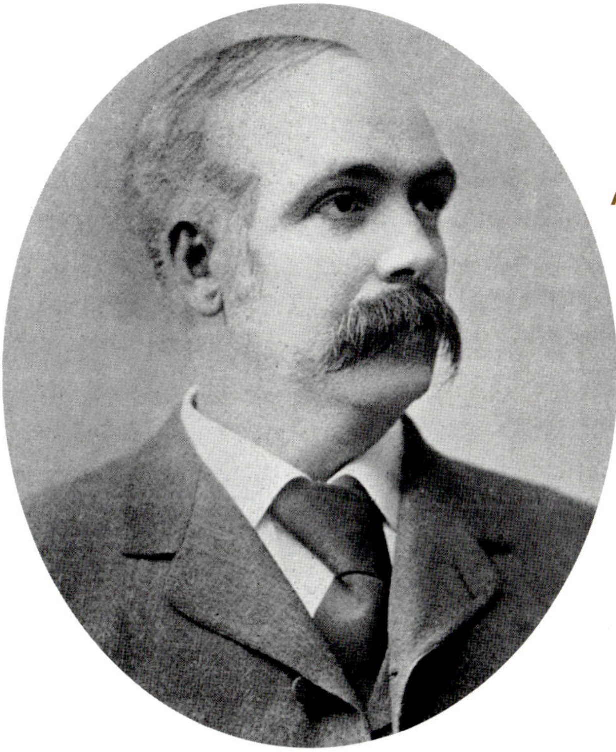

Albert Rockwood Choate
Choate (1843–1919) was born in Tewksbury, Massachusetts. He was educated in the Tewksbury public schools, and went on to work as a machinist for the Abbot Worsted Company. He was elected to serve on the board of the school committee in 1889 and was instrumental in forming a hose company in Graniteville, which was named for him.

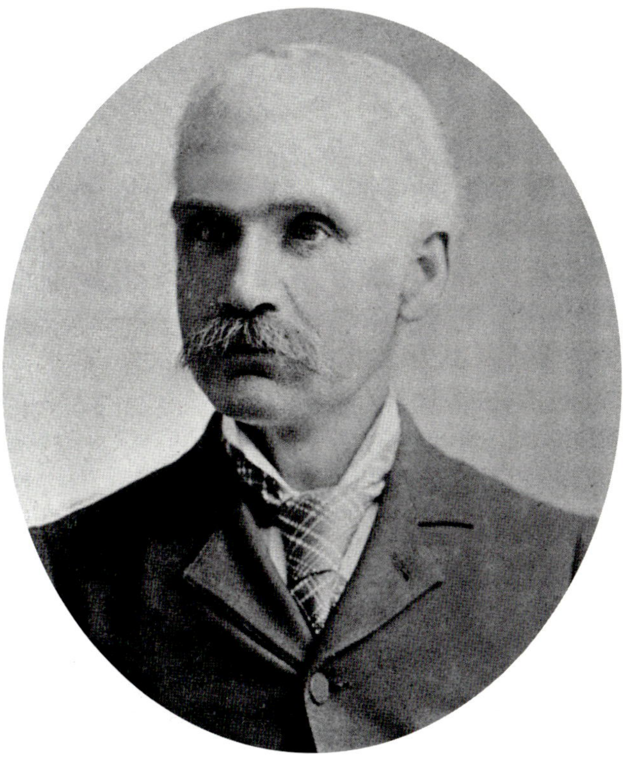

Alfred Woodbury
Woodbury (1844–1907) was born in Fitchburg, Massachusetts. He received his education in Fitchburg and Lancaster public schools and later came to Westford, where he made his living as a local farmer. He served on the Westford School Committee.

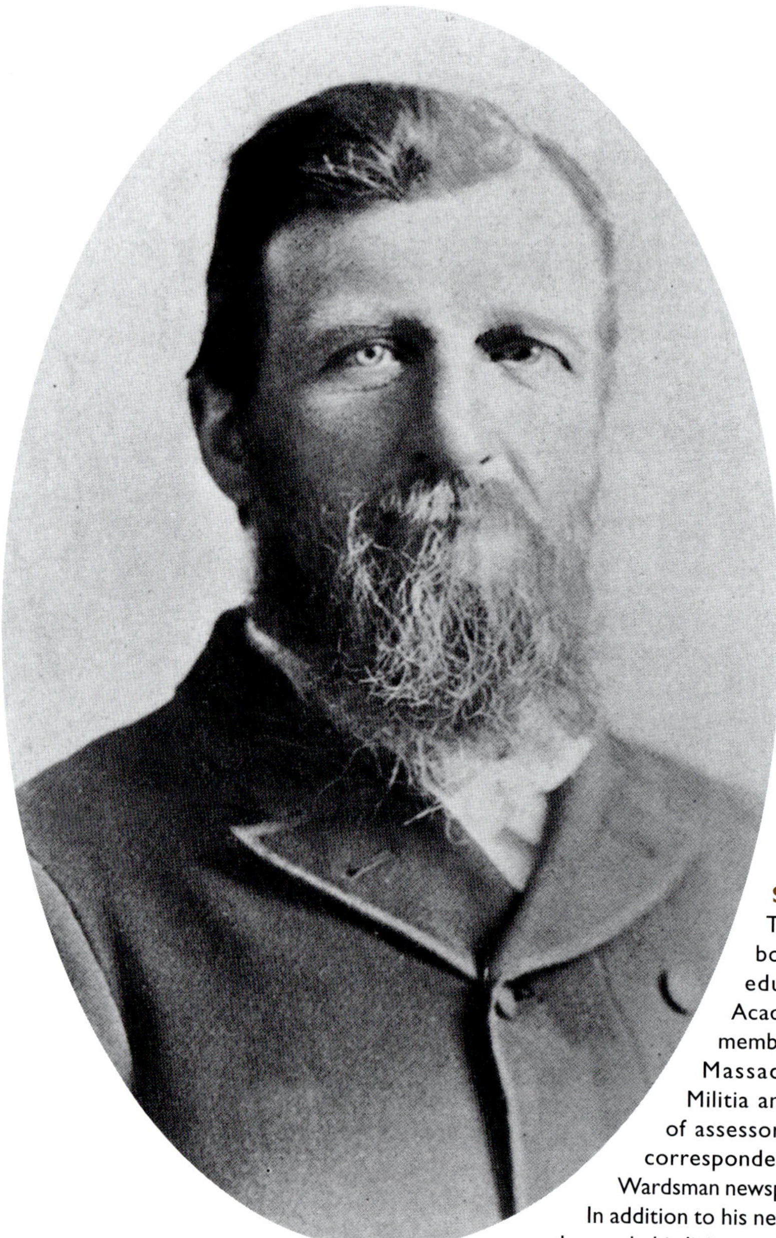

Samuel Law Taylor

Taylor (1845–1932) was born in Westford and educated at Westford Academy. He served as a member of Troop F Cavalry, Massachusetts Volunteer Militia and was on the board of assessors. He was a regular correspondent for the Westford Wardsman newspaper during the 1910s. In addition to his newspaper work, Taylor also made his living as a farmer.

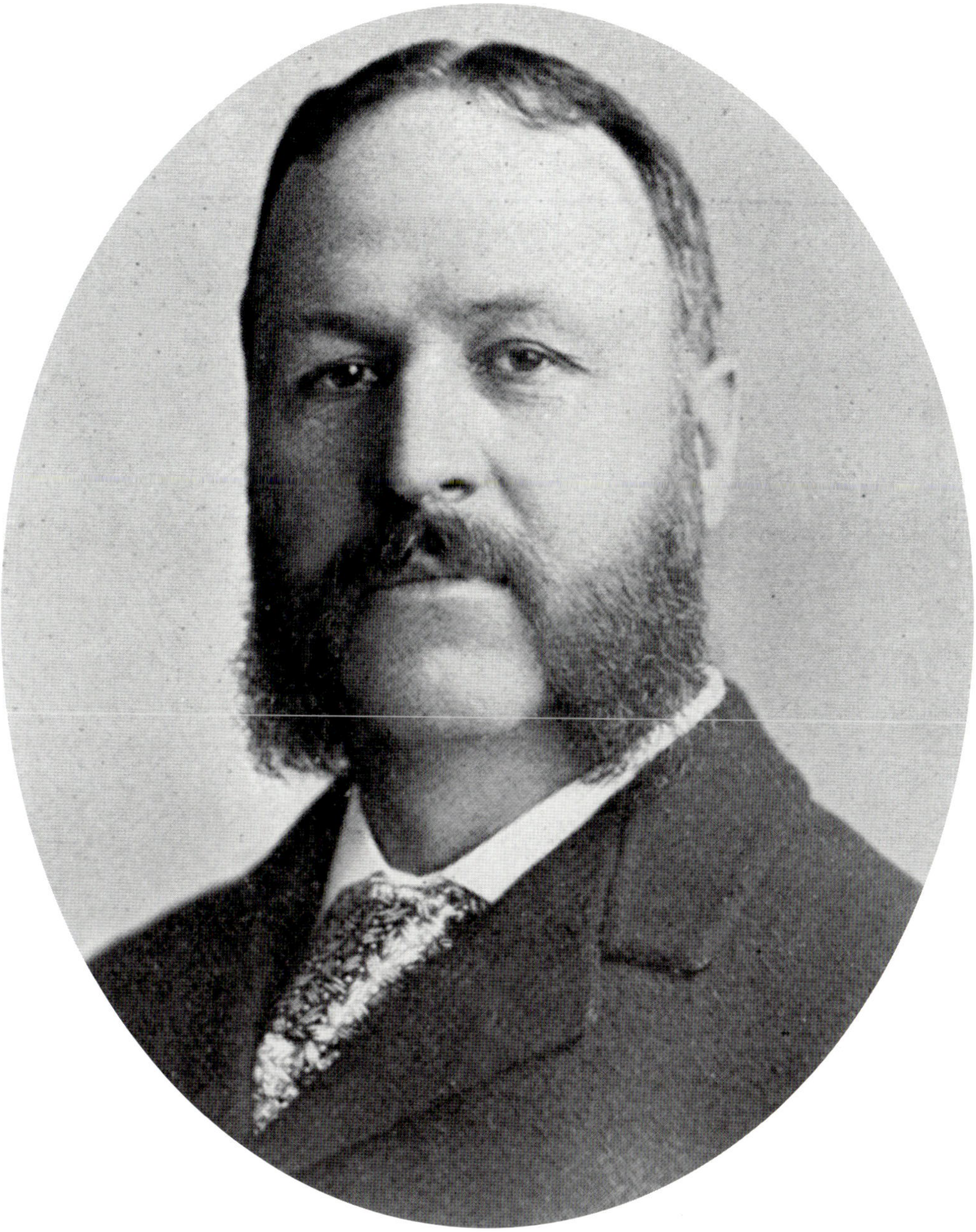

Abiel Jacob Abbot

Westford native Abbot (1850–1921) was educated at Westford Academy and continued his education at Highland Military Academy, Philips Exeter Academy, and the Massachusetts Institute of Technology. His contributions to the town of Westford were numerous. He served as chairman of trustees of the Westford Public Library, chairman of the school committee, and trustee of Westford Academy. As treasurer of the Abbot Worsted Company, he also served on the executive committee of the National Association of Wool Manufacturers. His donation of Abbot family portraits to the town of Westford has helped ensure the preservation of the town's rich history. The portraits hang on the walls of town hall to this day.

George Henry Hartford

Born in Newfield, Maine, Hartford (1852–1922) received his education from Lowell public schools. Not unlike many residents of Westford at the time, he made his living as a farmer. He served as a member, and eventually chairman, of the Westford Board of Assessors.

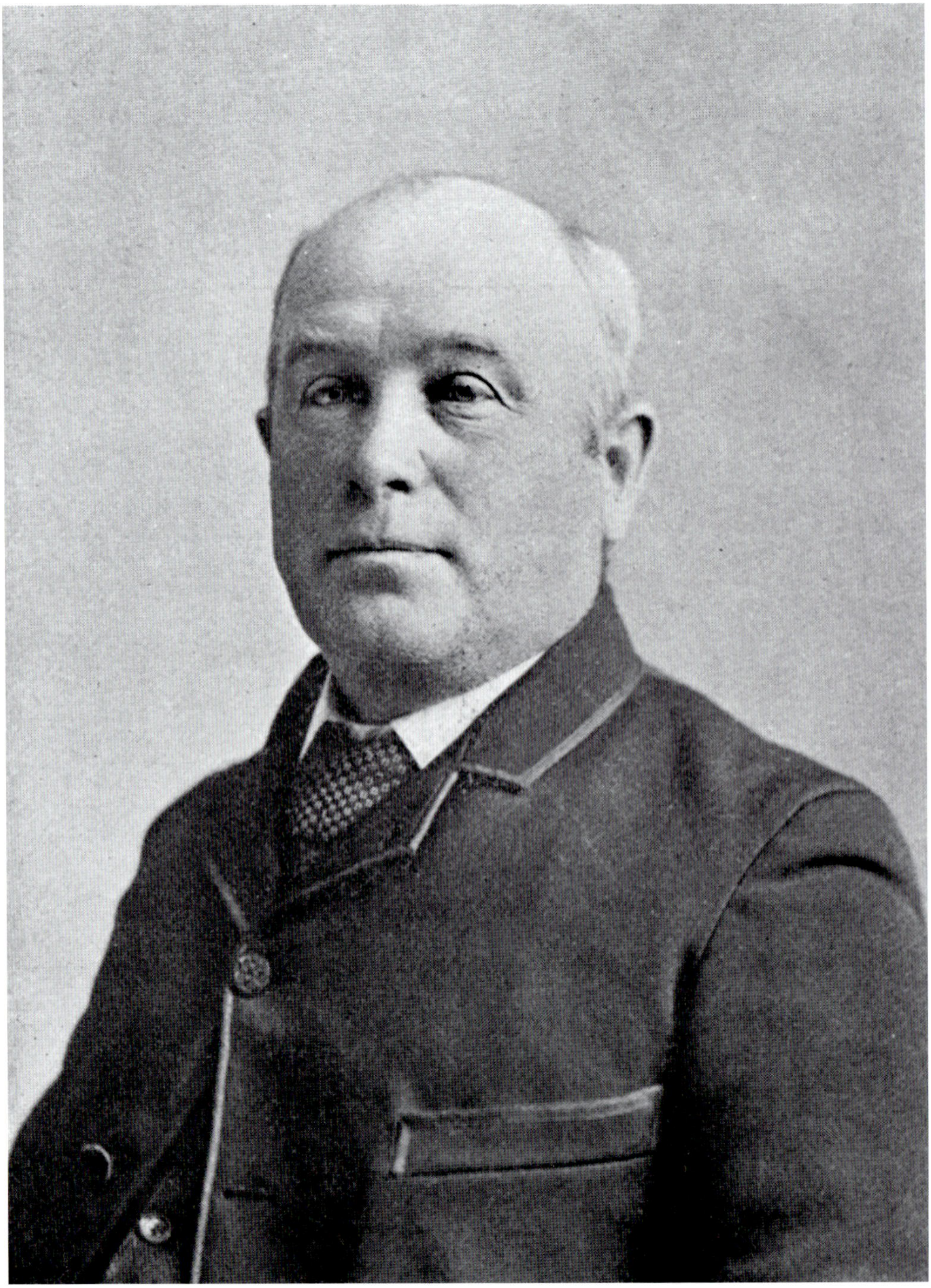

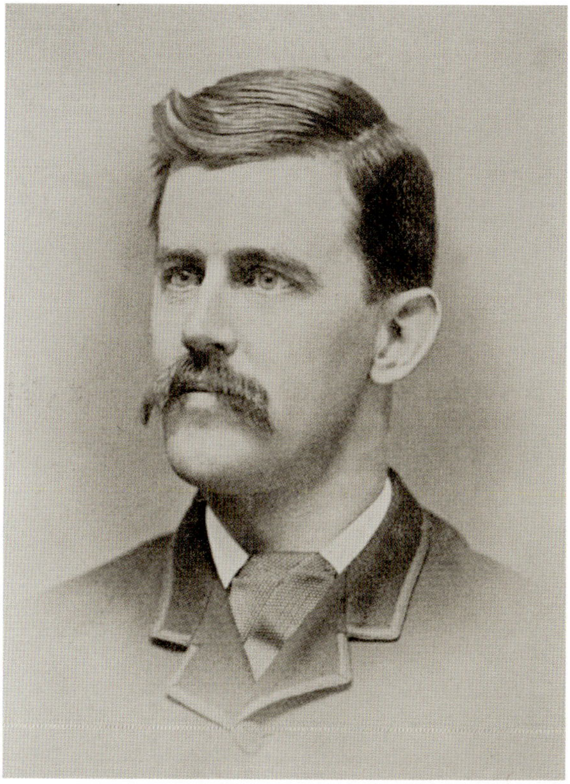

Hammett Delette Wright
Wright (1856–1920) was born in Westford and received his education at Westford Academy. Wright made his living as a granite dealer at the quarry in Graniteville and was elected to serve on the board of Overseers of the Poor in 1891.

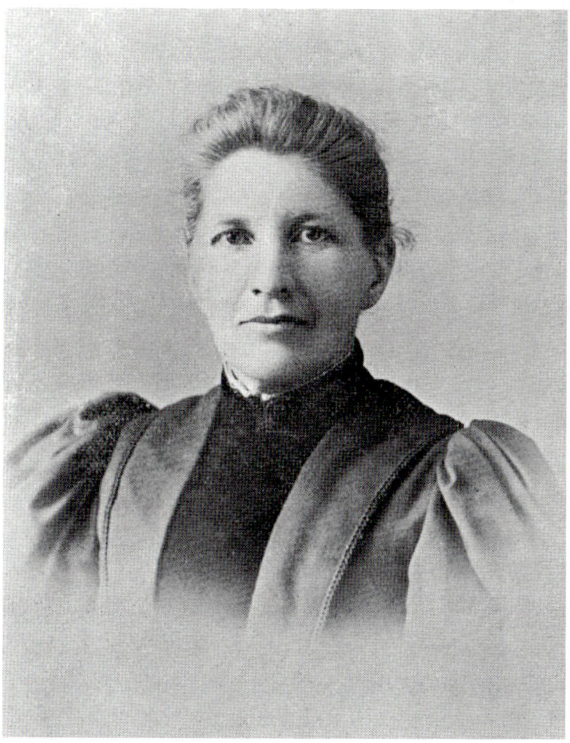

Alta Mahala (Schellenger) Taylor
Taylor (1858–1922) was born in Stockholm, New York, and educated in public schools there. She later relocated to Westford, where she married Samuel L. Taylor. She made her living as a housekeeper and was elected to serve as a member of the Westford School Committee.

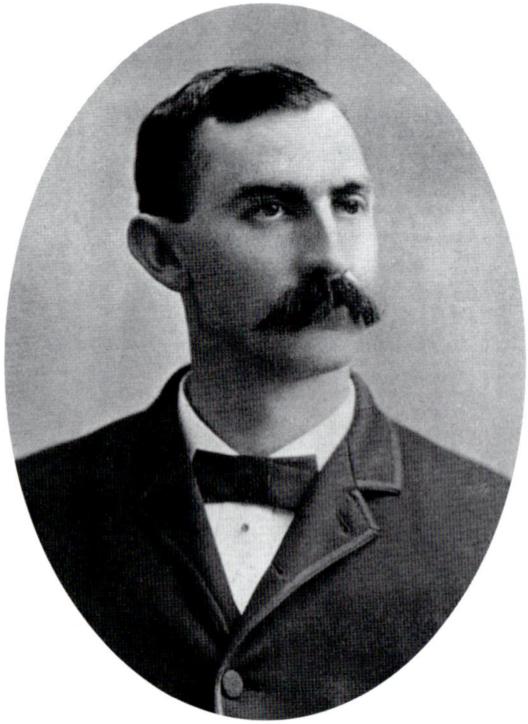

Frank Henry Hildreth
Hildreth (1861–1920) was born in Westford and received his education in the Westford public schools. Like most of his contemporaries, he earned his living as a local farmer. He was elected to serve on the board of school committee in 1893.

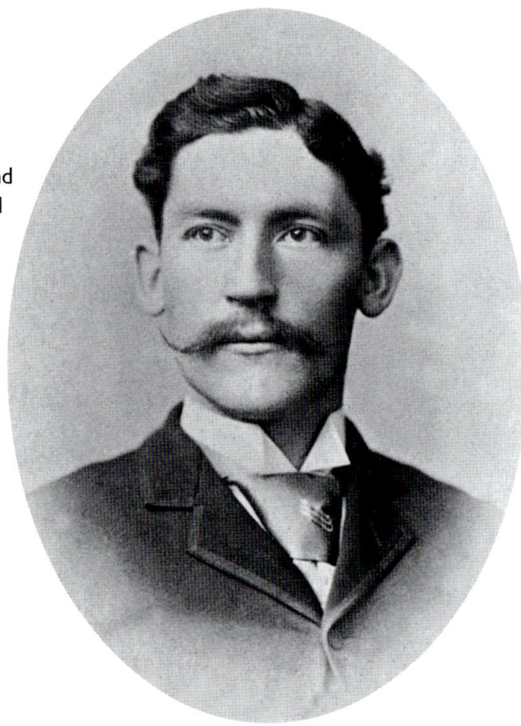

Walter Cummings Wright
Wright (1865–1936) was born in Westford and attended Westford Academy. He received his postsecondary education from Bryant & Stratton's Commercial College in Boston, Massachusetts. In Graniteville, he made his living as a bookkeeper for Wright & Bemis general store, founded by his father, and served as postmaster. He was elected collector of taxes in 1893 and later served on the school committee.

CHAPTER THREE

The Library People

Established in 1797 as the Social Library, the town library has served the community for over 200 years. The library's motto, "Widening Westford's World," exemplifies the town's commitment to ensuring that its residents have access to a wealth of information. In 1881, the library was housed in a room in the town hall, and as the collection approached 4,000 volumes, it became apparent that the town would need to construct a suitable library building. A site was secured in 1894, and in 1896, the town was asked to erect a new library. Before action was taken, a letter was received from the Honorable J. Varnum Fletcher announcing his intentions to donate nearly $10,000 for the purpose of constructing a new library building. He later donated an additional $4,000, bringing his total donation to $14,000. The town raised an additional $5,000 to complete the construction and to furnish the building and immediately voted to name the library the J.V. Fletcher Library. The building was dedicated on June 4, 1896, and as part of that dedication a commemorative pamphlet was published. The pamphlet, which sold for 10¢, served as a who's who of prominent local residents of the day and provided biographies of those who served on the library building committee as well as other residents who were committed to public service.

This chapter pays tribute to the efforts of the people who made the J.V. Fletcher Library possible, and to the pamphlet commemorating the dedication in 1896. All of the images contained in this chapter are reproduced from that pamphlet in order to share them with another generation. Additional images from the 1896 pamphlet appear throughout this book.

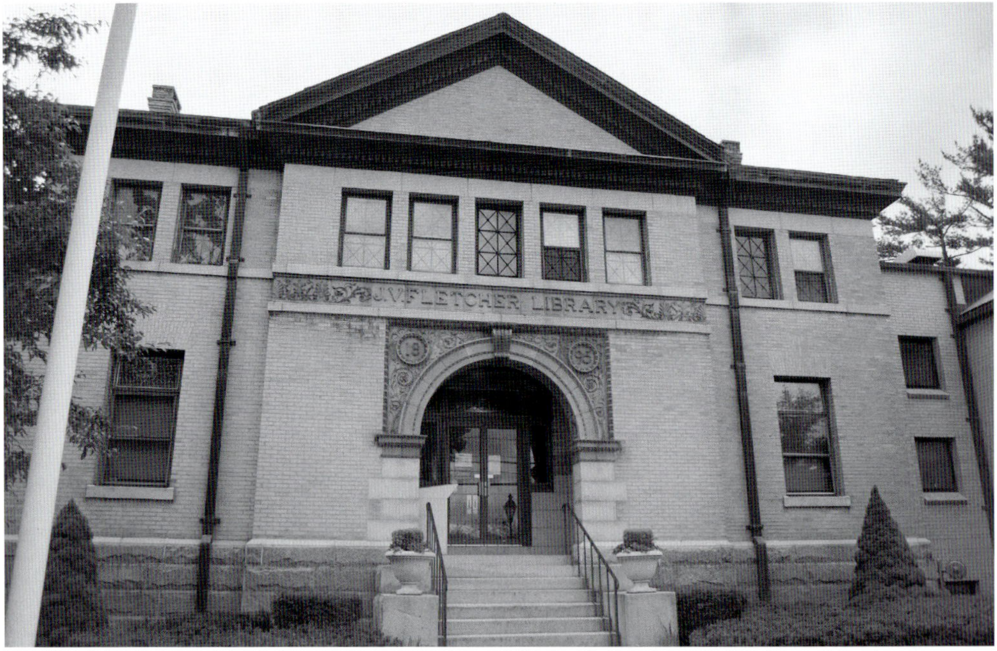

J.V. Fletcher Library

Built in 1895 with funds donated by J. Varnum Fletcher, this library building has served the residents of Westford for over 100 years. It has seen several additions and improvements in that time and has kept pace with advancements in technology and the ever-growing collection of works housed within and beyond its walls. Through library consortiums and virtual collections and subscriptions, the library continues to be a valuable asset to the residents of Westford. (Author's collection.)

J.V. Fletcher Library Commemorative Pamphlet

The image to the right shows the cover of the 1896 commemorative pamphlet that was published for the dedication of the J.V. Fletcher Library. The Westford town seal can be seen in the image. The souvenir pamphlet, which sold for 10¢ at the time, contained a wealth of information, including portraits of the key people in government and the core supporters of the effort to construct the new library.

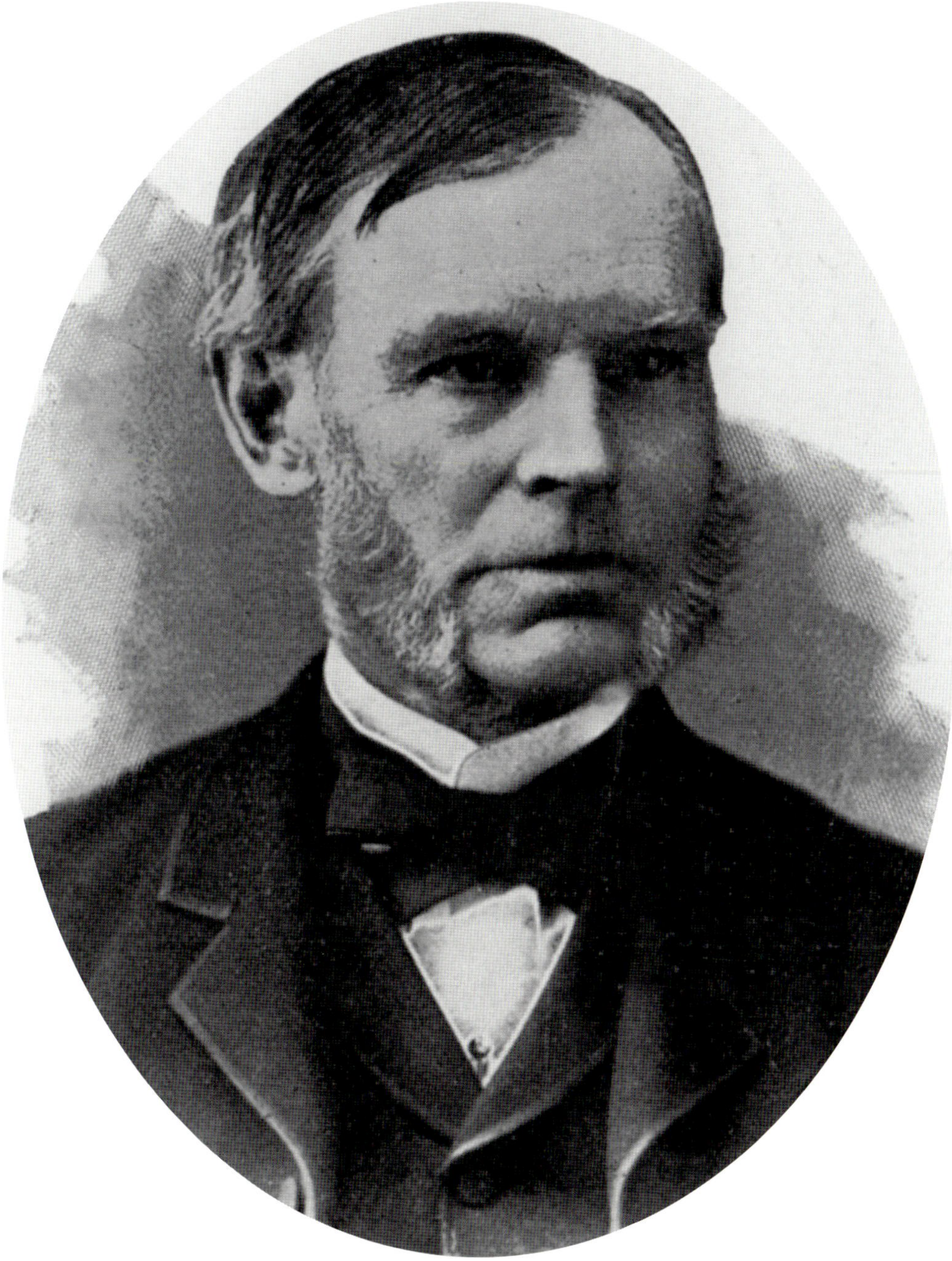

Jonathan Varnum Fletcher

Westford native Fletcher (1812–1899) lived most of his life in Belmont, Massachusetts, but maintained a summer residence in Westford. He made his living in the banking industry in Boston and Belmont and was also president of the Quincy Cold Storage Company. He served as representative to the general court and went on to serve as a state senator. In 1896, Fletcher donated nearly $14,000 for the construction of a new public library in Westford. It was decided by a unanimous vote that the Westford Social Library should be renamed the J.V. Fletcher Library, a name it retains to this day.

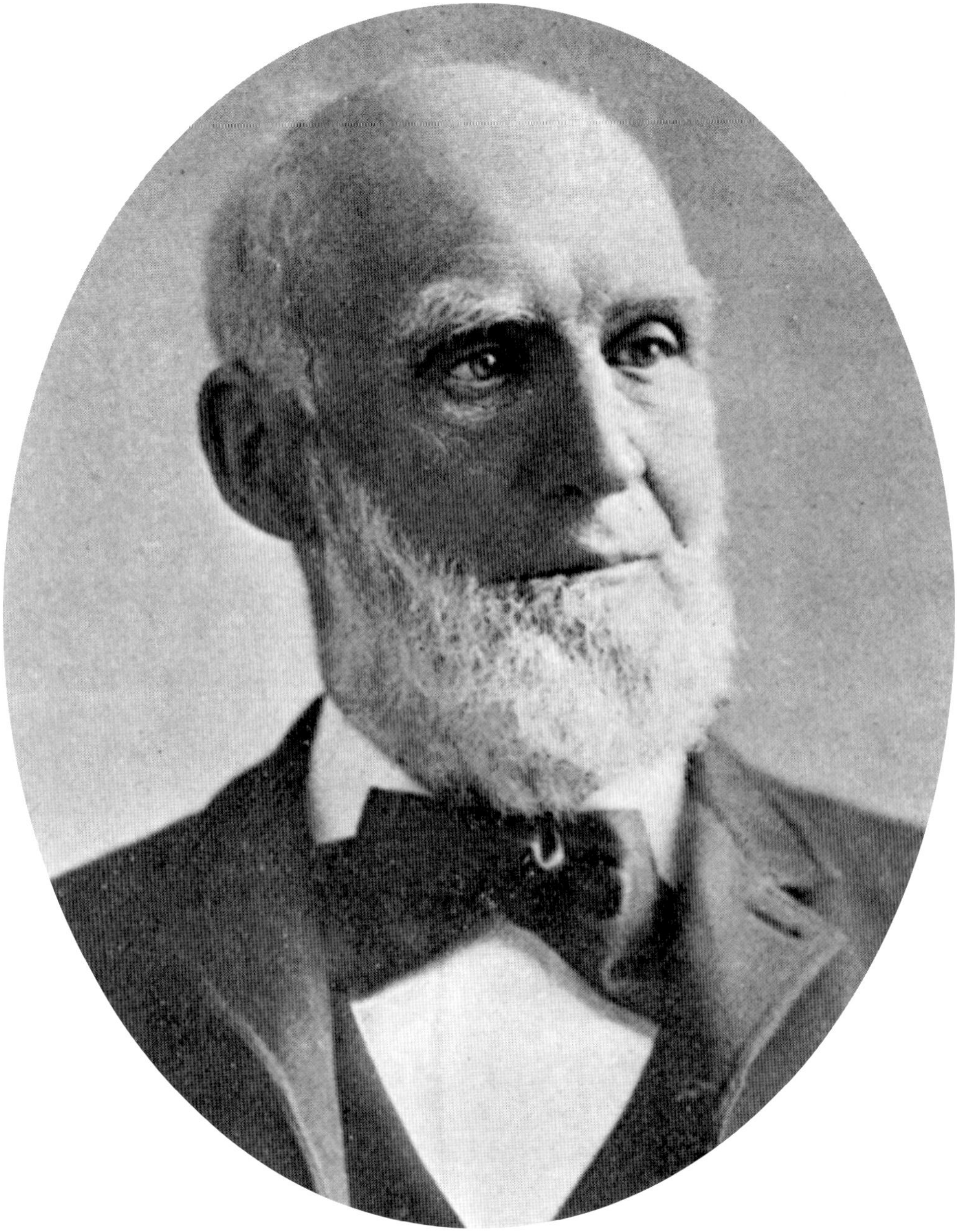

George Washington Heywood
Heywood (1829–1914) was born in Westford and educated in Westford public schools. He made his living as a principal owner of Heywood and Burbeck grain dealers and held several positions in the line of public service. He was a member of Troop F Cavalry, Massachusetts Volunteer Militia, served as a representative in the state legislature in 1868, and held the position of selectman from 1871 to 1874 and again in 1891. He also served as chairman of commissioners of public burial grounds and was a member of the building committee of the J.V. Fletcher Library. Appropriately, Heywood's tombstone is a millstone from his grist mill on the Stony Brook at Depot Street.

George Thomas Day

Day (1833–1918) was born in Westford and received his education from South Grammar School in Lowell, Massachusetts, and Westford Academy. Like many of his contemporaries, he was a local farmer, but truly made his mark on the town and the region through his public service. He served as a member of Troop F Cavalry, Massachusetts Volunteer Militia. He was a Massachusetts State Representative in 1859 and 1863 and served as a Westford selectman from 1865 to 1869 and from 1886 to 1890. He served on the Westford School Committee from 1856 to 1857 and from 1862 to 1867. He was the director of the public library from 1872 to 1874 and was a trustee of Westford Academy. From 1890 to 1896, he served as agent for burial of deceased soldiers and sailors and also as commissioner of public burial grounds. His long list of positions also included serving as the agent of board of health for suppression for contagious diseases among domestic animals and inspector of animals and provisions. He also served as a member of the building committee for the J.V. Fletcher Library.

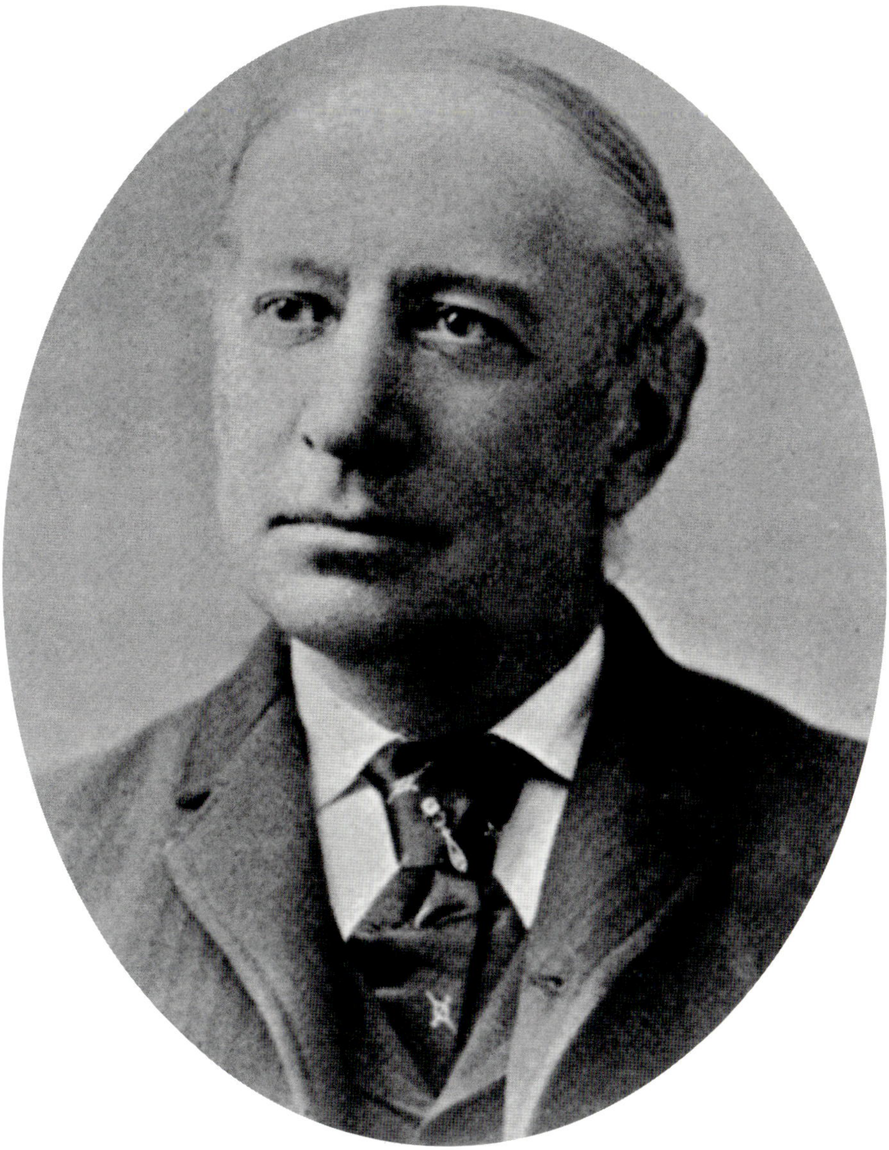

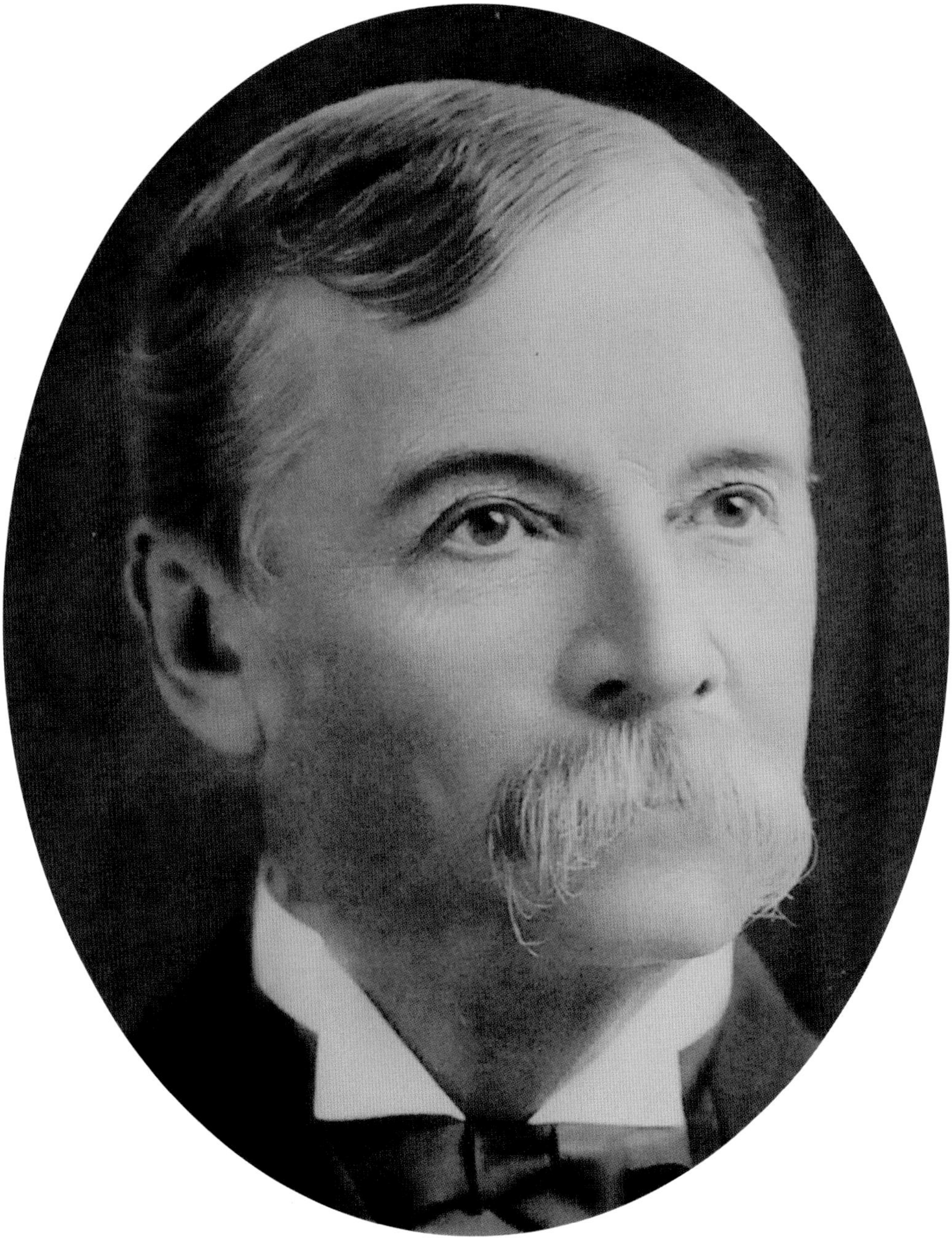

William Edwin Frost
Frost (1842–1904) was born in Norway, Maine. He received his education at Norway Liberal Institute, Maine Wesleyan Seminary, and Edward Little Institute. He graduated from Bowdoin College in 1870. He served as a corporal in Company H, 23rd Regiment, Maine Volunteers during the Civil War, and later served as president of the Westford Veteran's Association. He was chairman of the trustees of the J.V. Fletcher Library and a member of the building committee of the J.V. Fletcher Library. He is best known as the longtime preceptor of Westford Academy (1872–1904). Frost Elementary School, erected in 1908, was named in his memory.

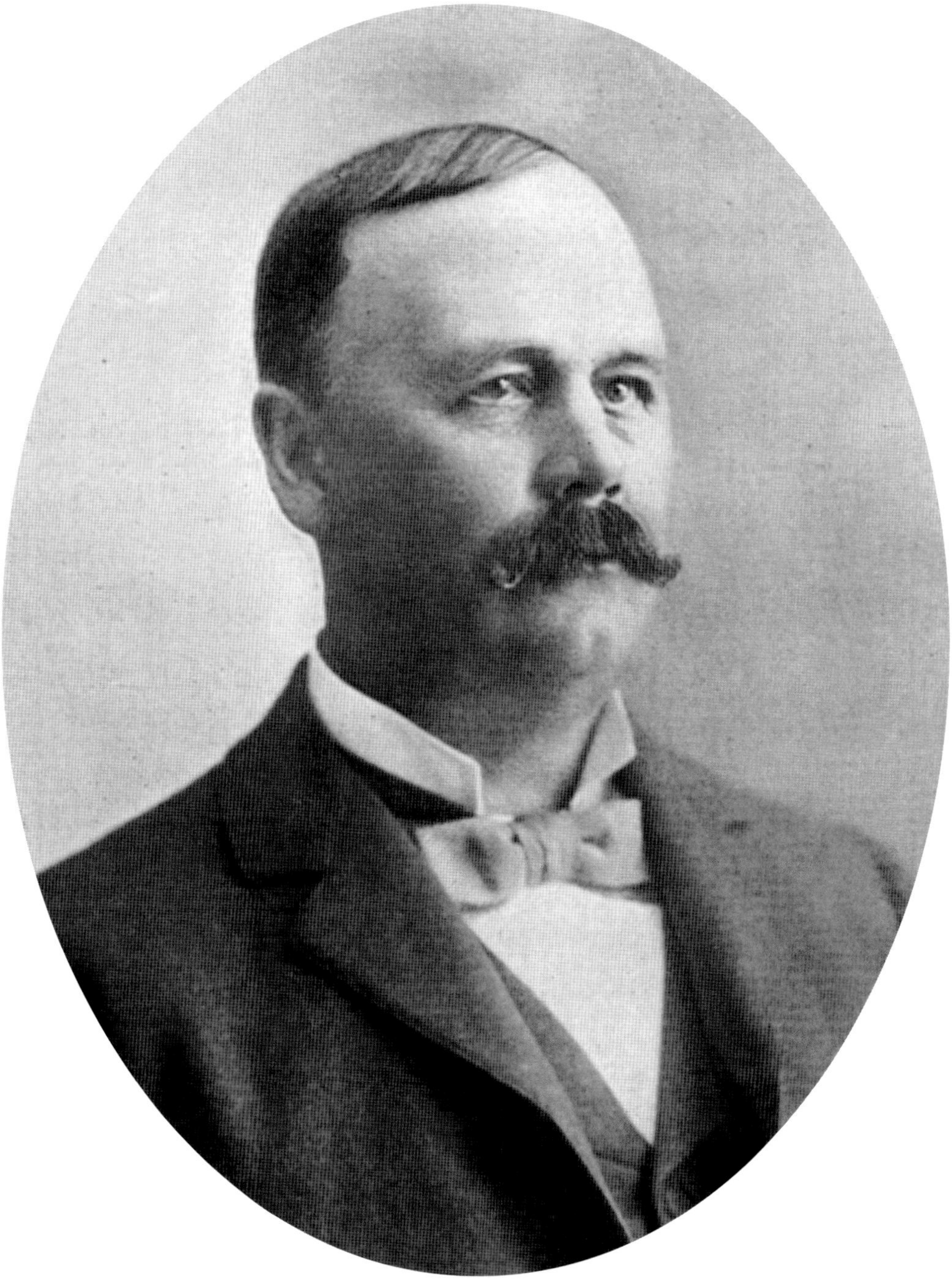

Albert Pierce Richardson
Richardson (1843–1903) was born in Jaffrey, New Hampshire. He received his education at Westford Academy and served in Troop F Cavalry, Massachusetts Volunteer Militia. He served as a selectman in Westford from 1879 until 1891. He held many positions in town, including inspector of animals and provisions and superintendent of burial grounds. He also served on the building committee of the J.V. Fletcher Library. He made his living as an undertaker and as a farmer.

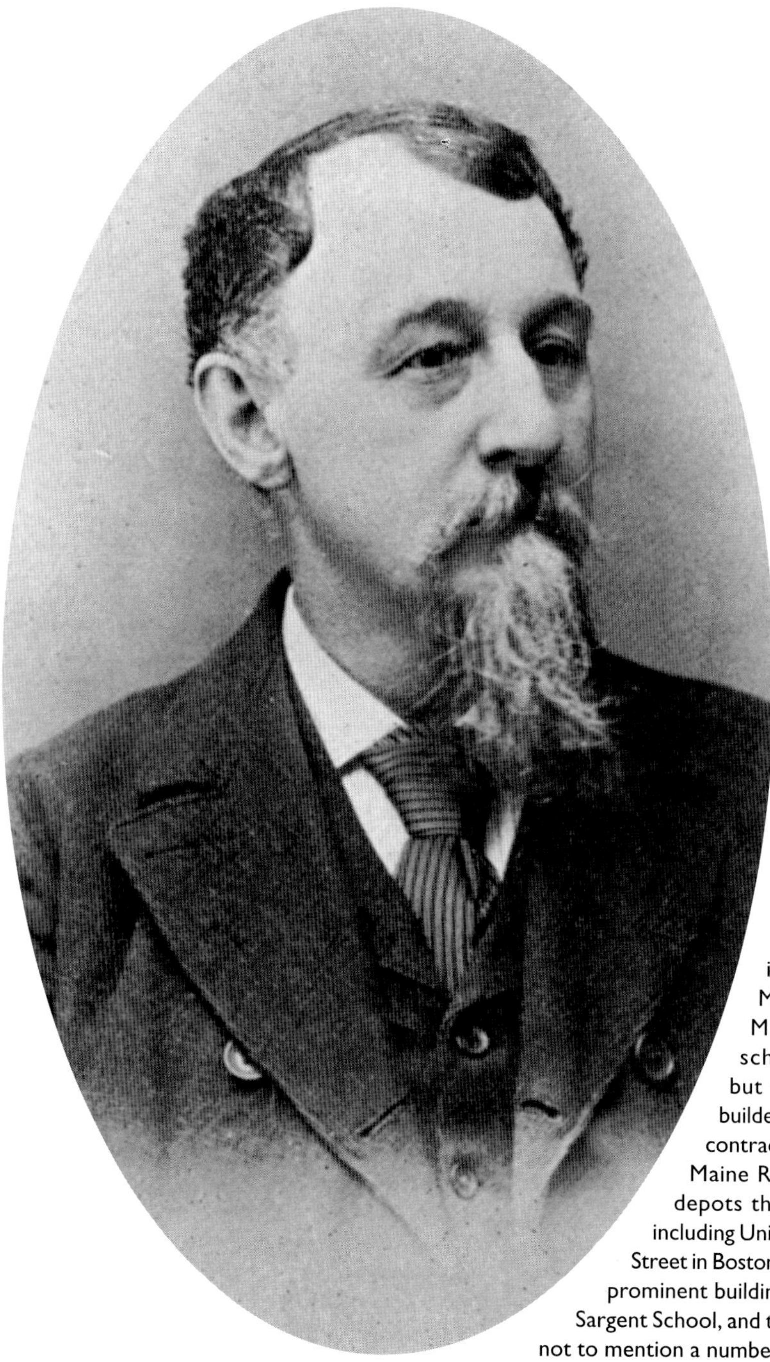

William C. Edwards

Edwards (1845–1929) was born in Westford and served 12 years in Troop F Cavalry, Massachusetts Volunteer Militia. He served as a school committeeman, but was best known as a builder and contractor. While contracted with the Boston & Maine Railroad, he built many depots throughout the system, including Union Depot on Causeway Street in Boston. Locally, he built several prominent buildings, including town hall, Sargent School, and the J.V. Fletcher Library, not to mention a number of Westford homes.

Sherman Heywood Fletcher

Fletcher (1846–1928) was born in Westford and attended Westford Academy. He made his living as a member of the firm of the Wright & Fletcher General Store in Westford, but like many townspeople of the time, he spent several years serving in public capacities. Among his positions were the following: member of Troop F Cavalry, Massachusetts Volunteer Militia from 1864 to 1888; captain of the troop from May 1877 to 1888; representative to the Massachusetts Legislature in 1882; director of the public library from 1878 to 1879; town selectman starting in 1891; and member and chairman of the building committee of the J.V. Fletcher Library.

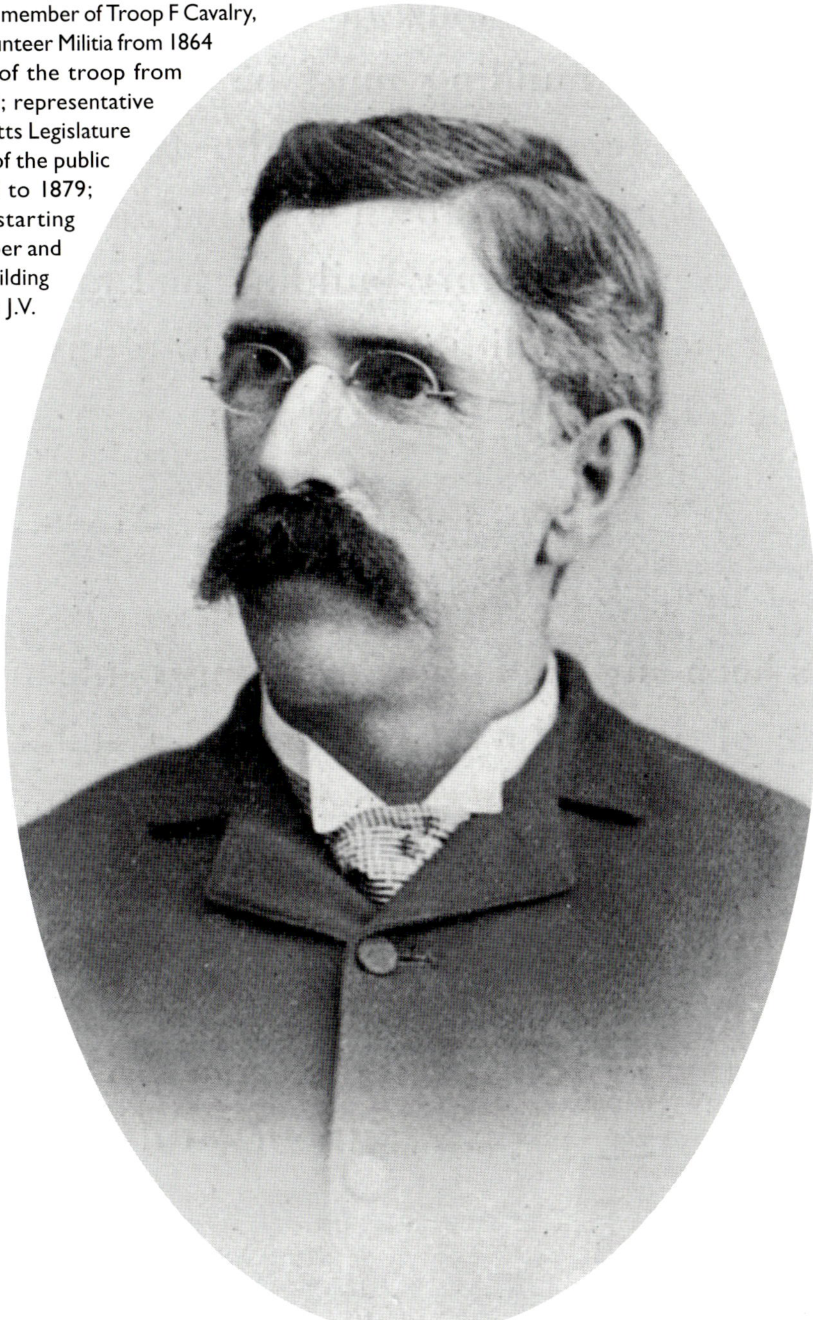

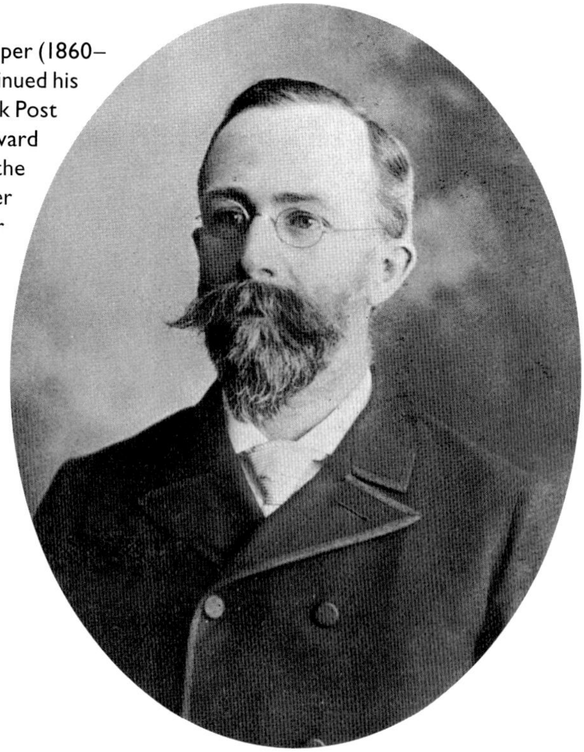

Walter Julian Sleeper, M.D.

A Manchester, New Hampshire, native, Sleeper (1860–1908) was educated in Manchester and continued his education at Dartmouth College, New York Post Graduate Medical College, and finally Harvard University. He served as the secretary of the Westford School Committee and as a member of the building committee of the J.V. Fletcher Library. He made his living as a practicing physician and surgeon in Westford.

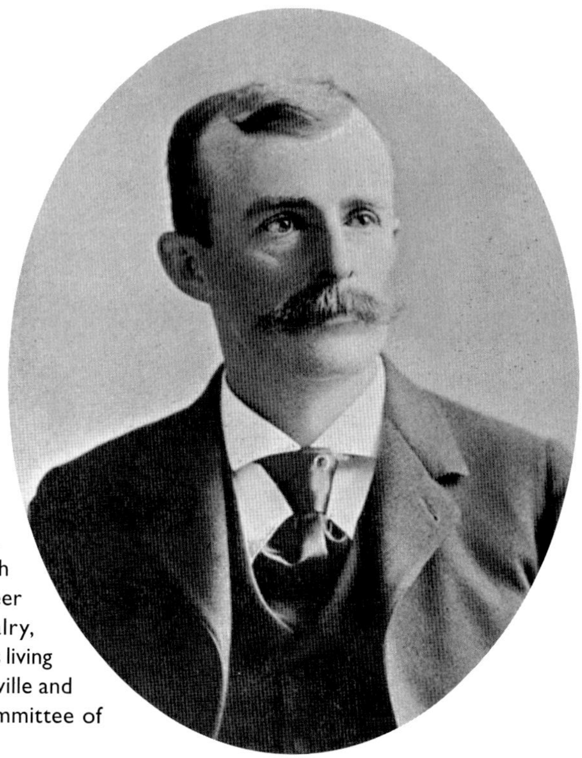

Herbert Victor Hildreth

Hildreth (1863–1934) was born in Westford and received his secondary education at Westford Academy. He went on to attend the Massachusetts Institute of Technology. He served as a lieutenant in Company L, 8th Regiment of Infantry, Massachusetts Volunteer Militia, and a sergeant in Troop F Cavalry, Massachusetts Volunteer Militia. He made his living as a granite dealer at the quarry in Graniteville and served as the secretary of the building committee of the J.V. Fletcher Library.

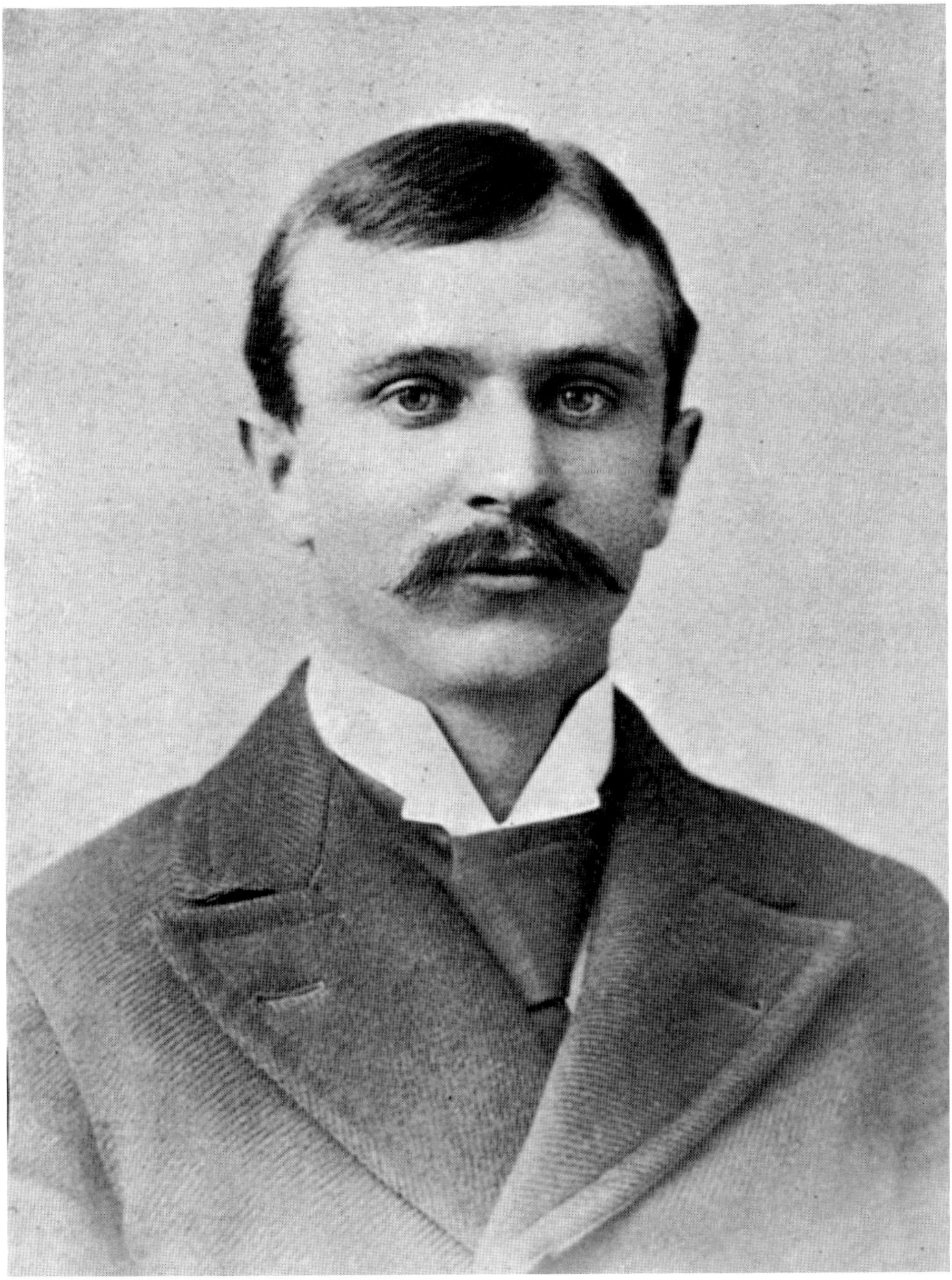

Julian Abbot Cameron

Cameron (1866–1949), born in Westford, attended Westford Academy and continued his education at the Massachusetts Institute of Technology. He made his living as superintendent and, in 1900, president of the Abbot Mills at Forge Village and also as manager of the Sugden Press Bagging Company in Chelmsford, Massachusetts. He served as a member of the board of selectmen and on the building committee of the J.V. Fletcher Library.

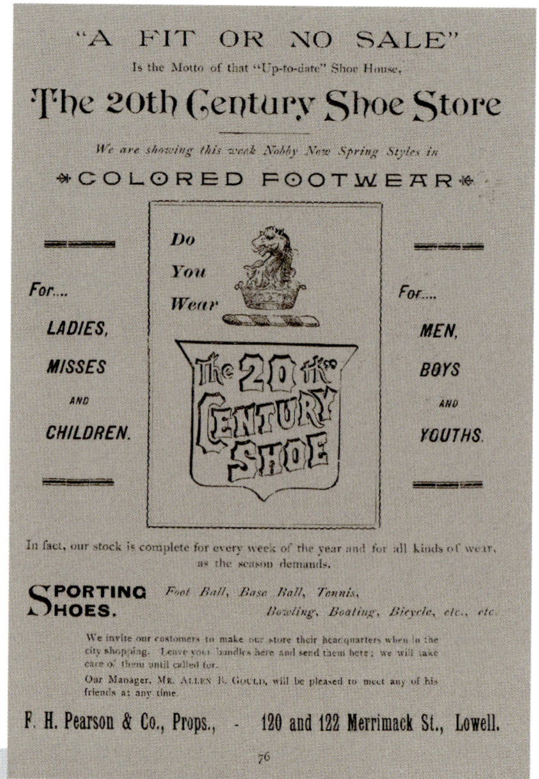

Advertising
These advertisements are a sampling of the ones used to fund the publication of the library dedication pamphlet and are examples of the advertising of the period. These advertisements for the 20th Century Shoe Store and Putnam & Son Men's Wear in neighboring Lowell, Massachusetts, were located at the back of the publication.

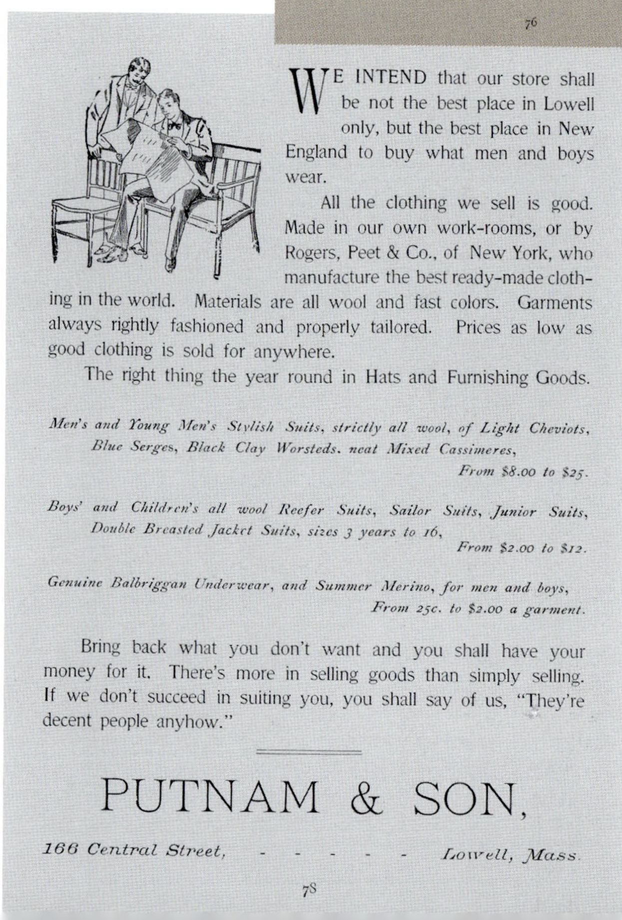

CHAPTER FOUR

The Authors, Athletes, and Artists

Perhaps it is the well-preserved, picturesque atmosphere in Westford, or perhaps it is the community-minded nature of the people who live here. Whatever the reason, Westford seems to foster creativity and a striving for excellence. There is no shortage of historians, many of whom have been inspired to share their work with the community at large through their writing. June Kennedy, a 54-year resident, has dedicated many years to compiling stories that document the rich history of the town. Edgar Allan Poe, who spent time in Westford in 1848, was inspired by his relationship with a local girl to write a well-known poem. David Brody, a local real estate attorney, was motivated to begin writing in 1997 and has written five popular novels, using many local legends and topics as subject matter for his work. Westford has also been home to many nationally successful athletes. Olympic skier Pamela Fletcher got her start at Nashoba Valley Ski Area, her family's business located in Westford. Pat Bradley, LPGA Hall of Famer, got her start with her golfing family here in Westford. Many nationally renowned artists also got their start in Westford, including award-winning watercolor artist Andrew Kusmin and prolific painter William Millett, who continued his training in Paris and Venice. Whether authors, artists, athletes, or entertainers, it goes without saying that Westford has and continues to produce its share of creative genius.

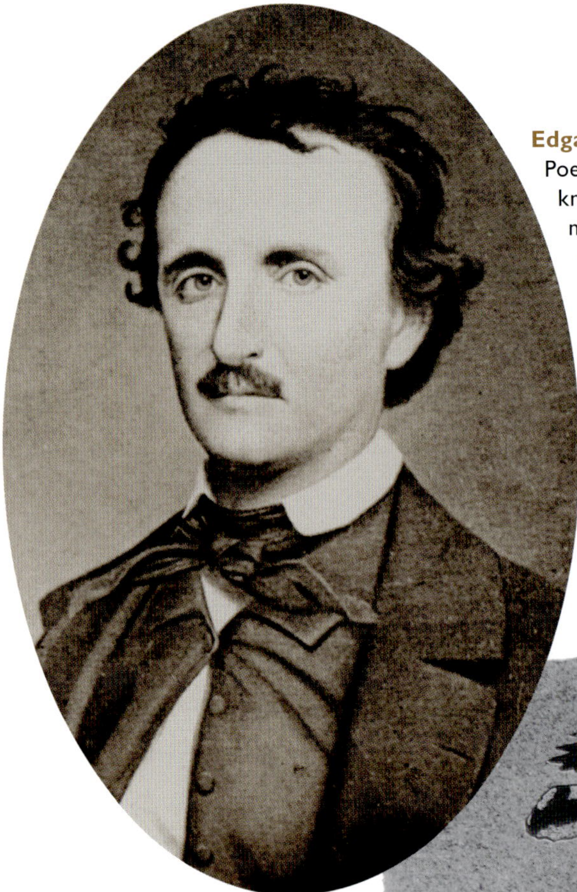

Edgar Allan Poe

Poe (1809–1849) was an American author best known for his grotesque tales of horror and mystery. A master of the short story, Poe was the first prominent American writer to support himself solely from his writing. While visiting Lowell, Massachusetts, Poe became friends with Nancy (Heywood) Richmond (1820–1898) of Westford. He came to stay in Westford for a short time in 1848 and 1849. It is said that his poem "For Annie" was written for Richmond. A marker commemorating his time in Westford is located at 11 Graniteville Road. (Left, courtesy of Library of Congress; below, Brian Herzog.)

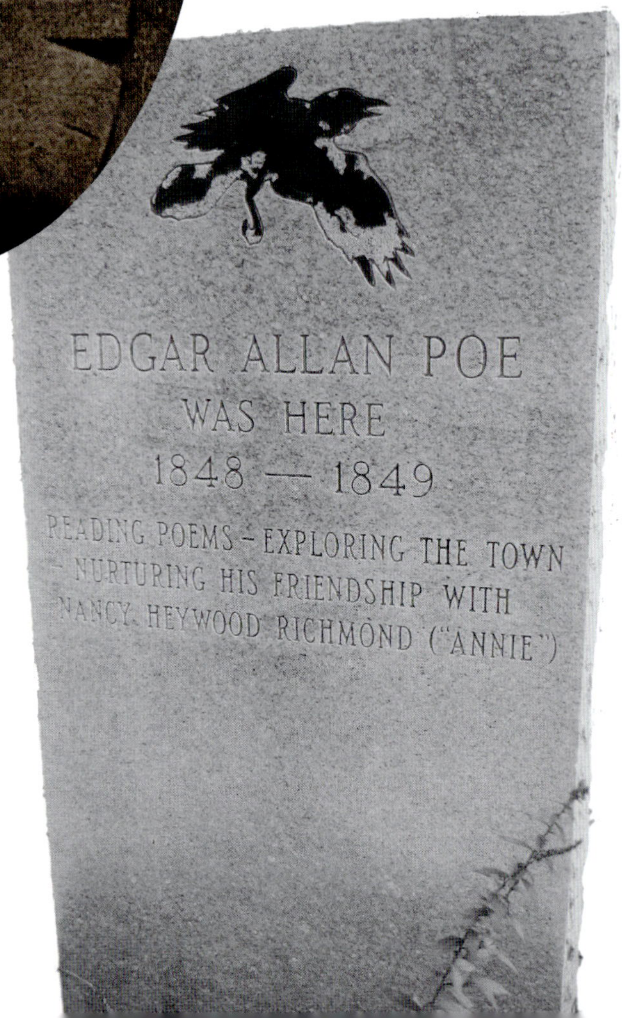

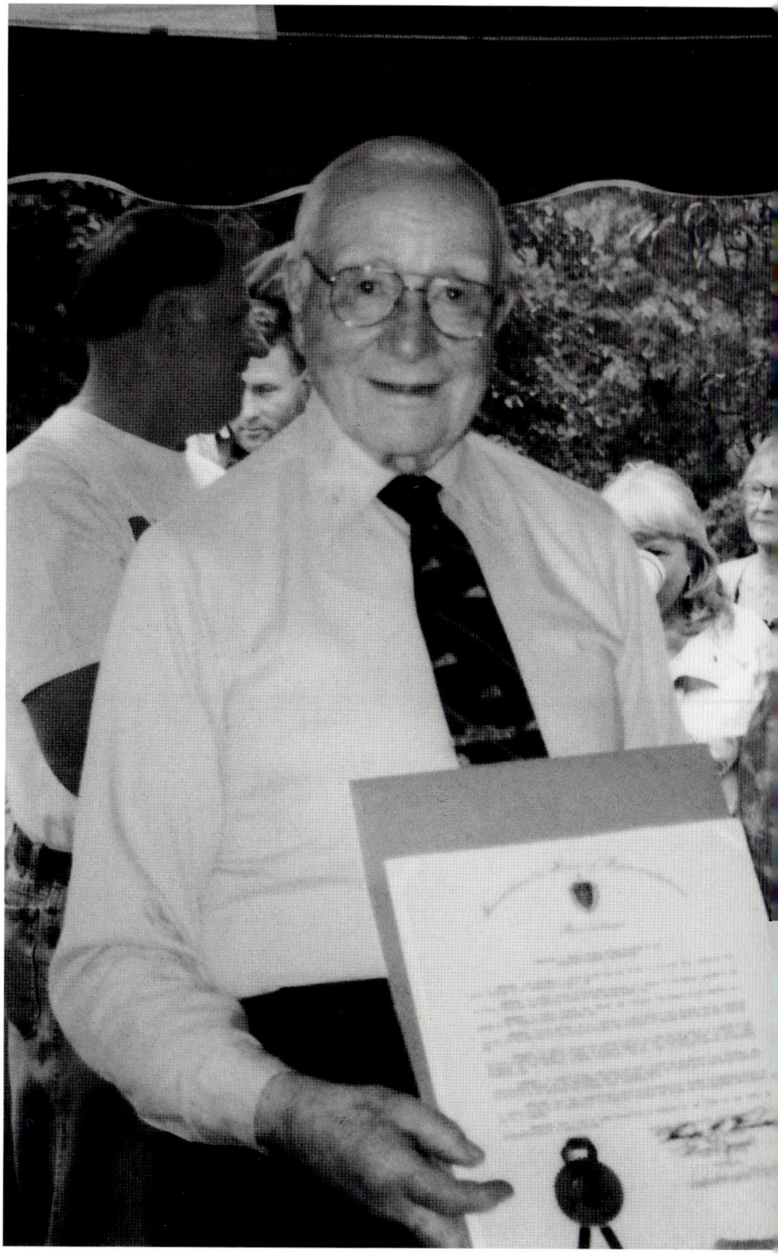

Henry Arnold Wilder
Wilder (1909–2009) moved to Westford in 1923 at the age of 14. A 1927 graduate of Westford Academy, he received his degree in mechanical engineering from Northeastern University in 1966. His local employment included jobs at the Wright & Fletcher General Store from 1928 to 1934 and the Abbot Worsted Company from 1935 to 1956. Wilder was known to be an expert on railroads in New England and wrote the definitive Westford railroad history. For being the oldest living Westford resident at the time, and for being what people described as a walking history book, he was honored by the Westford Kiwanis at the 41st Apple Blossom Festival. (Courtesy of George Fletcher.)

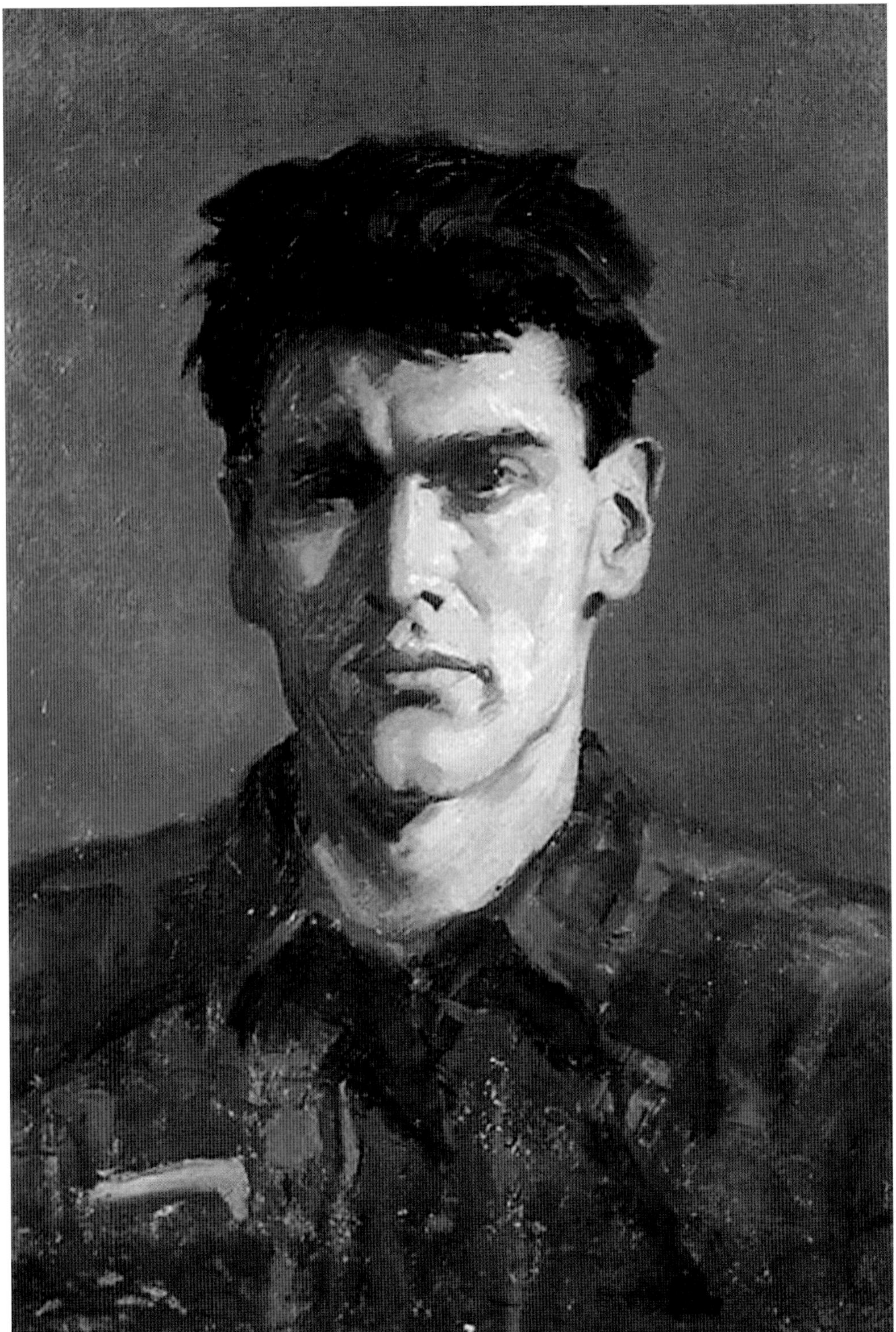

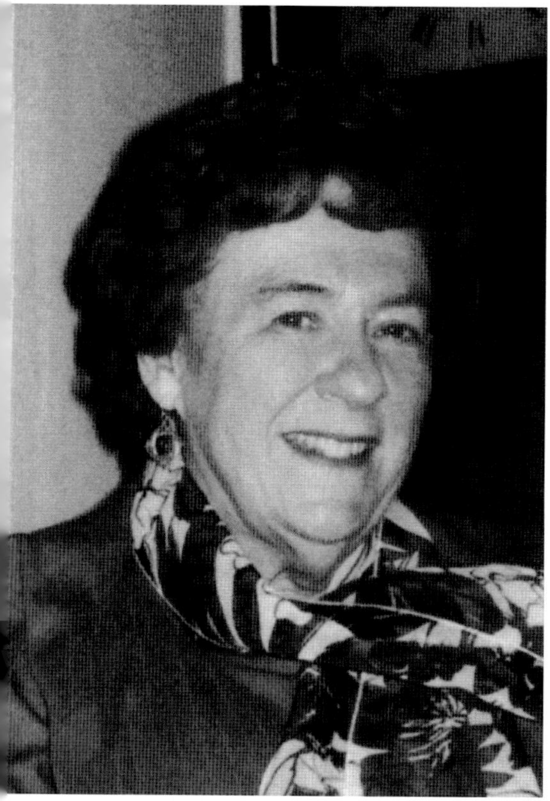

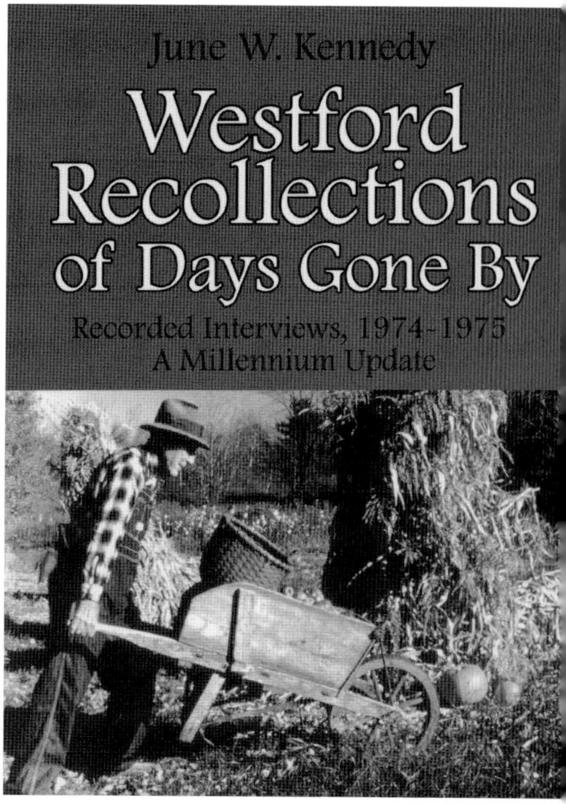

June Wilson Kennedy
Kennedy (1935–present) has been a resident of Westford since 1958. She is a local historian who has dedicated her life to preserving the history of Westford for future generations. Her passion has propelled her to document in writing Westford's rich history. She is the author of the book *Westford Recollections 1729–1979*, written for the town's 250th anniversary, and *Westford Recollections of Days Gone By*, a collection of interviews with Westford residents conducted in the 1970s. She serves as historian at the First Parish Church United, is a founder of the Westford Museum, and is founder of the Friends of Parkerville Schoolhouse. She and her husband, Charlie, were the recipients of the Massachusetts Historical Commission 2000 Preservation Award for 35 years of historic preservation efforts in Westford. (Courtesy of June Kennedy.)

William Millett (OPPOSITE PAGE)
Millett (1922–2007) was born in Brockton, Massachusetts. He attended the Scott Carbee School of Art and the Vesper George Art School in Boston. He studied under Aldro Hibbard in Rockport, Massachusetts, and with the painter Bernard M. Keyes and spent several years studying painting in Paris and Venice. While studying in Paris at the Academie Frochot, Millet lived in the studio of the famed Toulouse Lautrec. He exhibited his work at the Ross Gallery in Boston and the Parker Gallery, and spent time painting at the historic Fenway Studios. In the 1960s, he moved to his family home in Westford, where he continued to paint but declined to sell his work, instead choosing to maintain the pieces for his personal collection. Today, his sizable collection of works has been shown at the Parish Center for the Arts in Westford; individual pieces are available for sale. (Courtesy of Deborah Stein Sharpe.)

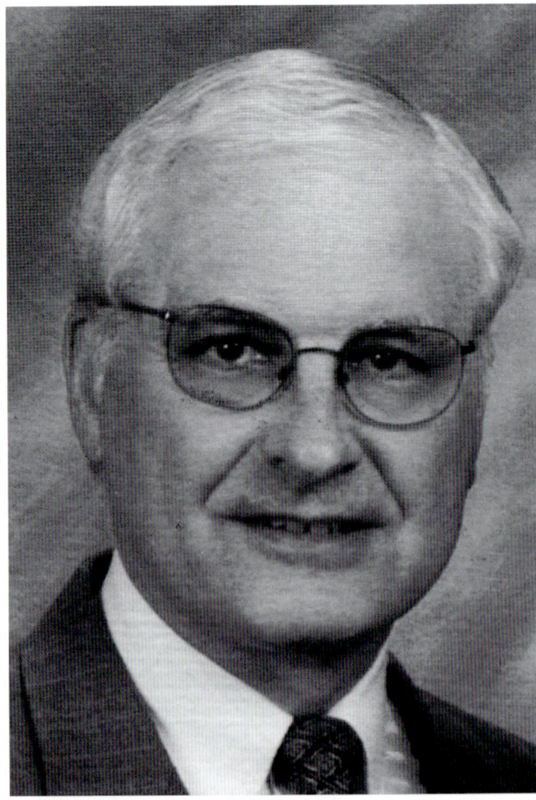

Dr. Robert Walter Oliphant
Oliphant (1942–present) was born in Oberlin, Ohio, and moved to Westford in 1977. He received his bachelor of science degree and master of science degree in metallurgy from Case Institute of Technology and his doctorate in metallurgy from Case Western Reserve University in 1969. He worked as director of business development and as program manager for BBN Technologies before his retirement in 2006. Oliphant's contributions to the preservation of Westford's history and local genealogy are many. He has served as vice president for the Westford Historical Commission, historian for the United Methodist Church of Westford, as a member of Westford's Records and Archives Management Committee, and as a member and board member of the Westford Museum and Historical Society. He and his wife, Bonnie, have served as board members of the Friends of Parkerville Schoolhouse. His contributions in those capacities are numerous, but arguably his most visible work on behalf of the history of Westford is his publication of the *Westford Gazetteer, A History of Westford, Massachusetts In Its Place Names*. Oliphant also writes the weekly "Museum Musings" column in the *Westford Eagle* newspaper, which features extracts of historic items from the *Westford Wardsman* of a century ago. (Courtesy of Dr. Robert Oliphant.)

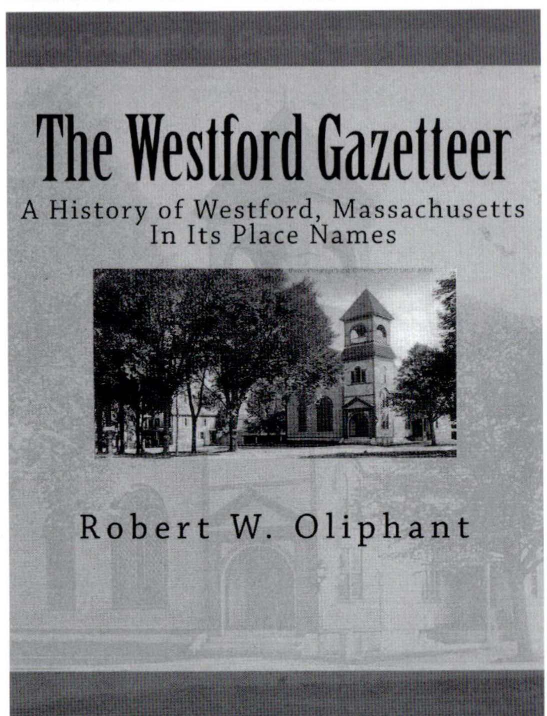

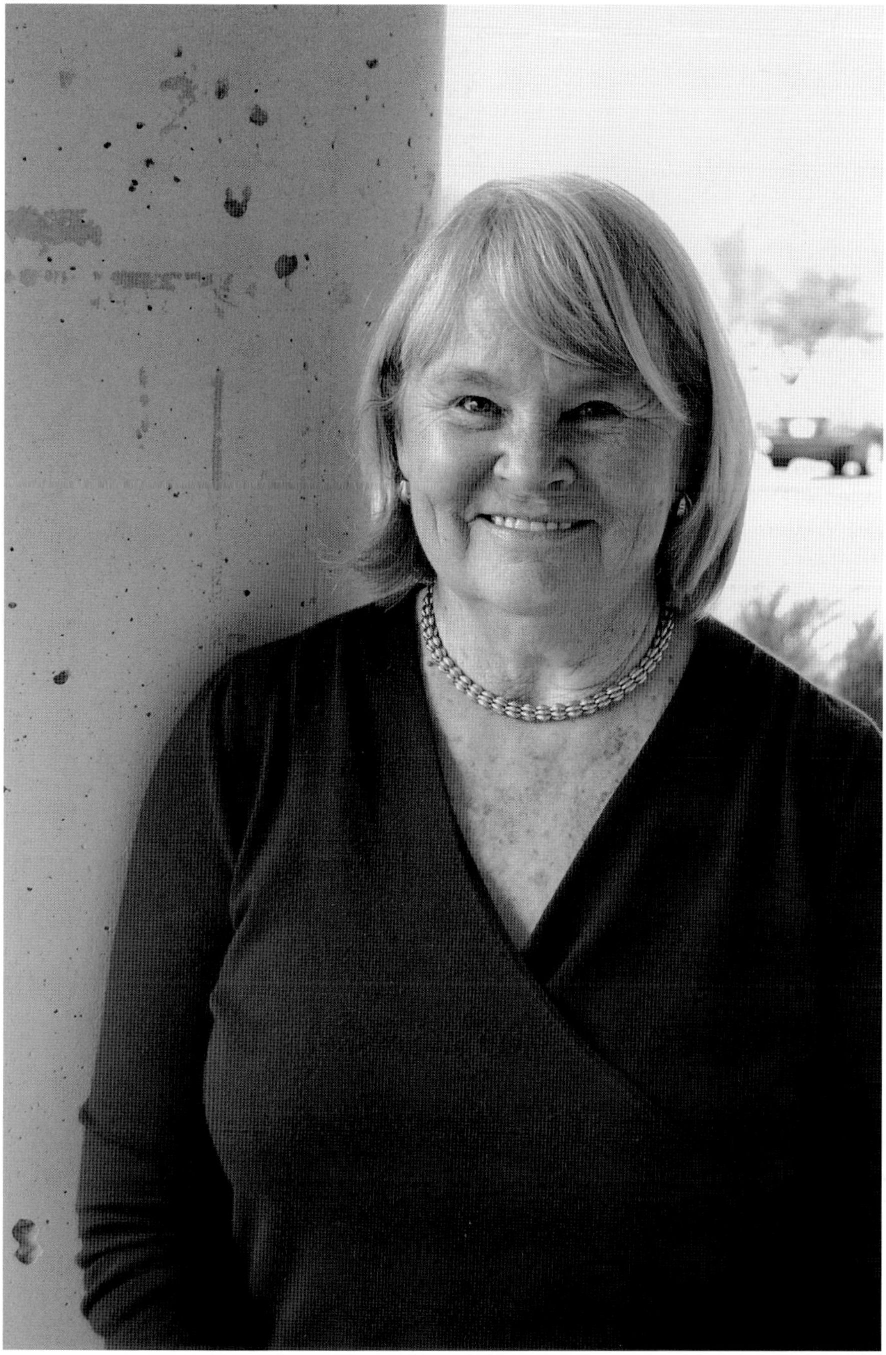

Nancy Russo
Russo (1944–present) was born in West Barnstable and moved to Westford in 1978. She got her start as an artist in 1973 and developed into not only a well-known watercolor artist, but also a popular art teacher. She taught for many years at the Roudenbush Community Center, giving many new artists their start, including nationally renowned painter Andrew Kusmin. (Author's collection.)

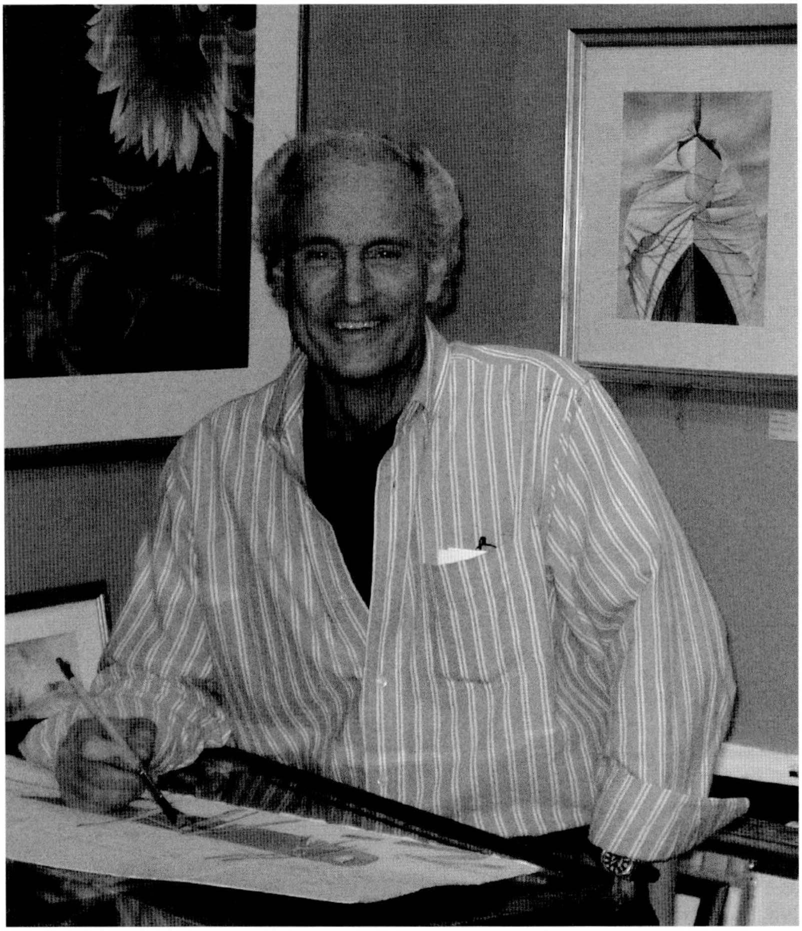

Andrew Kusmin

Born in Quincy and raised in Plymouth, Massachusetts, Kusmin (1945–present) is a 1963 graduate of Bates College and a 1971 graduate of Tufts University School of Dental Medicine. Following two years in the Navy, Kusmin and his family settled in Westford, where he opened his dental practice. Restoring a Colonial-era farmhouse at 72 Main Street as a residence and the barn as a dental office, he discovered a passion for both preserving Westford's history and contributing to the growth of the community. In nearly three decades of residence in Westford, he restored three additional historic buildings: 20 Boston Road (School House No. 1 and the Tadmuck Club); 40 Main Street (Wright and Fletcher General Store); and 38 Main Street (residence). He was instrumental in the revitalization, restoration, and governance of the Roudenbush Community Center and the Parish Center for the Arts. While working in many capacities for the development of the Roudenbush Community Center, he was led to take his first art class there. This awakened a passion in him that drew him to his second career, as a full-time artist and teacher. Although his work, widely exhibited, garnered over 90 local and national awards, he remained committed to public service through working with numerous Massachusetts art organizations, serving as president of the New England Watercolor Society, and teaching painting. After returning to Plymouth, Massachusetts, in 2000, he opened his own gallery, continued historic restorations and, in 2007, founded the Plymouth Center for the Arts. Kusmin feels the Westford community gave him the experience and confidence to move forward with these projects. His mark can be seen through the revitalized historic structures and the many paintings that remain in public and private collections. (Courtesy of Kusmin Art.)

Pat Bradley

Bradley (1951–present) was born in Westford and is a 1969 graduate of Westford Academy. Raised in a golfing family, she was the 12th woman to be inducted into the LPGA Hall of Fame. Bradley competed in 627 tournaments, garnering 312 top-10 finishes and 208 top-five finishes. She shattered top earnings records for women, bringing in over $2 million in 1986, $3 million in 1990, and $4 million in 1991. She was the first woman to win all four major golf championships. She retired in 1995 and has had the pleasure of watching her nephew Keegan Bradley turn professional in 2008 and win the PGA Championship in 2011. He was also named PGA Tour Rookie of the Year. (Courtesy of Associated Press.)

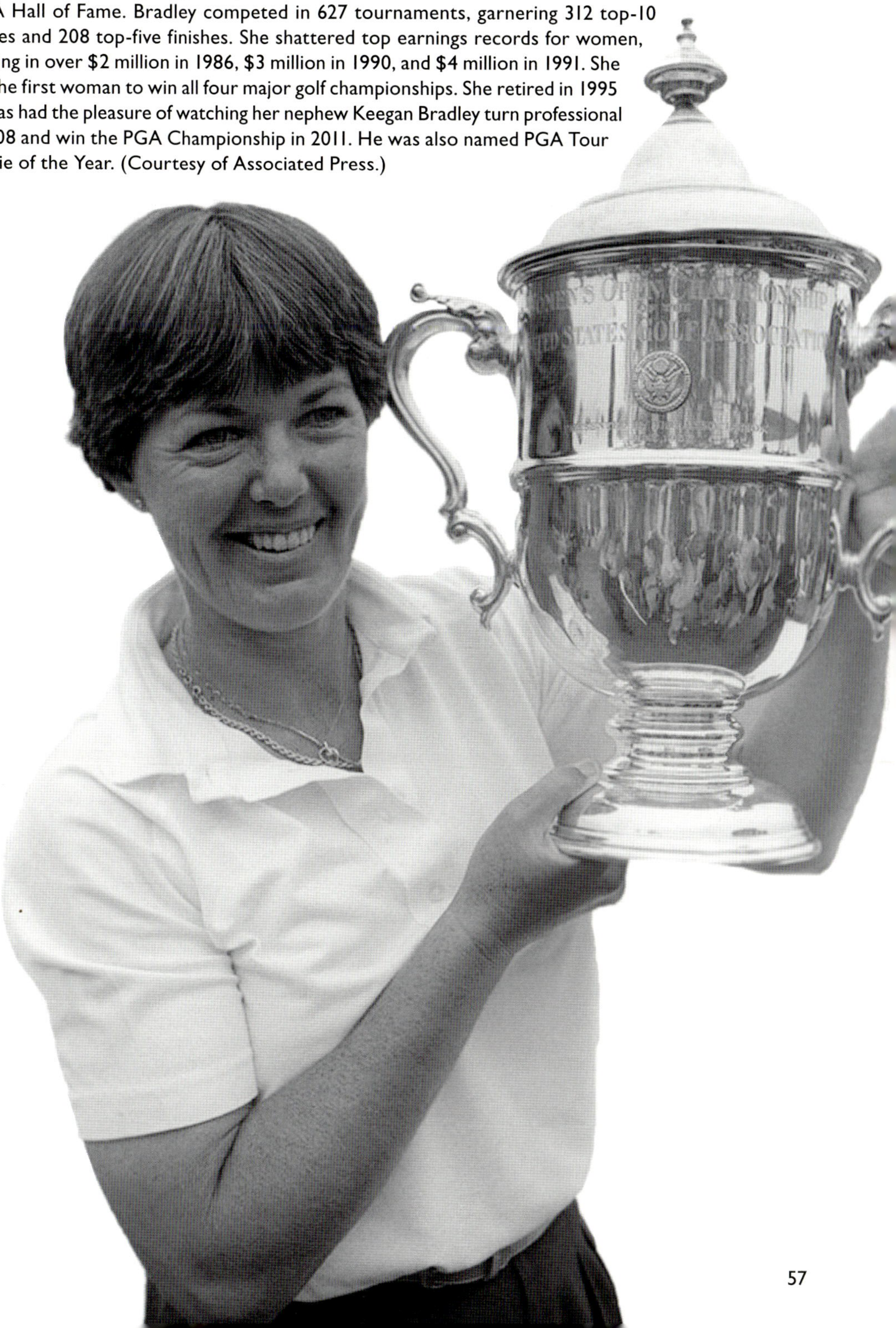

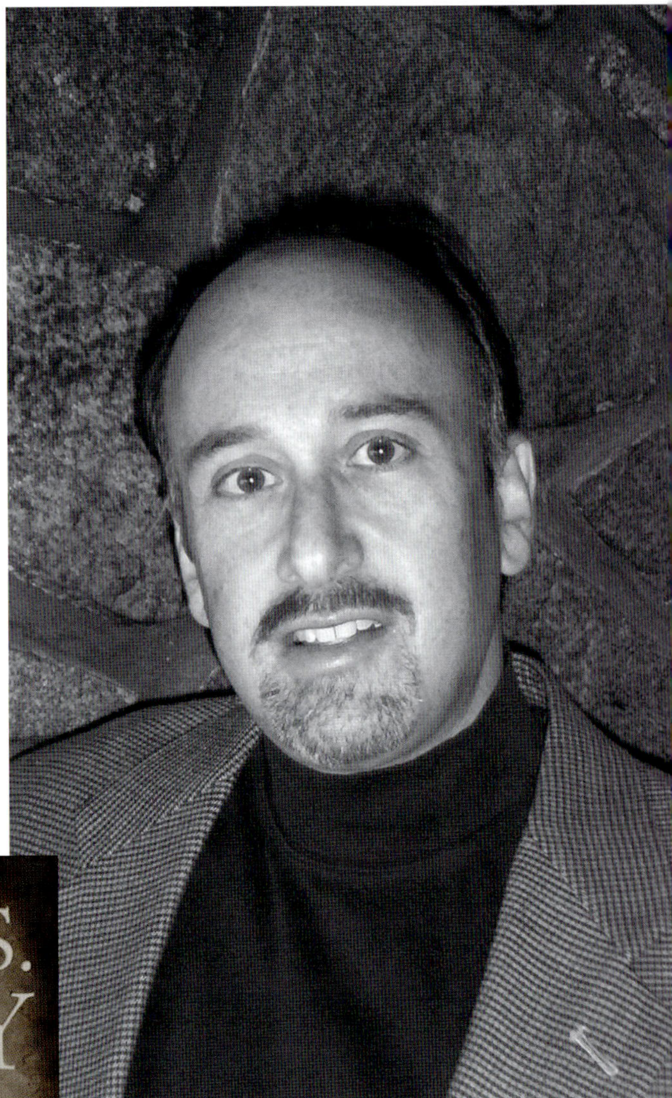

David Brody
Brody (1962–present) was born and raised in Laconia, New Hampshire, and moved to Westford in 1998. He graduated from Tufts University and received a law degree from Georgetown Law School, going on to practice real estate law. He began writing in 1997 and has published five novels. He was recognized as Best Local Author by the *Boston Phoenix* in 2003. His works include *Unlawful Deeds* (best seller), *Blood of the Tribe, The Wrong Abraham, Cabal of the Westford Knight* (best seller), and *Thief on the Cross.* He has served as director of the New England Antiquities Research Association and is widely considered an expert on pre-Columbian exploration in New England. In typical Westford fashion, Brody is active in his community, coaching youth sports and working with the Special Olympics. (Courtesy of David Brody.)

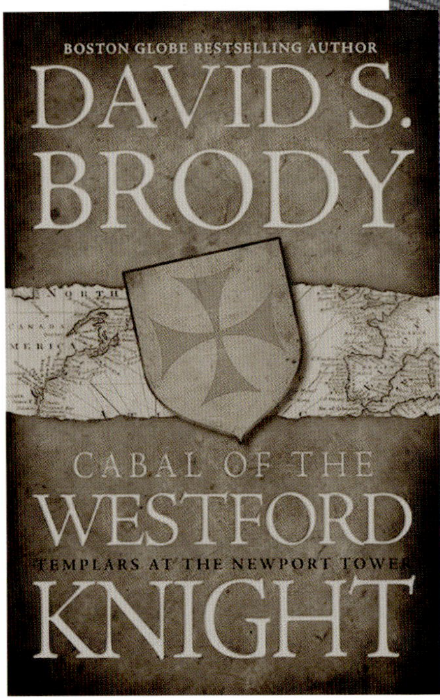

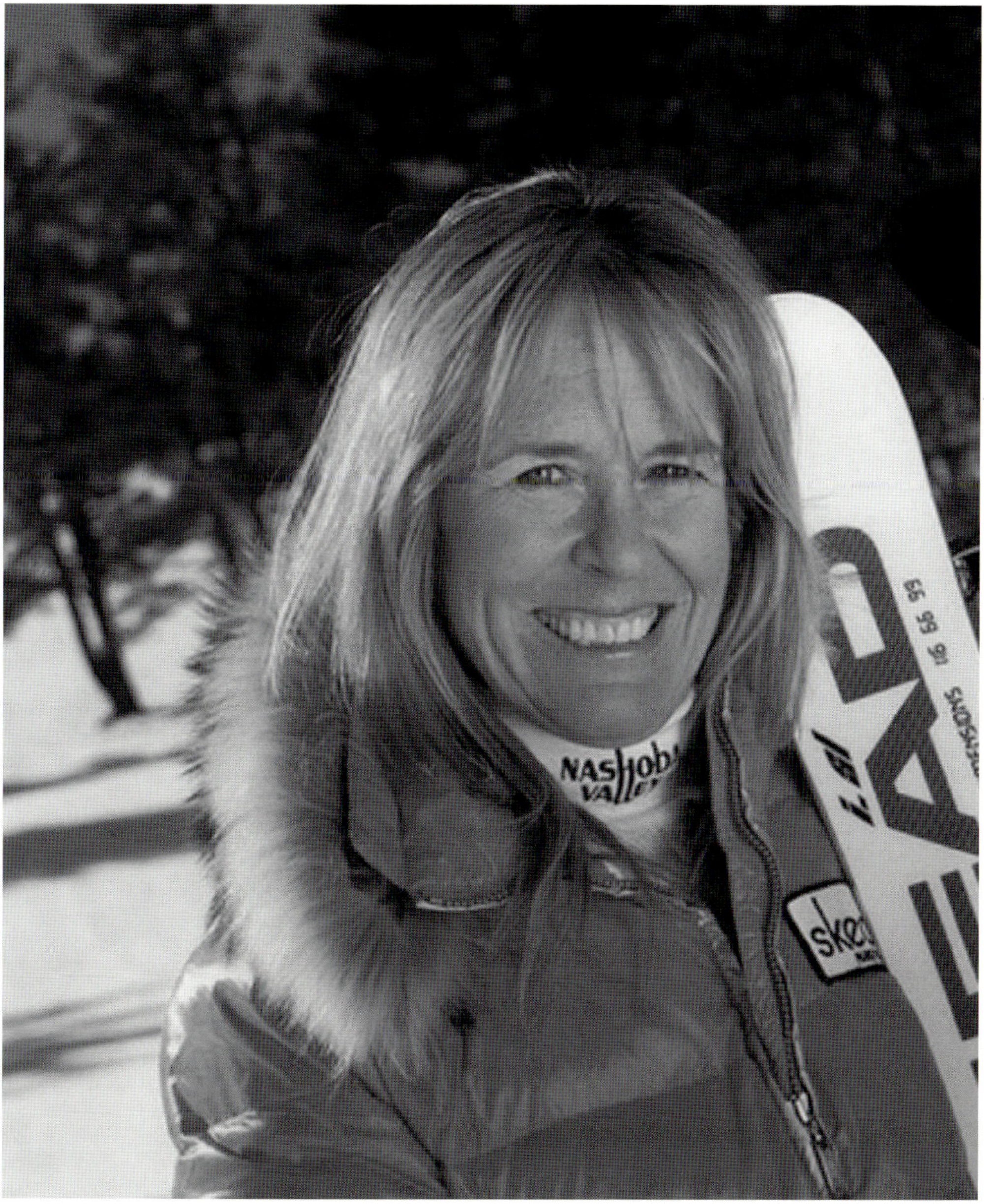

Pamela Fletcher

Fletcher (1963–present) is a nine-year US Ski Team veteran and represented the United States at the 1988 Winter Olympics in Calgary, where she was a favorite to win a medal in Alpine skiing. Although a freak accident shattered her leg and her hopes for an Olympic medal, she was named Outstanding Competitor of the Year by the US Ski Writers Association. In 1988, she began her career in broadcasting, covering skiing events for ABC, CBS, NBC, FOX Sports, and the Outdoor Life Network, going on to host *New England Living* on the WB and TV38 in Boston. Fletcher's life continues to revolve around the slopes, as she hosts corporate ski outings and gives motivational speeches telling her story to audiences across the nation. She currently serves as events marketing and sales manager for Nashoba Valley Ski Area, which was founded by her father, Alan Fletcher Sr. (Courtesy of Pam Fletcher.)

Aaron Stanford

Stanford (1976–present) was born in Westford, graduated from Westford Academy in 1995, and went on to graduate magna cum laude from Rutgers University's Mason Gross School of the Arts in 2000. In his first major role, he played Oscar Grubman opposite Sigourney Weaver in the independent film *Tadpole* (2002), a role for which he was nominated for the Golden Satellite Award. He appeared on the television series *Third Watch* as Sergei, a Russian teenager. Stanford was named one of the "Top Ten Actors to Watch" by *Daily Variety* in 2002. He is best known for his role as Pyro in the 2003 film *X2*, based on the Marvel Comics *X-Men*, and his continuation of the role in the 2006 film *X-Men: The Last Stand*. As of the publication of this book, he has a current ongoing role as the techie Seymour Birkhoff on the CW television series *Nikita*. (Courtesy of Aaron Stanford.)

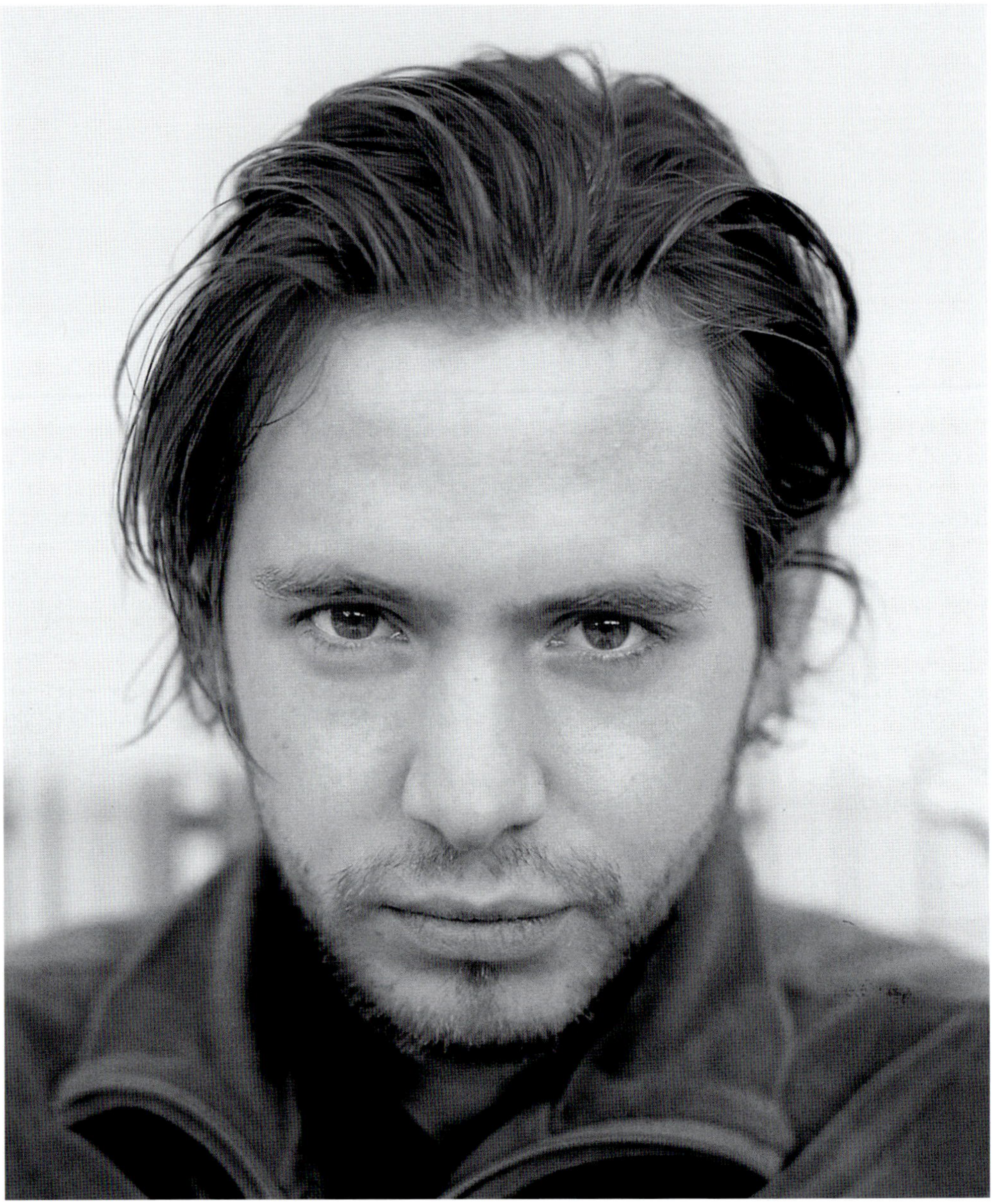

CHAPTER FIVE

The People Who Serve

Public service has been a hallmark of life in Westford since before its founding in 1729. The town has produced many state legislators and military leaders, and countless residents have stepped up to serve in leadership roles in town government. What makes Westford truly unique is the large number of people who give of their time without compensation. An army of volunteers weaves together to form the fabric of Westford. Over 300 locals left home to serve during the Civil War, solidifying Westford's place in the events that formed a young nation. After serving on the local level for nine years, Geoffrey Hall went on to serve in the Massachusetts House of Representatives for 18 years. Ellen Harde, town moderator and 45-year resident, has earned the nickname "Mayor of Westford" due to her many years of volunteer service and innovation on behalf of the town she loves. Even the town's furry friends have stepped up to do their part to serve the residents. Cinder the Fire Dog served the local fire department for 14 years, acting as a liaison and public greeter to those visiting the center fire station. Whether serving the nation during times of war, representing the residents on many levels of government, or preserving the history of the town for future generations, countless people have answered the call to improve the community in which they live.

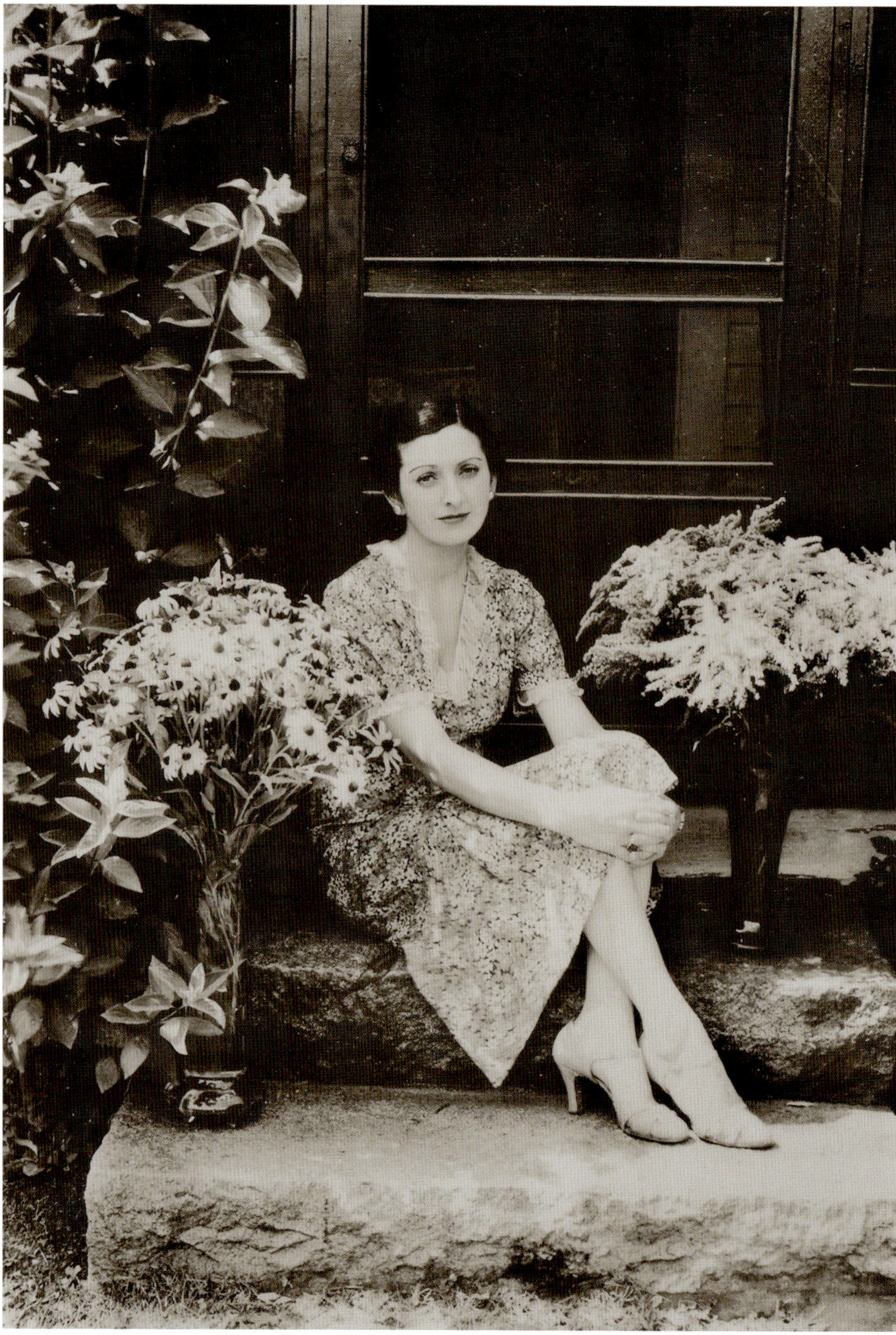

Alice Ann (Battersby) Hildreth
Hildreth (1905–1974), seen here on the steps of her home, served as the Westford town clerk. Her husband, Charles L. Hildreth (1879–1968), held the position prior, and upon his death in 1968, Alice assumed the role. She held the position and maintained the clerk's office in her home until her death in 1974.

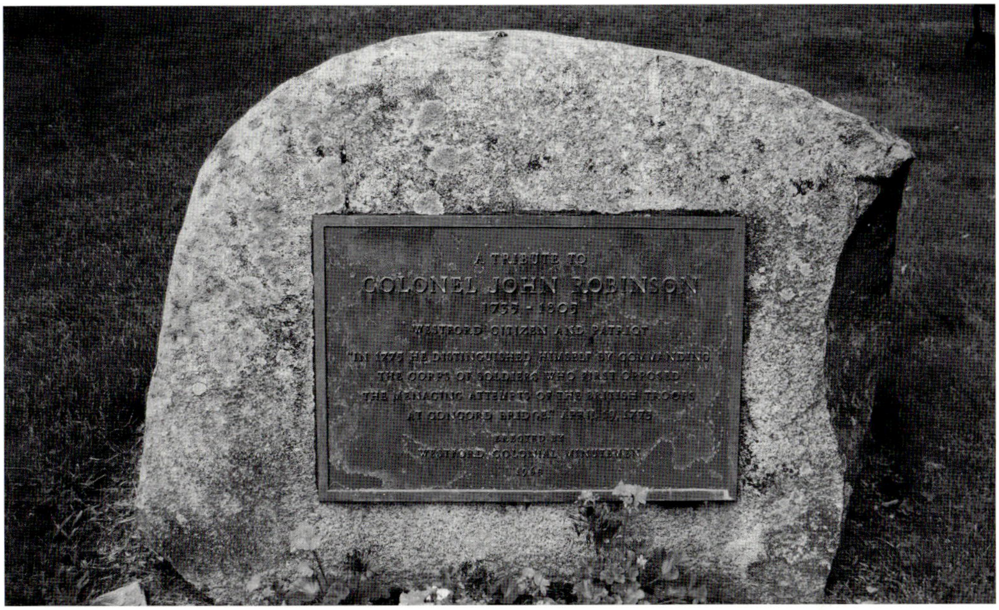

Col. John Robinson

Robinson (1735–1805) was born in Topsfield, Massachusetts, and moved to Westford in his twenties in search of open farmland. He was appointed lieutenant colonel with the Massachusetts militia and the Continental Army during the American Revolutionary War and was promoted to colonel in February 1776. Robinson was the highest ranking officer at the Battle of Concord but he relinquished command to Major Buttrick, as the majority of the troops present were from Buttrick's unit. Robinson also fought at the Battle of Bunker Hill, and served under Gen. George Washington during the Siege of Boston. A stone marking his service to the nation and placed by the Minutemen for the bicentennial in 1976 can be found on the town common. Another stone (see page 121) marks the site of his home on Robinson Road (seen in the bottom photograph), and the Col. John Robinson Elementary School was named in his honor.

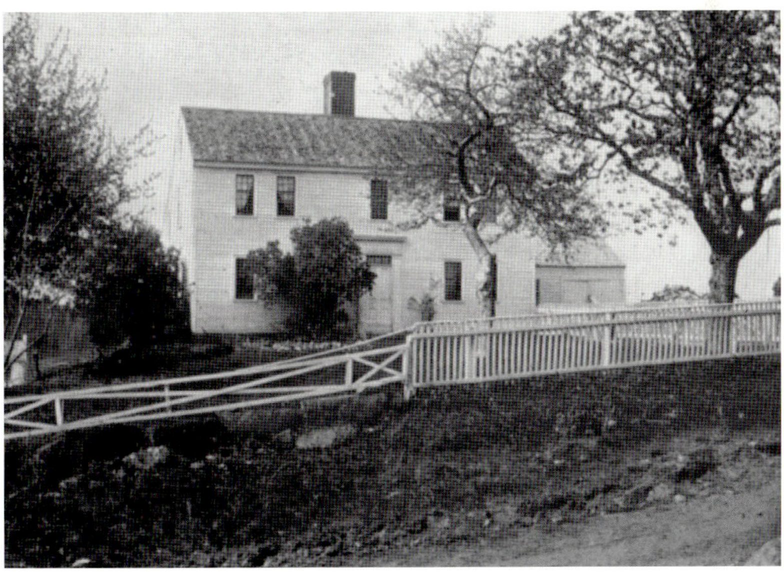

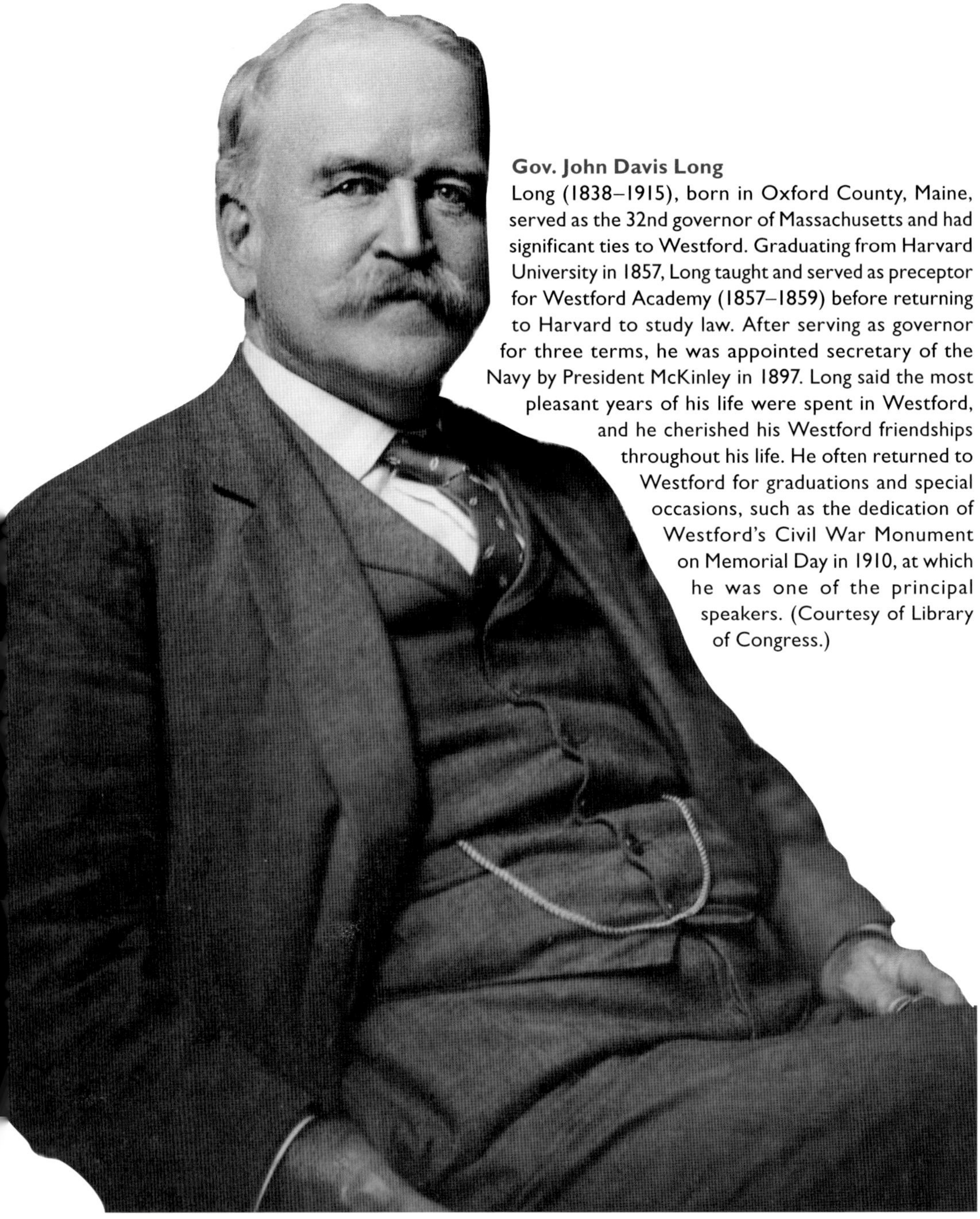

Gov. John Davis Long
Long (1838–1915), born in Oxford County, Maine, served as the 32nd governor of Massachusetts and had significant ties to Westford. Graduating from Harvard University in 1857, Long taught and served as preceptor for Westford Academy (1857–1859) before returning to Harvard to study law. After serving as governor for three terms, he was appointed secretary of the Navy by President McKinley in 1897. Long said the most pleasant years of his life were spent in Westford, and he cherished his Westford friendships throughout his life. He often returned to Westford for graduations and special occasions, such as the dedication of Westford's Civil War Monument on Memorial Day in 1910, at which he was one of the principal speakers. (Courtesy of Library of Congress.)

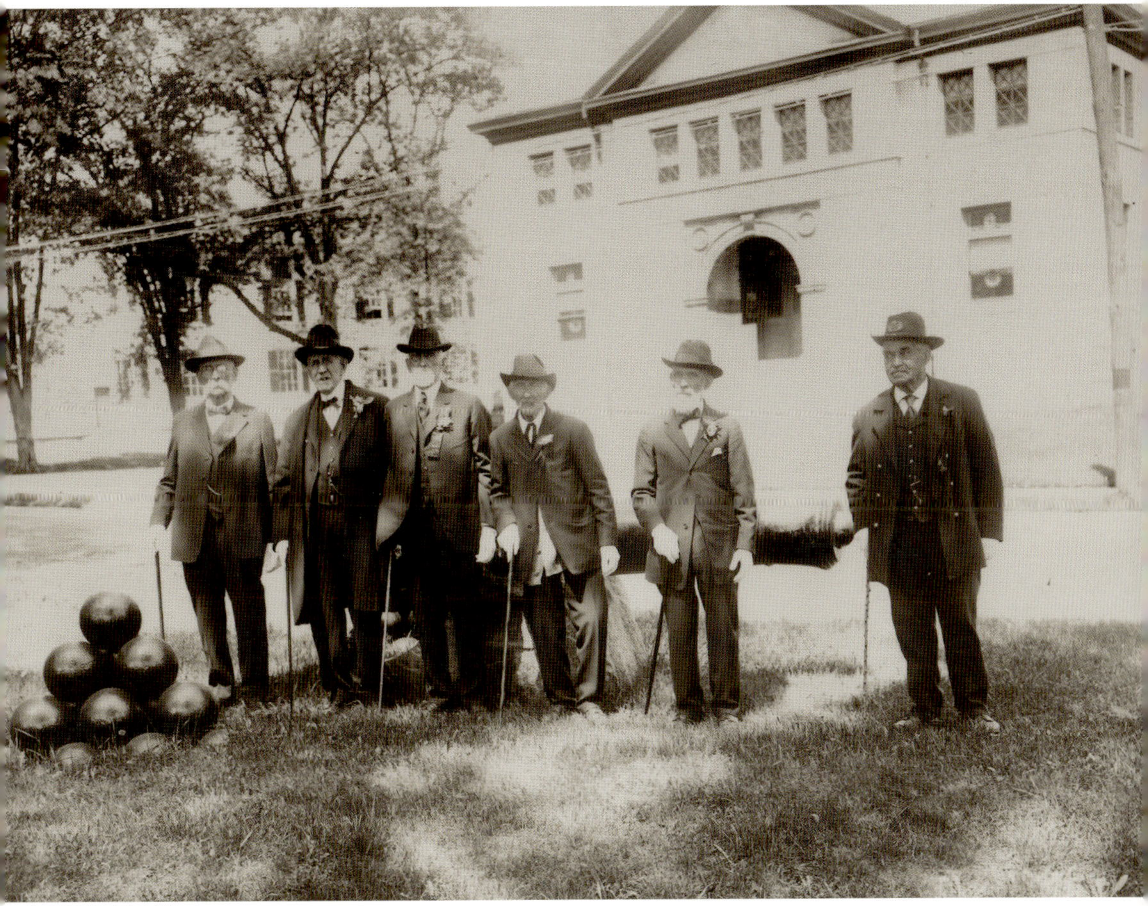

Civil War Veterans

Westford saw over 300 of its residents leave home to serve in the Civil War between 1861 and 1865. These six gentlemen, pictured around 1909, were among the surviving veterans after the turn of the century. In 1910, the Soldiers Monument was donated by Col. Edwin D. Metcalf, son of William Metcalf, formerly of Westford, who served as the only commissioned officer from the town in the Civil War.

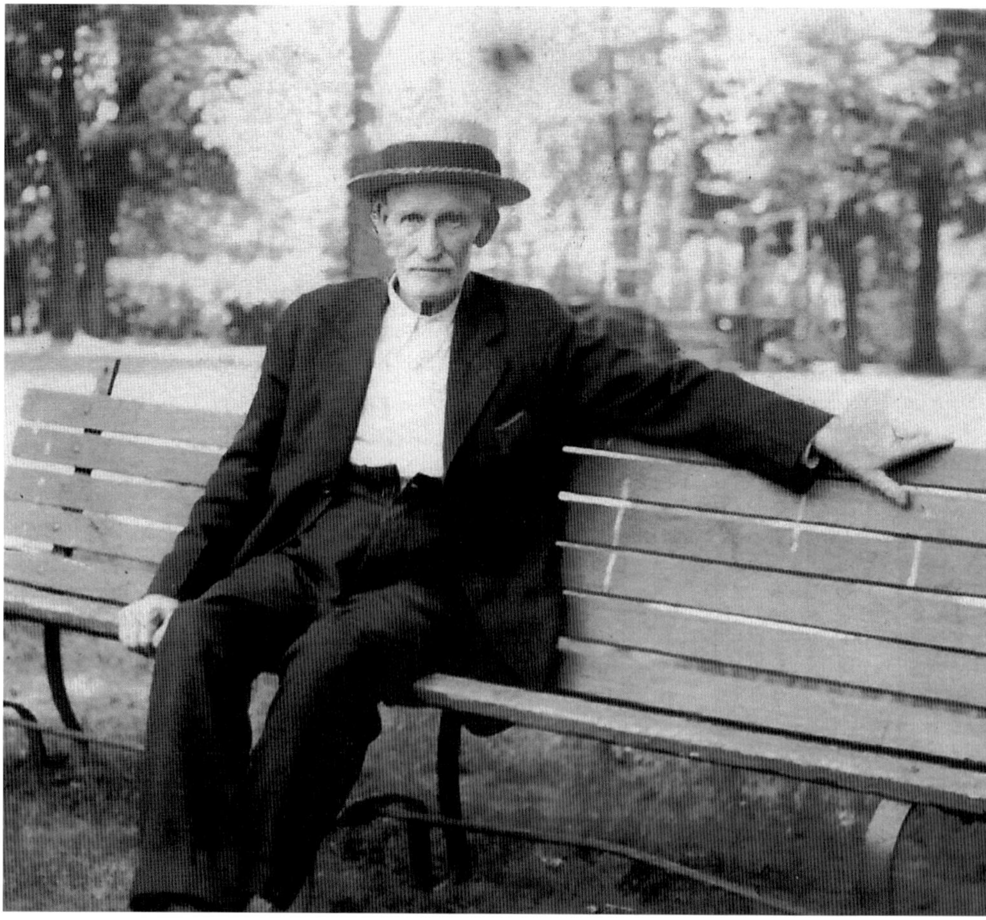

Joseph Willard Fletcher
Fletcher (1856–1936), seen here relaxing on a bench on the town common, was born in Almond, Wisconsin, but later relocated to Westford. Once settled here, he founded the Fletcher Farm, which employed four generations of Fletchers until its closing in the 1980s. Very active in the community, Fletcher served as a town assessor and was also the first Master of the Westford Grange, founded in 1895.

George Fletcher (OPPOSITE PAGE)
Fletcher (1933–present), a native of Westford, attended the Frost School, Westford Academy, and the University of Massachusetts, Stockbridge School of Agriculture. Fletcher is synonymous with public service in the town of Westford. He has held countless public and volunteer positions and continues to give back to the community he calls home. As a third-generation farmer, he ran his family's Stony Brook Dairy Farm, the last dairy farm in Westford, until its closing in 1989. He served with the Westford Fire Department for 43 years and held the position of deputy fire chief for over 20 years. He served as animal inspector, animal control officer, and the sealer of weights and measures. He was instrumental in the development of the town's master plan, served on the highway garage building committee, and served for three years on the board of selectman. He was a founding board member of the Westford Conservation Trust and served on the conservation commission for five years. In recent years, he has been working actively with the East Boston Camps and has served as a member of the East Boston Camps Master Plan Committee. (Author's collection.)

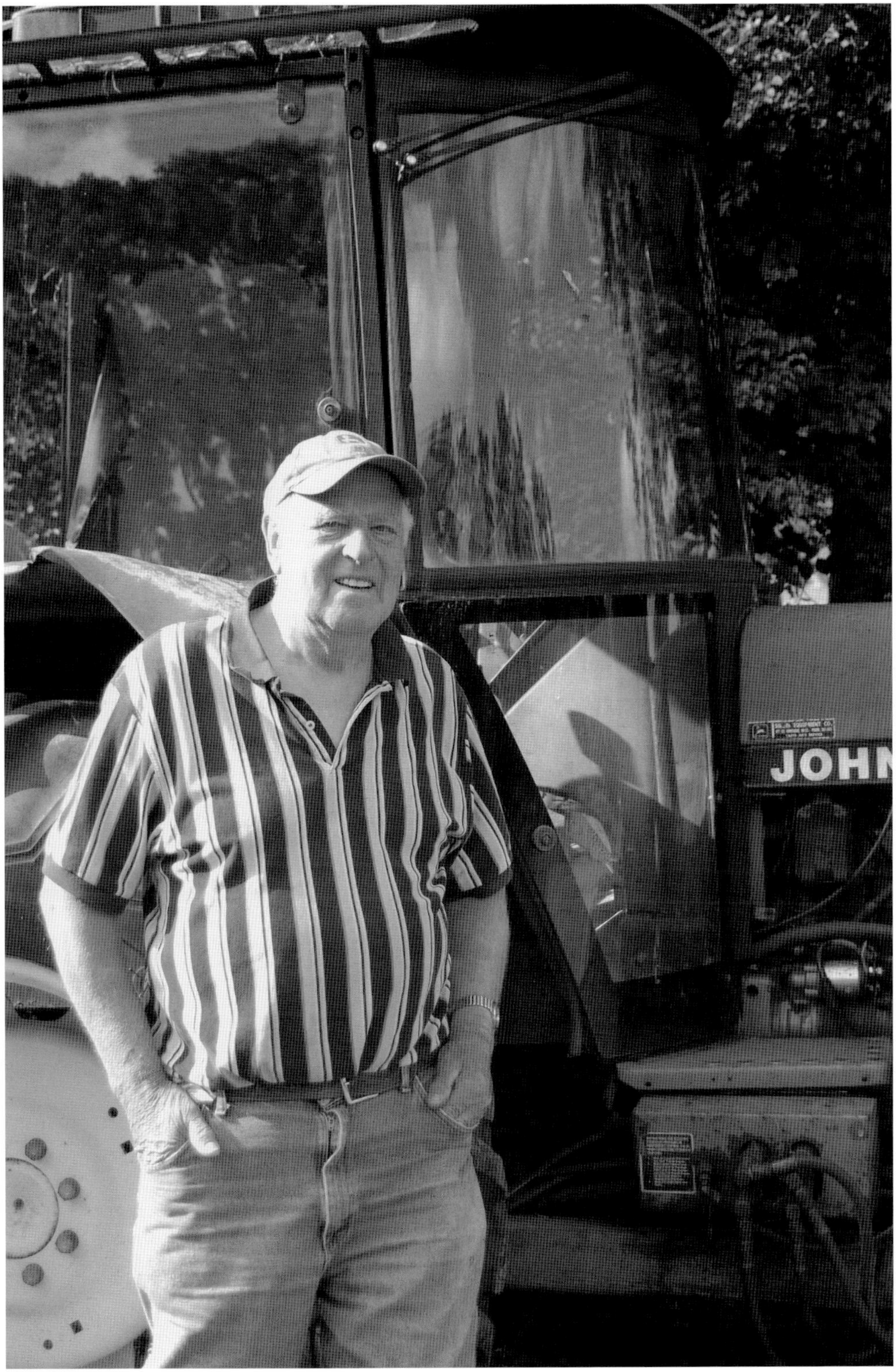
JOHN

Beth Shaw

Shaw (1942–present) was born in Needham, Massachusetts, and moved to Westford in 1972. She attended Skidmore College in New York, and earned her master's degree in public health from Boston University and her doctorate in education from the University of Massachusetts–Lowell. She went on to teach nursing at Fitchburg State University and has been a very active member of the Westford community. She, along with 11 others, was a founding member of the Westford Museum in 1982 and has been instrumental in preserving and promoting the history of Westford. She is currently the president of the Westford Historical Society. (Author's collection.)

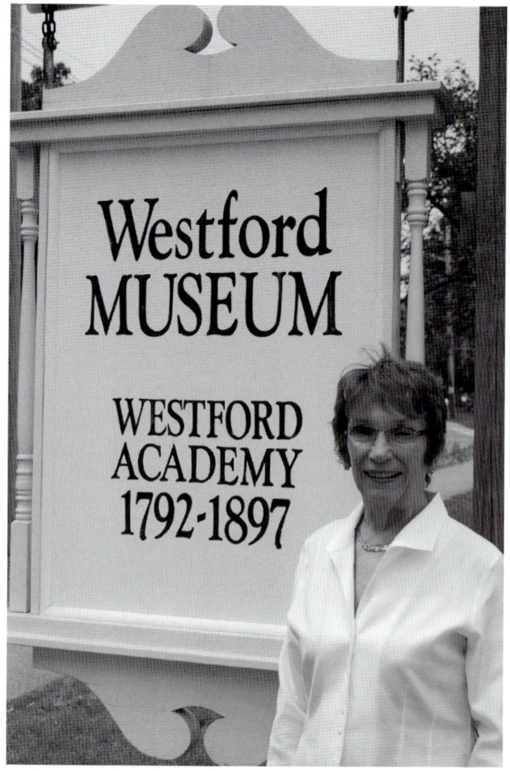

Newell F. Tillman

Tillman (1943–present) was born in Providence, Rhode Island, and moved to Westford in 1975. He attended Wentworth Institute of Technology in Boston, Massachusetts, where he studied electronics and nuclear engineering and worked as a customer support manager for Oxford Instruments America until his retirement in 2004. As an avid volunteer in Westford, he serves on the board of directors of the Westford Historical Society. He has also volunteered with the J.V. Fletcher Library, the Parish Center for the Arts, and the Westford Farmers Market. He has produced two historical videos about Westford, documenting the history of Route 110 and the renovation of the Abbot Mill in Forge Village. He, like so many others, is passionate about the town he lives in, and stands out as a committed and enthusiastic resident. (Author's collection.)

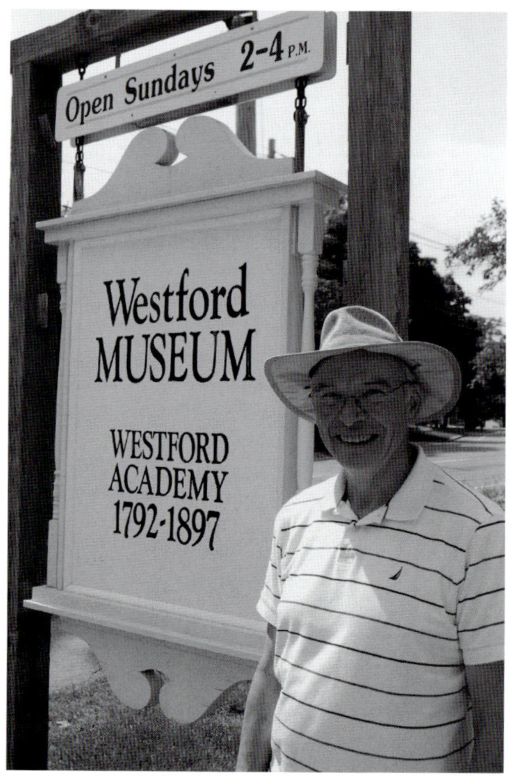

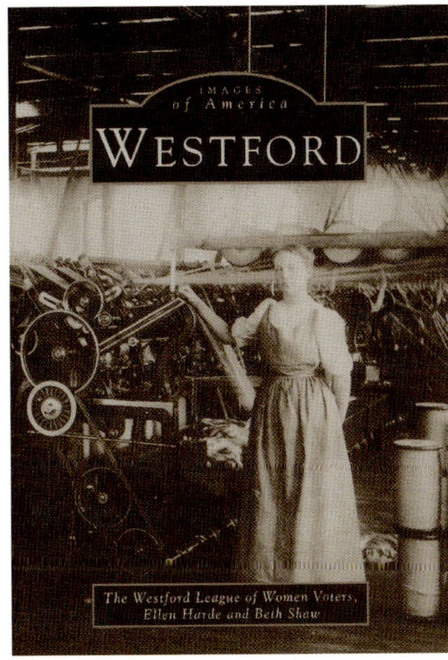

Ellen Harde

Harde (1945–present) moved to Westford in 1967. If anyone in Westford is asked, "Who has made a significant impact on the town?" most will not hesitate to mention Ellen Harde. A career volunteer, Harde has built her life around improving the lives of others in her community. She was instrumental in the founding of the Roudenbush Community Center in 1973, started the town-wide recycling program in 1988, created the Westford Directory, and spearheaded the town common restoration project. Also a noted local author, Harde has several books to her credit, including *The New Old Houses of Westford* (2011, coauthor), Images of America: *Westford* (coauthor), and *The True Story of Cinder the Westford Fire Dog*. Harde was Westford's first female selectman, has served on numerous town boards, and was elected to the position of town moderator in 1993, a position she still holds today. Many affectionately refer to her as the "Mayor of Westford" due to her lifelong commitment to the community she calls home. (Author's collection.)

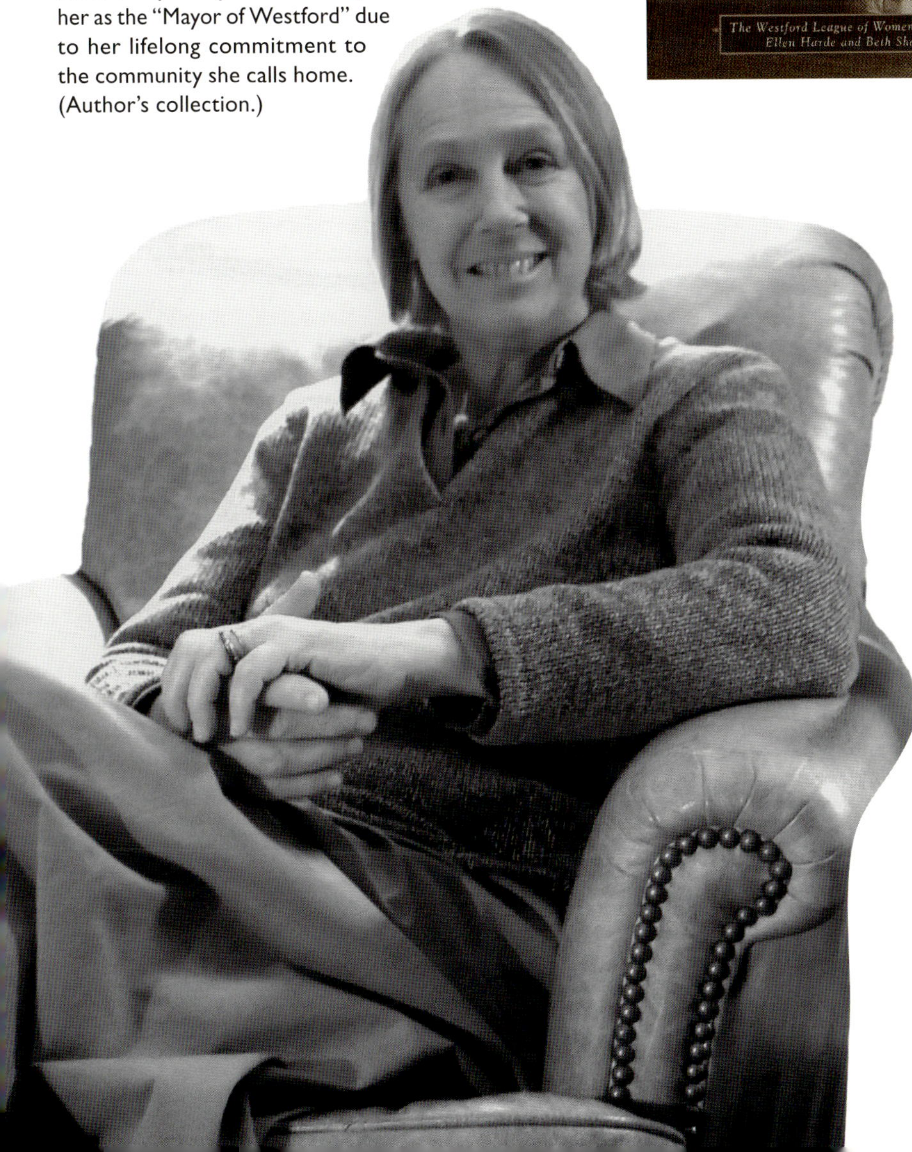

Geoffrey Hall
Hall (1948–present), a third-generation, lifelong resident of Westford, has dedicated his life to public service. Hall graduated from Salem State in 1970 with a degree in social sciences and immediately began his 38-year career as a social studies teacher. He served on the Westford Board of Selectmen from 1983 to 1989 and as chairman of the board from 1985 to 1986. He served on the Westford Housing Authority from 1989 to 1992 and as chairman from 1991 to 1992. In 1991, Hall was elected to the Massachusetts House of Representatives, representing the Second Middlesex district, a position he held until his retirement in 2009. He remains active in Westford as a volunteer and currently serves on the board of the Westford Historical Society. (Author's collection.)

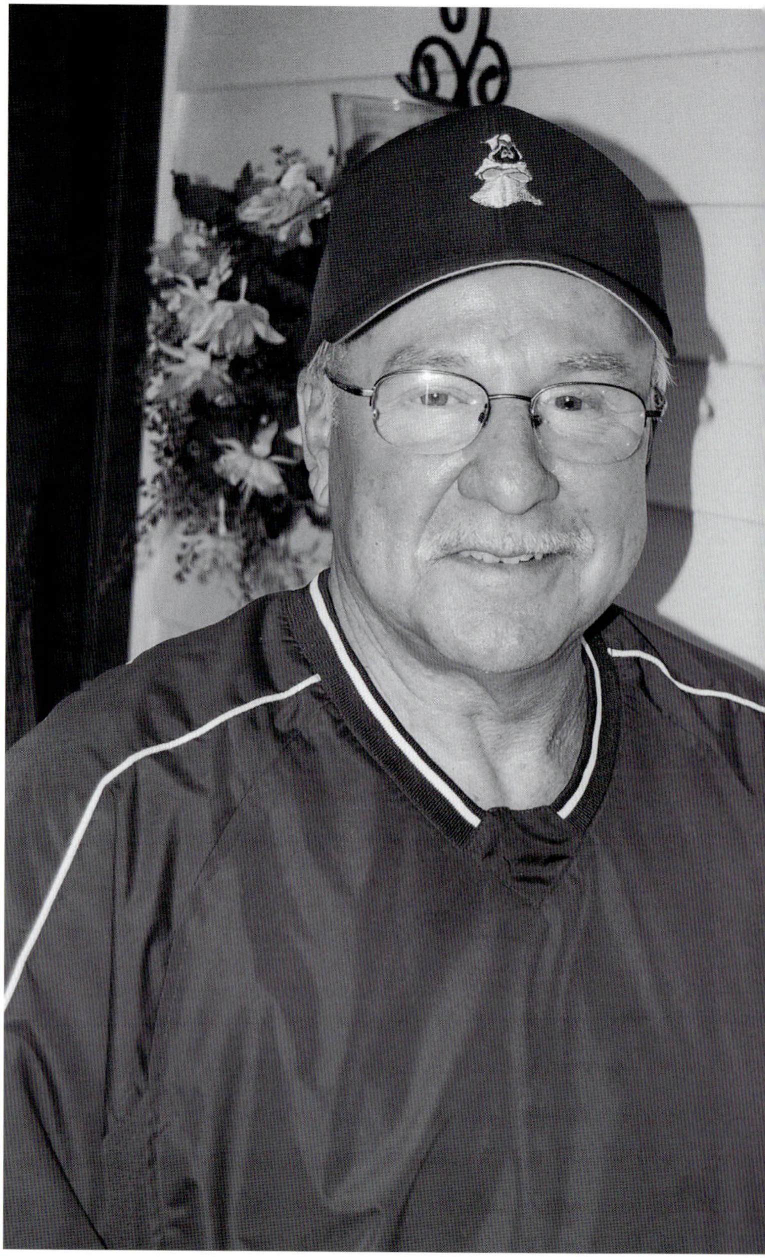

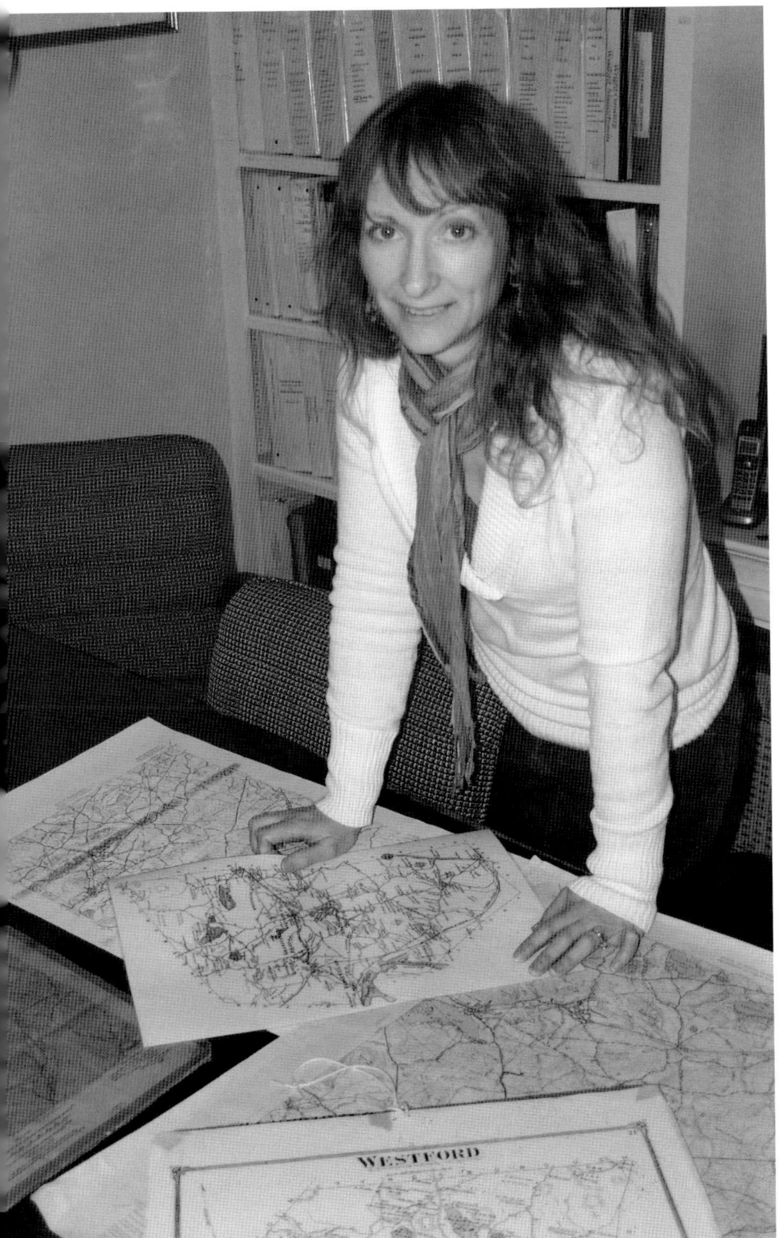

Penny Lacroix
Lacroix (1962–present) was born in Frankfurt, Germany. She attended Clarence Central High School in Clarence, New York, and Kristiansand Katedralskole in Krisiansand, Norway. She attended college at Colgate University, majoring in physics, and started her professional career as a systems engineer for MITRE Corporation. She moved to Westford in 1987; having lived in Westford longer than anywhere else, she considers it her hometown. She was hired as the director of the Westford Museum in 2006, and has worked tirelessly to oversee proper preservation and display of Westford's long and rich history.

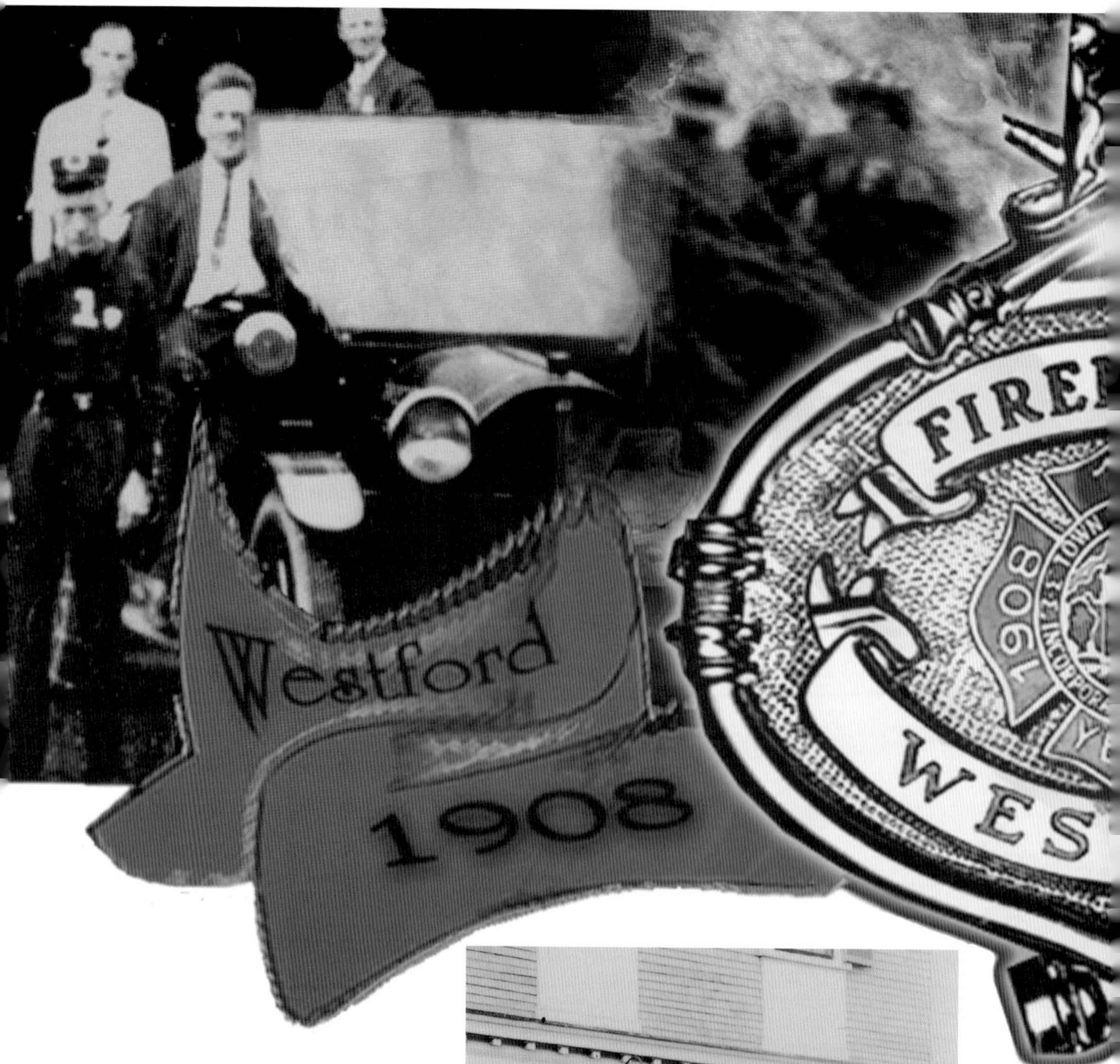
Westford
1908

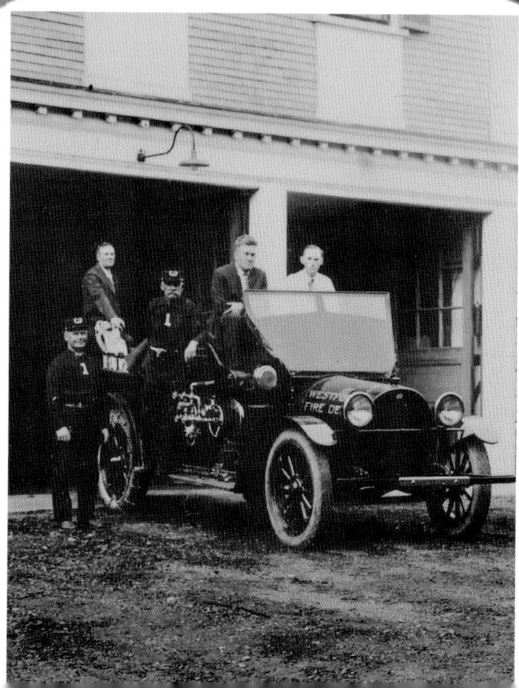

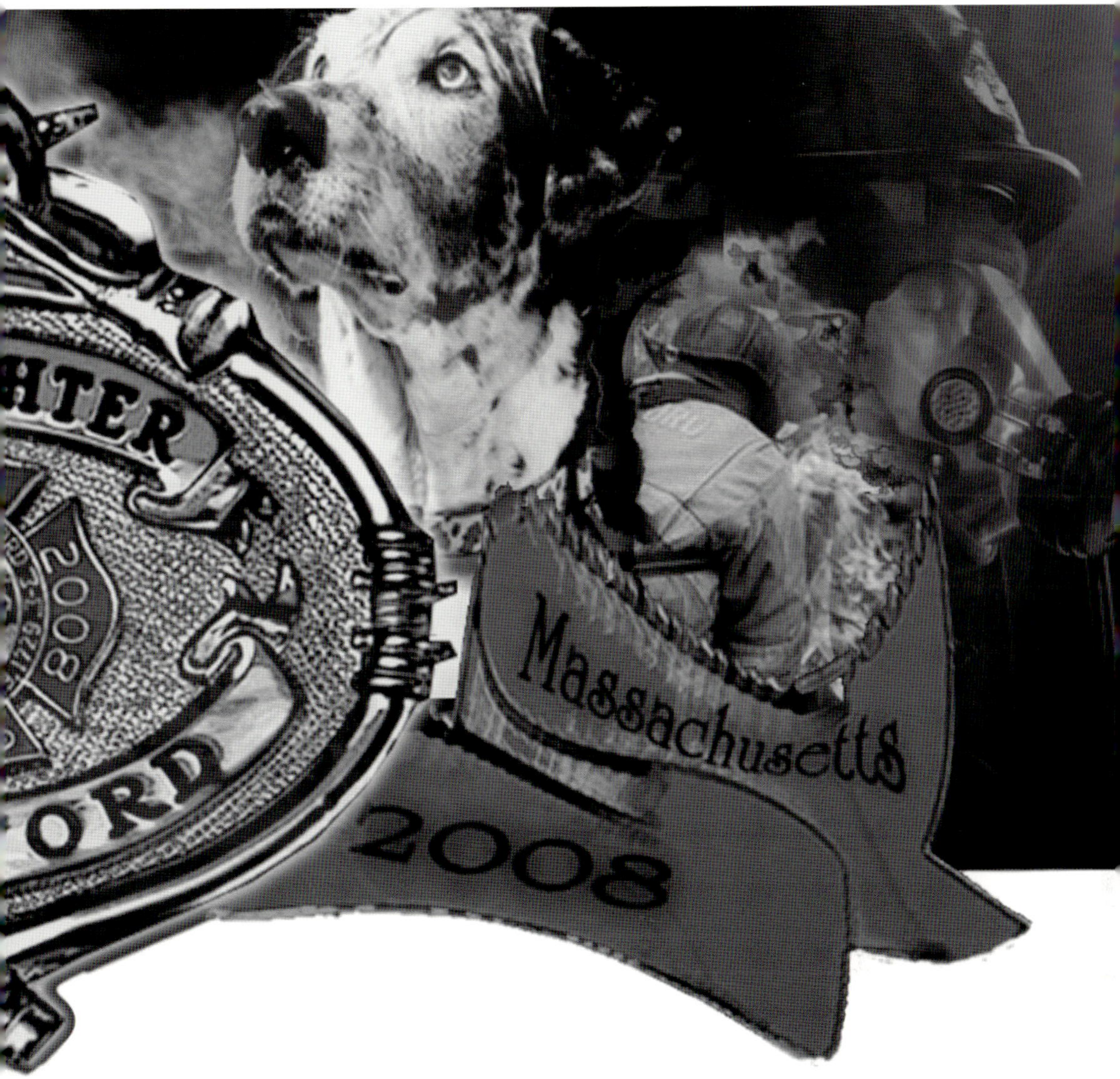

Westford Fire Department

Although officially established in 1908, with the organization of hose companies in Westford's three main villages, the Westford Fire Department's history dates back to 1892, when the town established the first recorded fire-related positions. It appointed George Heywood and Edward Prescott as the first forest fire wards. A year later, the town built three firehouses, in Westford Center, Graniteville, and Forge Village. In 1907, the town appropriated $250 to build a firehouse at Brookside Mill in Nabnasset, and in 1909, Westford lost its first firefighter to an injury in the line of duty. Lt. Daniel Harrington, after sustaining a head injury during a barn fire, laid in a coma for six days before succumbing to his injuries. In 1913, Edward M. Abbot was appointed as the department's first chief engineer, and in 1914, a new firehouse was built in Graniteville. In 1916, the town approved plans to turn the original Westford Academy building into the new Center Fire House, at a cost of $6,100, where it remained until the new police-fire station was built in 1974. The vacant building was then restored to its original appearance and became what is now the Westford Museum. (Courtesy of Westford Fire Department.)

Cinder the Fire Dog

Cinder (1987–2001) was abandoned as a puppy and found by town dog officer George Fletcher. Noting her Dalmatian markings, Fletcher decided to bring her for a visit to the Westford Fire Department. She was welcomed with open arms and remained at the firehouse for the next 14 years, where she was a welcoming host to everyone who came to visit. As a young dog, she rode the trucks to fire calls and frequently accompanied the fire prevention officer to complete inspections. She was beloved by the community, and even earned her own locker alongside veteran firemen of the department. A granite marker under her favorite tree in front of the central fire station stands as a reminder of the joy she brought to the residents of Westford. A book, *The True Story of Cinder the Westford Fire Dog* by local author Ellen Harde, tells her story. (Courtesy of Westford Fire Department.)

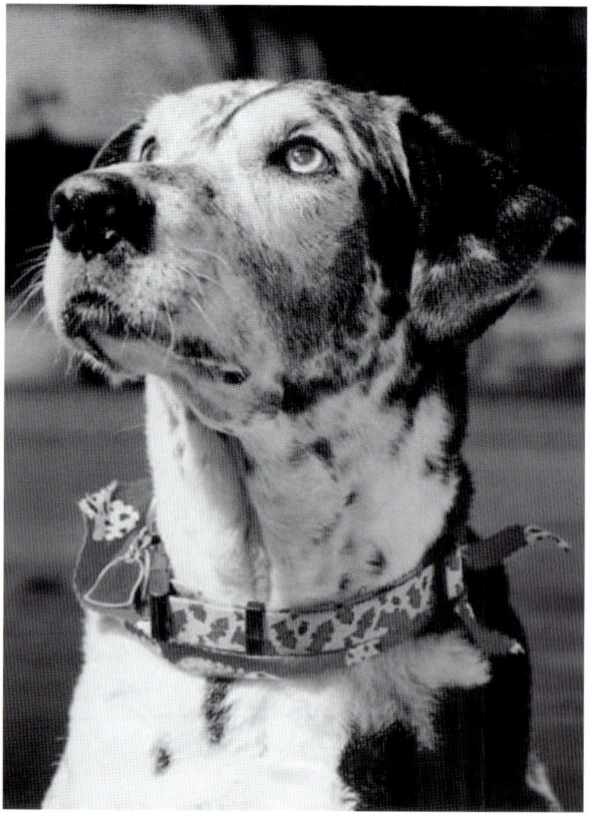

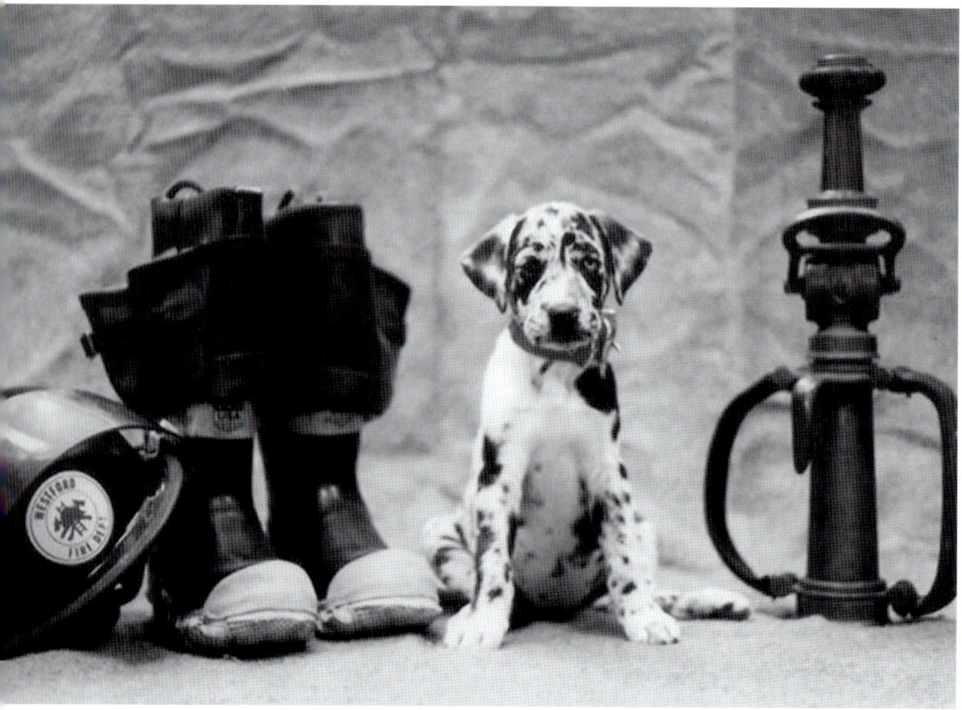

CHAPTER SIX

The Entrepreneurs

Since its earliest days, Westford has been home to a long line of innovative entrepreneurs. With the town's abundance of granite deposits and its proximity to mill cities such as Lowell, Westford saw people with vision capitalizing on local resources from day one. As early as 1676, Jonas Prescott of Groton built a gristmill and sawmill on Stony Brook where it runs out of Forge Pond, and in 1710, he built the first iron forge there, giving Forge Village its name. Westford saw its first granite quarry open in 1826, and the manufacturing industry got its foothold in 1853, when Jonas Prescott and John W.P. Abbot started the Westford Forge Company. John W.P. Abbot went on to cofound the Abbot Worsted Company, which by the 1870s was the prominent industry in town. Although the manufacturing industry has faded into history with changing times, recent days have seen other entrepreneurs make their mark on the local economy. The Kimball family, founders of Kimball Farm Ice Cream, started their venture when they purchased their farm in 1913. They began selling ice cream in 1939, and today, the business, having expanded to four locations, has become a regional destination. Alan Fletcher, seeing the potential in the area, began the Nashoba Valley Ski Area in 1964 on Nashoba Hill. With his partners, he pushed through difficult early days and built the ski area into a successful business that continues to expand to this day. Although Westford has seen many successful sizable businesses, it is also home to countless small businesses that provide a full range of goods and services to the people who live and visit here.

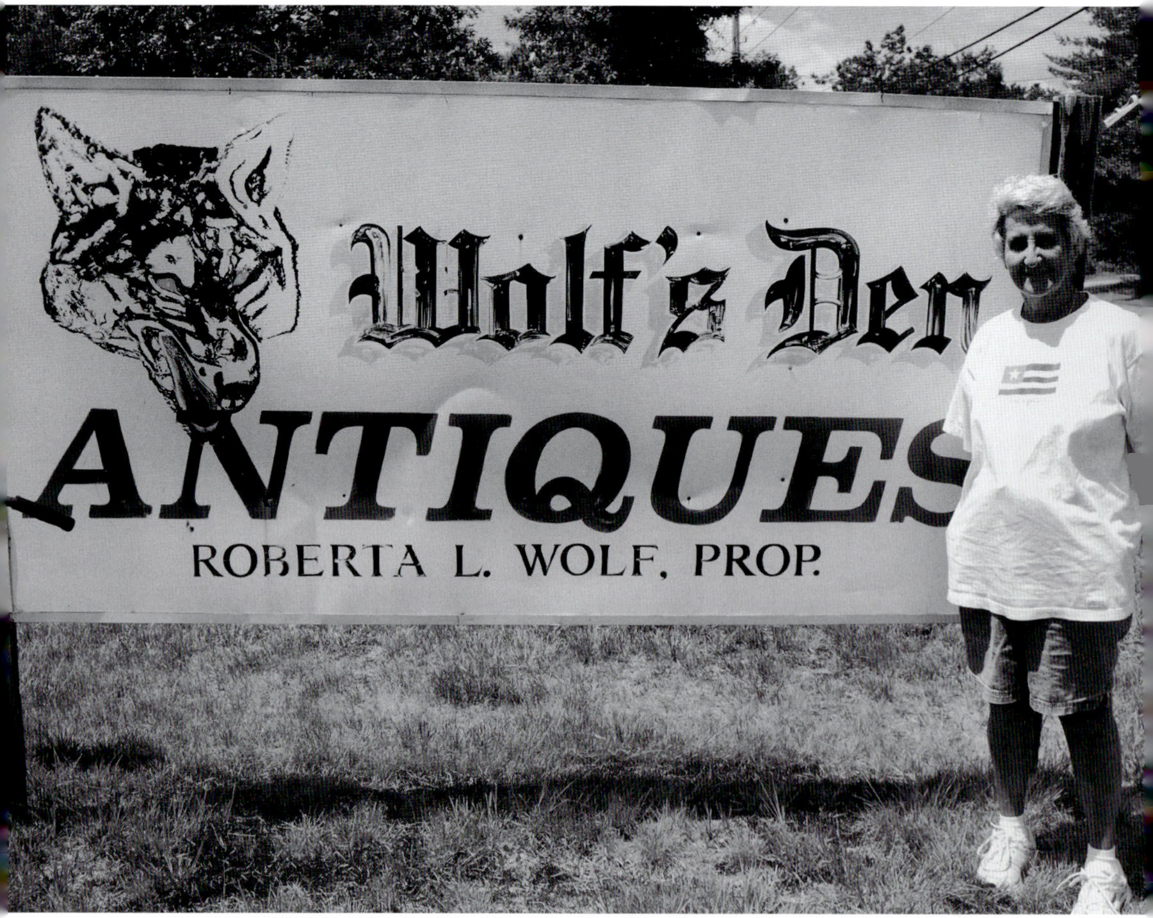

Roberta "Bette" Wolf

Wolf (1938–present) was born in Malden, Massachusetts. Since 1976, Roberta Wolf has purchased and sold antiques from her two-story barn in Westford, Wolf's Den Antiques. She specializes in Victorian marble-top furniture and accessories, and she sells to individuals and dealers from across the country who come to her for unique New England antiques. (Author's collection.)

Dr. Benjamin Osgood (OPPOSITE PAGE)

Osgood (1781–1863) was born in Westford. In 1804, at the age of 23, he went to Groton to study medicine under Dr. Amos Bancroft. He practiced medicine in Littleton for a short time before returning to Westford, where he spent the rest of his life. He married his first wife, Nancy Cumings, in 1810. Cumings died in 1831, and Osgood married his second wife, Eliza Cummings, Nancy's niece, in 1833. Although Dr. Osgood resided on Main Street, it is believed that he often attended to his patients by carrying his medicines in saddlebags and visiting them on horseback or by horse and carriage. Fees charged for his medical services were recorded as late as 1860. His saddlebags are on display at the Westford Museum.

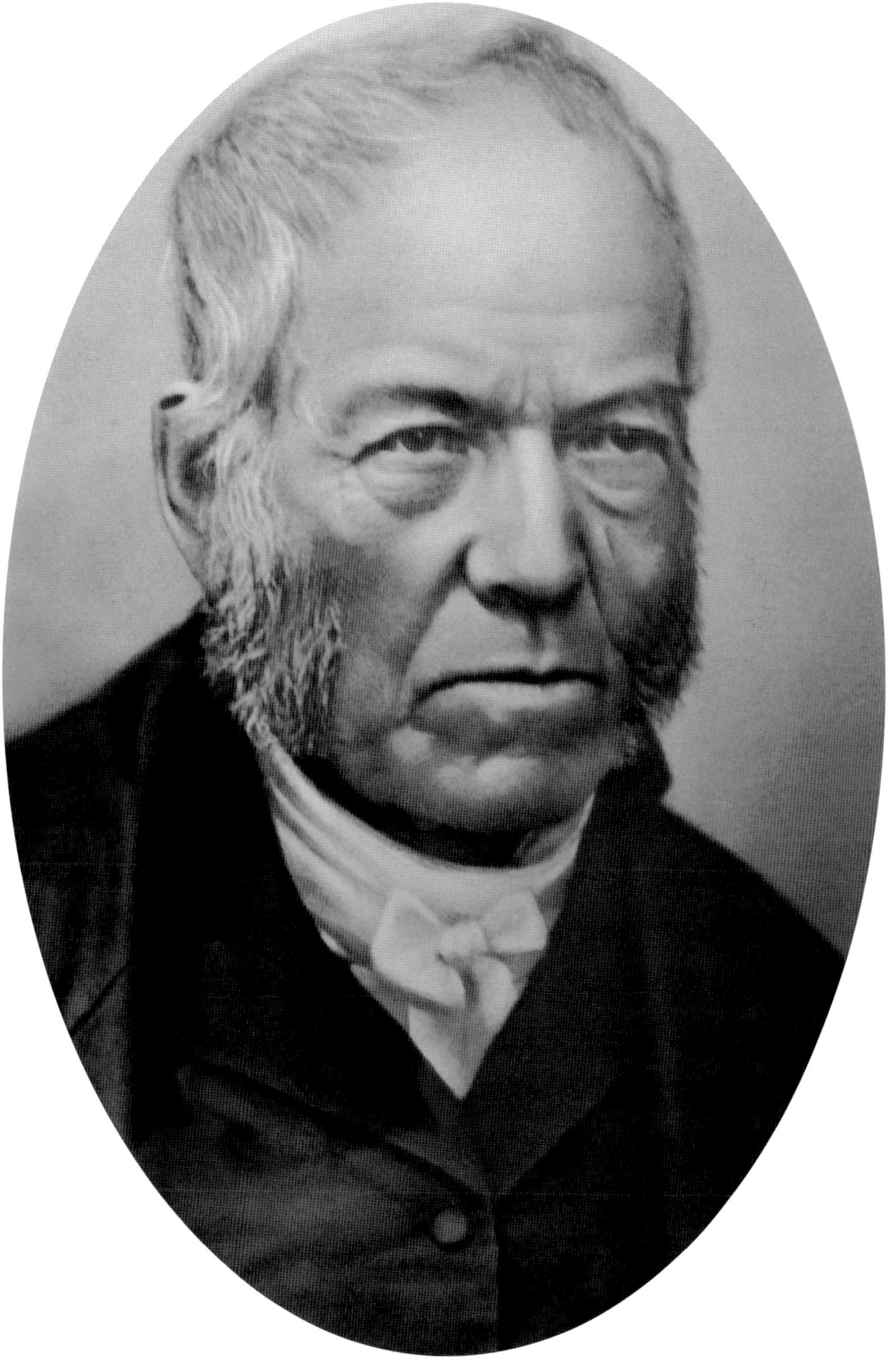

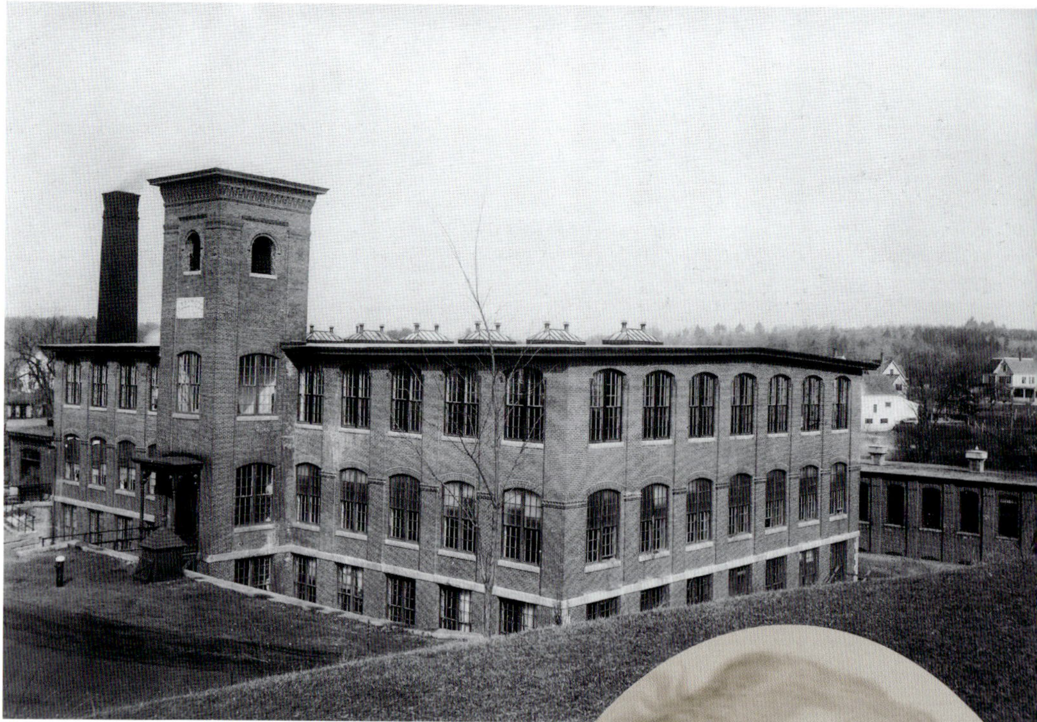

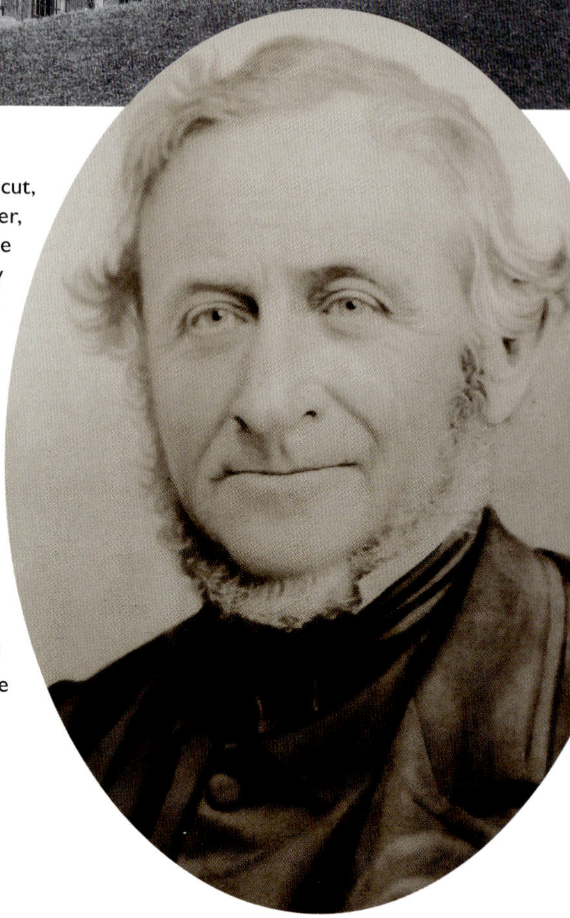

John William Pitt Abbot

Abbot (1806–1872) was born in Hampton, Connecticut, the home of his mother's family. A few weeks later, he was brought to Westford, where he lived the rest of his life. He attended Westford Academy and followed in his father's footsteps, graduating from Harvard in 1827. He received his law degree from Cambridge and joined his father's law practice. Active in public service, Abbot served as a Westford selectman, town clerk, treasurer of Westford Academy, judge for Northern Middlesex, and Massachusetts state senator. Abbot was a principal investor in the Westford Forge Company in 1853. In 1855, he entered into a partnership with his son John W. Abbot and Charles G. Sargent, forming the Abbot Worsted Company (above), which processed worsted yarns and ultimately became the predominant Westford employer in its day. An image of Abbot's residence can be seen on page 118.

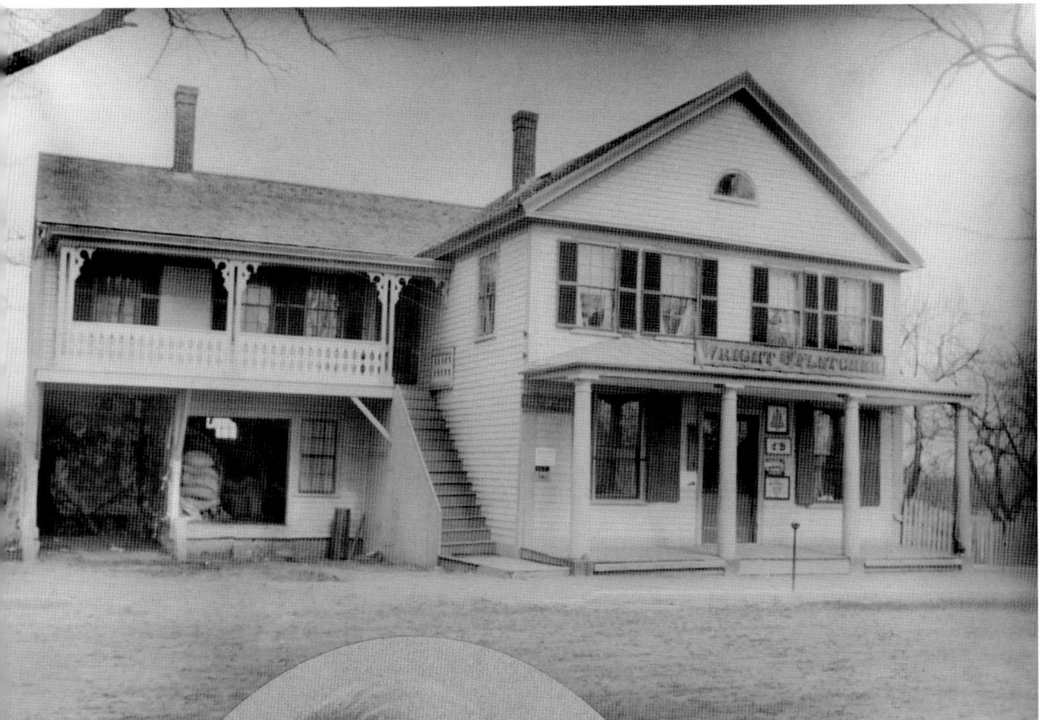

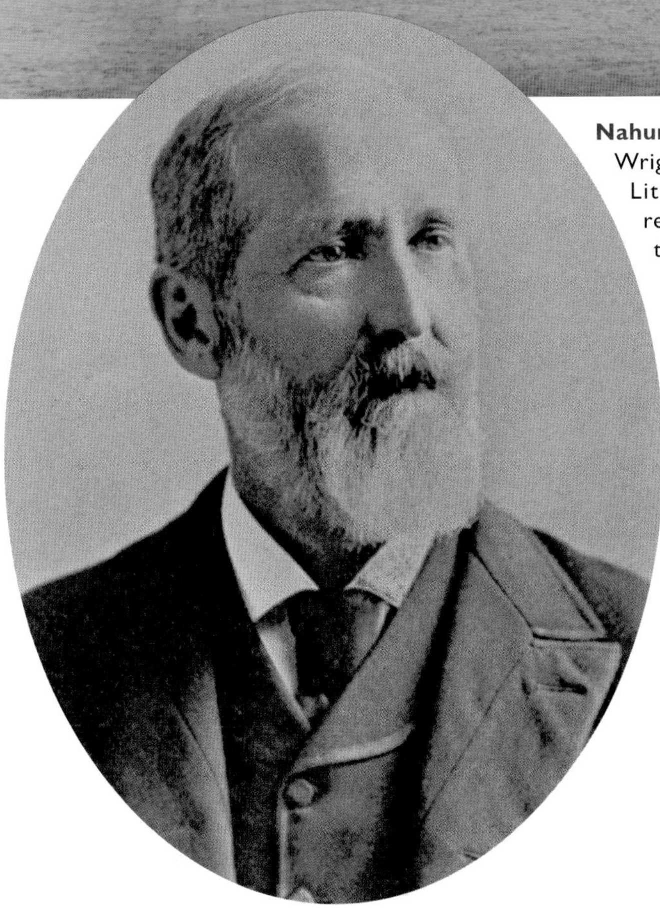

Nahum Harwood Wright
Wright (1831–1910) was born in Littleton, Massachusetts. He received his early education in the Littleton and Lowell public schools. In his early years, he served as an engineer on the Boston & Lowell Railroad. He ultimately made his living as a member of the firm of Wright & Fletcher General Store (above), and served the town both as a selectman and, for 23 years, as town treasurer. He lived the last 40 years of his life in Westford Town Center.

Ellen Henrietta Swallow Richards

Richards (1842–1911) was a true pioneer in the 19th century. Born in Dunstable, Massachusetts, and a graduate of Westford Academy, she was the first woman admitted to the Massachusetts Institute of Technology, the first female instructor at MIT, the first woman in America to be accepted to any school of science and technology, and the first woman to earn a degree in chemistry. Richards volunteered her services at MIT and donated $1,000 annually to develop programs for female students. From 1884 until her death, she served as an instructor at the Lawrence Experiment Station, where her work led to the first water-quality standards in the United States and the first modern sewage treatment plant in Lowell, Massachusetts. In 1909, she founded the American Home Economics Association, now the American Association of Family and Consumer Sciences.

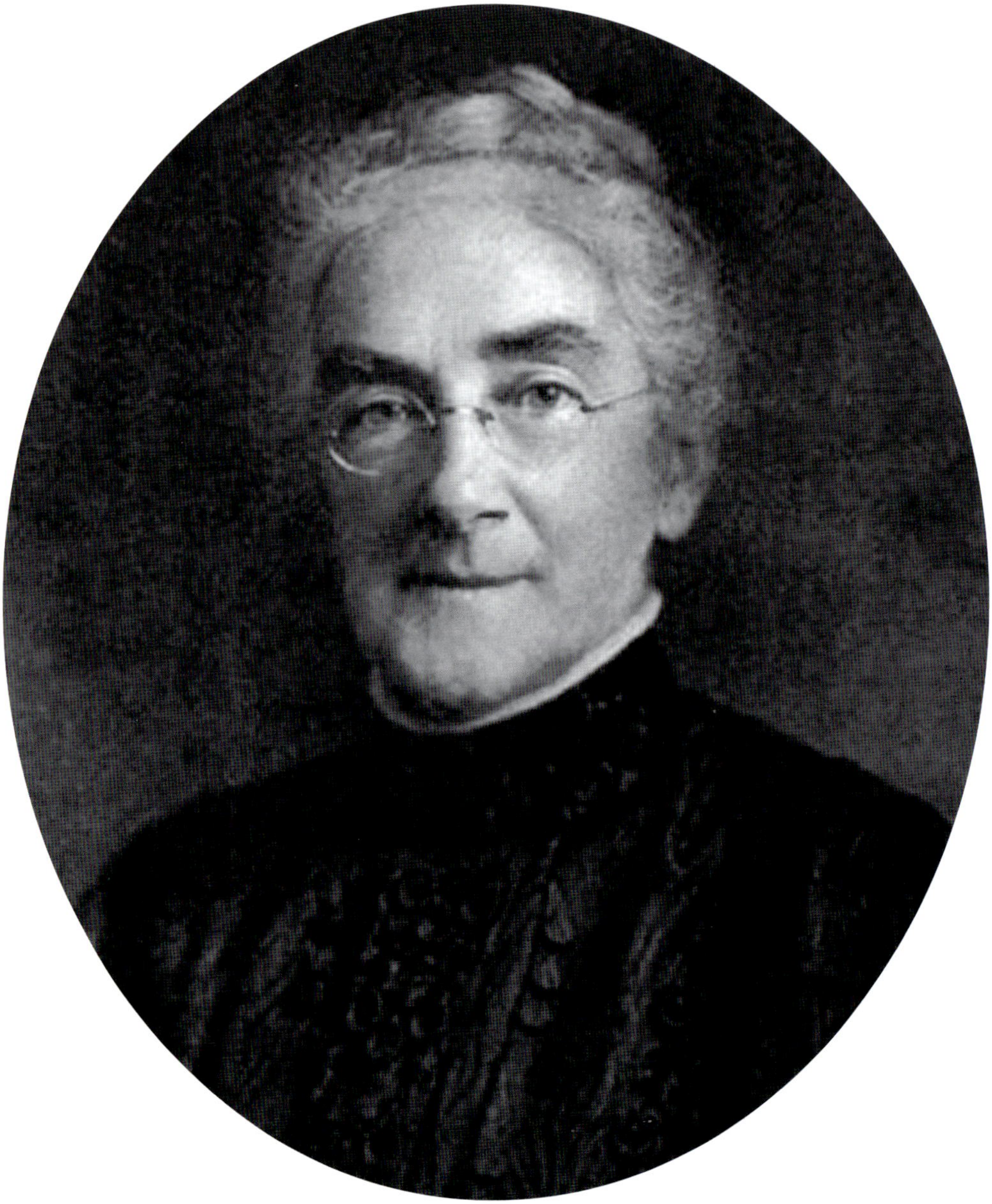

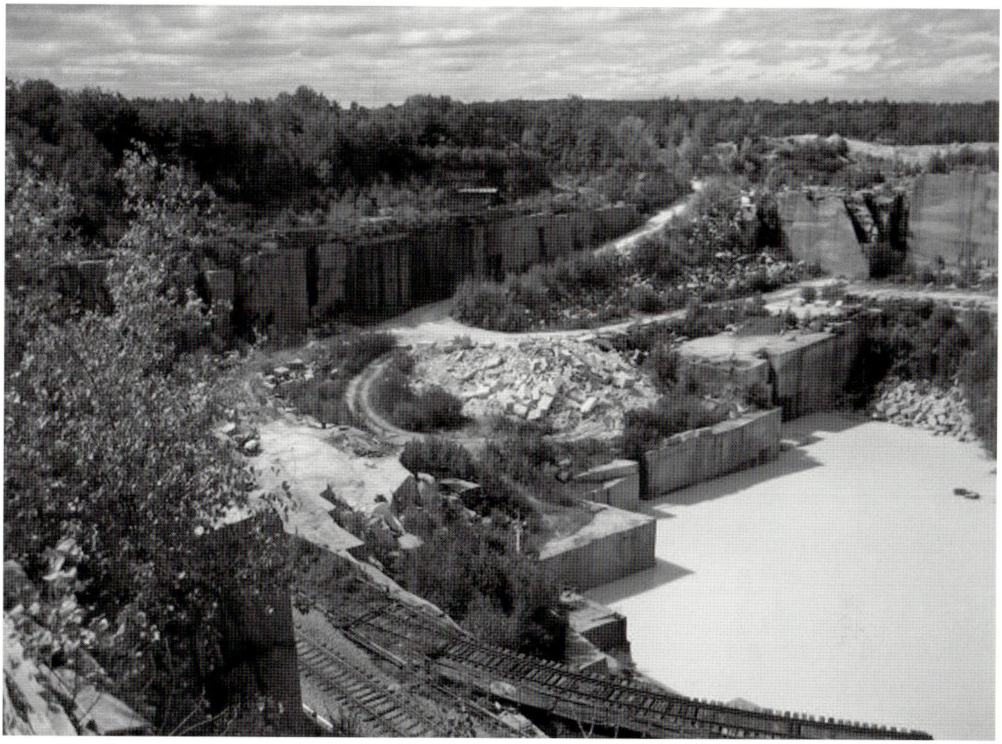

Herbert Ellery Fletcher

Fletcher (1862–1956), seen on the right in a family photograph, originally of Chelmsford, Massachusetts, founded Fletcher Granite Company, a granite quarry on Oak Hill in Westford, in 1881 at the age of 18. (The image above shows the quarry as it appears today.) The son of a prominent Chelmsford family, his ancestors included one of the original founders of Chelmsford in the 1600s. Fletcher Granite was in continuous operation from its founding until recent years, supplying granite to projects all over the country, including many prominent buildings in the nation's capital. Fletcher was an astute businessman, running not only the quarry operation but also a construction company and investing in other quarry operations in the area. He was a pioneer in the granite industry, having invented many new techniques for harvesting and processing stone. He was very active in local government, serving both as a state representative and a state senator. He lived to see three more generations of Fletchers running the business, until his death in 1956. Shown in the photograph to the right are, from left to right, (first row) Polly Fletcher and Edith Fletcher Flynn (children of Herbert Ellery Fletcher II); (second row) Herbert Ellery Fletcher II (1924–2008), Harold Hill Fletcher (1890–1960), and Herbert Ellery Fletcher (1862–1956). (Courtesy of Fletcher family.)

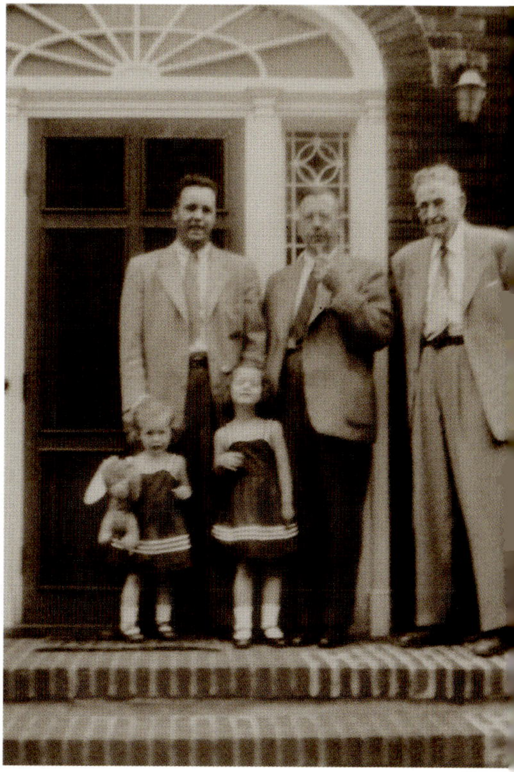

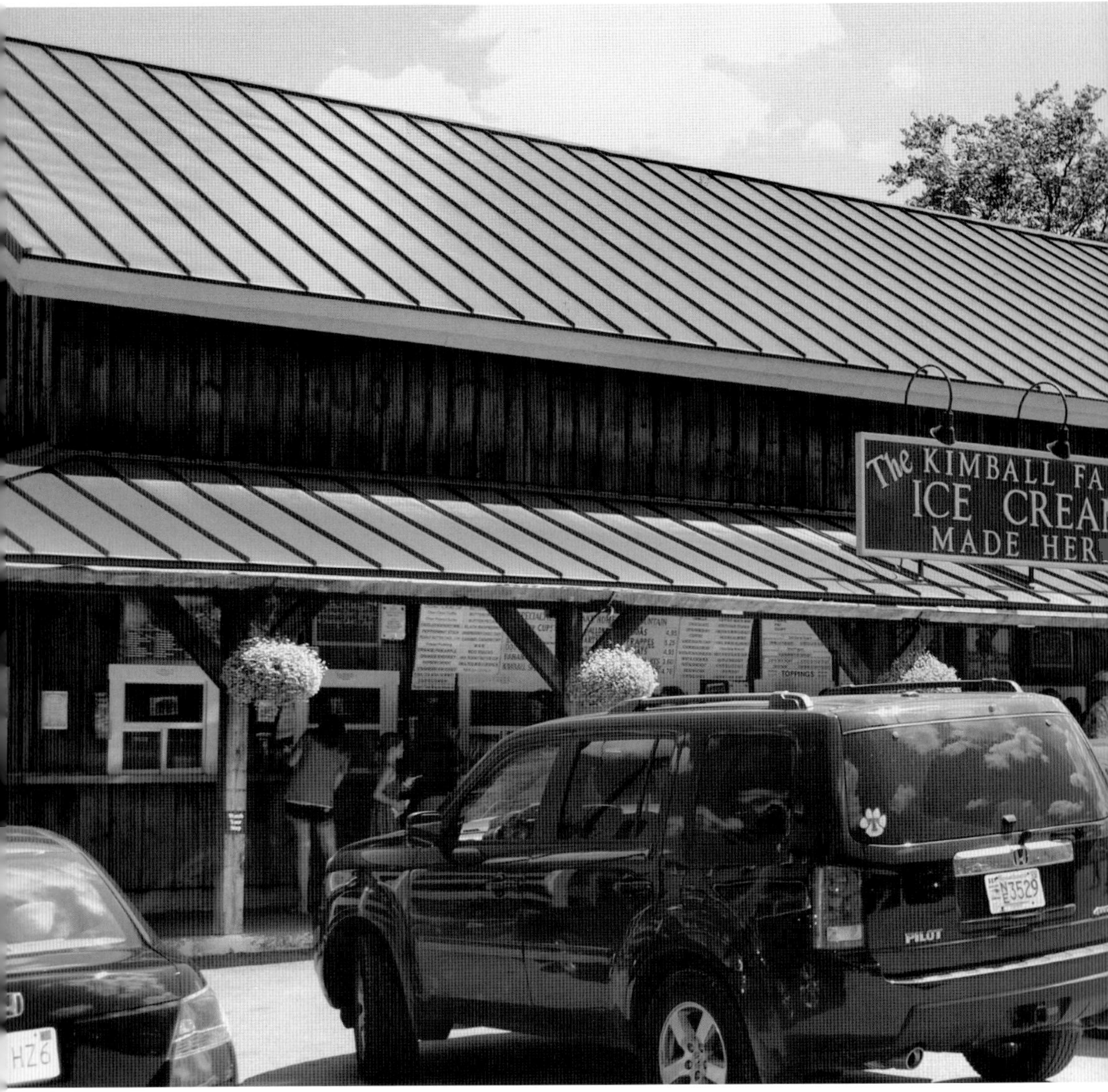

Kimball Family

Shown here are images of Kimball Farm Ice Cream, then and now. Clara and John "Jack" Kimball purchased what is now Kimball Farm in 1913 and began selling ice cream in 1939. When they turned the woodshed on the end of the house into an ice cream parlor, they never could have imagined what would come of their leap of faith. Today, Jack and Clara's grandsons Michael and Peter Kimball run four locations in both Massachusetts and New Hampshire, but still sell ice cream from what began as a dairy barn in Westford in 1908. They've since added a driving range, nine-hole pitch and putt golf course, miniature golf, a bumper boat pond, a country store gift shop, and an outdoor luncheon grill and seafood shack, but they have managed to maintain the hometown feel. Today, Kimball Farm Ice Cream is known throughout New England as a fixture of Westford. (Courtesy of Kimball Farm.)

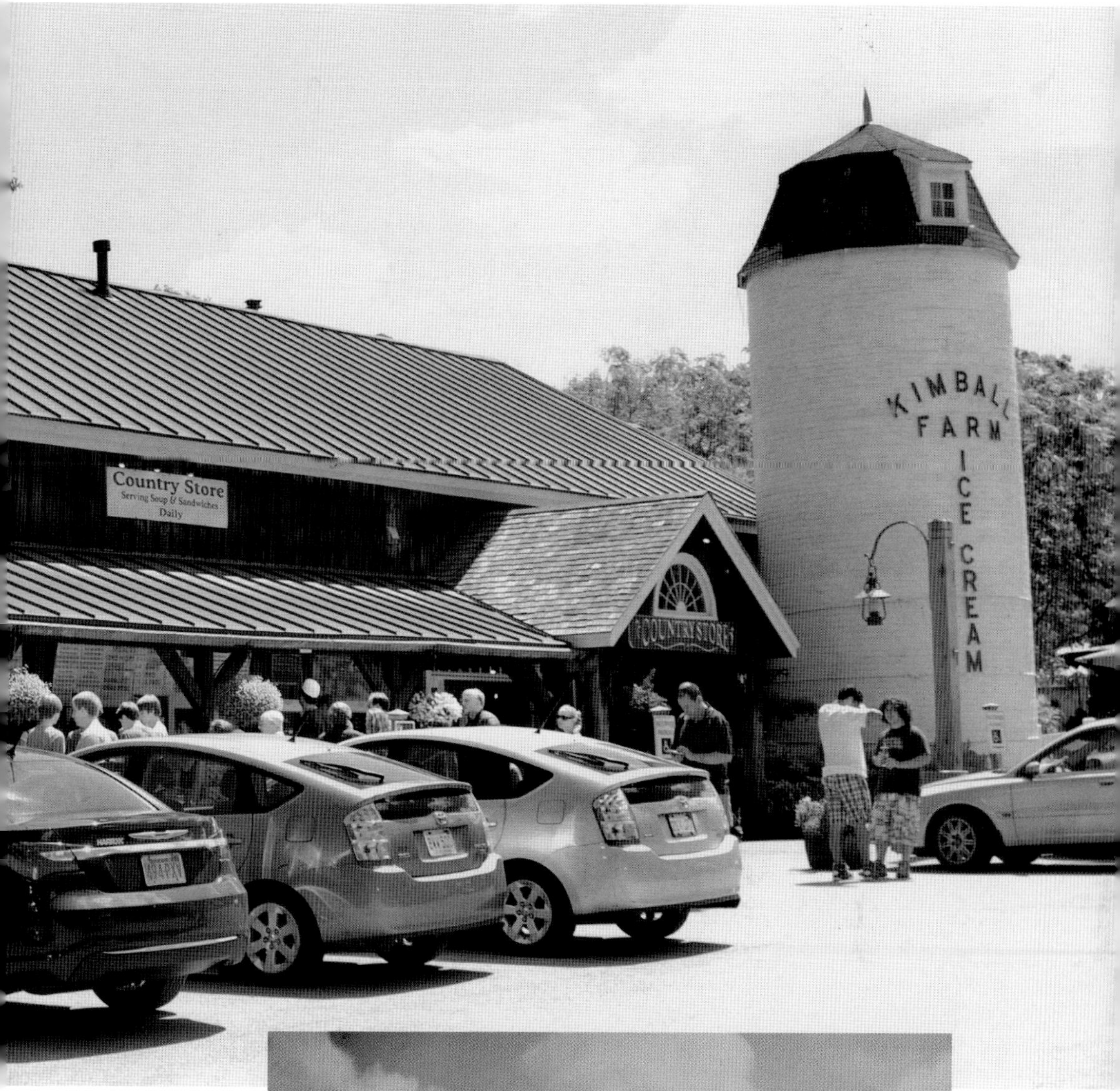
Country Store
Serving Soup & Sandwiches
Daily
COUNTRY STORE
KIMBALL FARM ICE CREAM

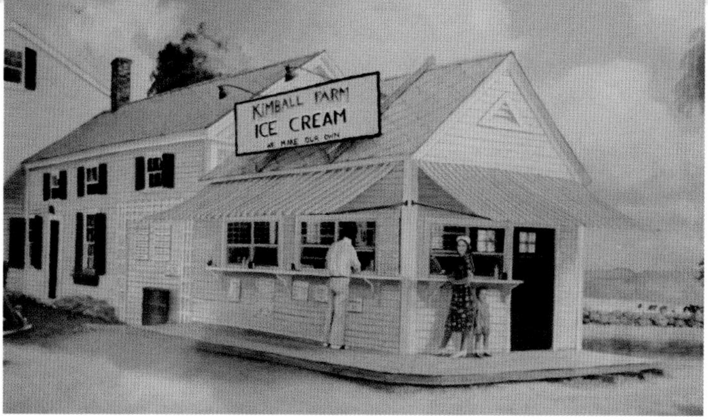
KIMBALL FARM
ICE CREAM

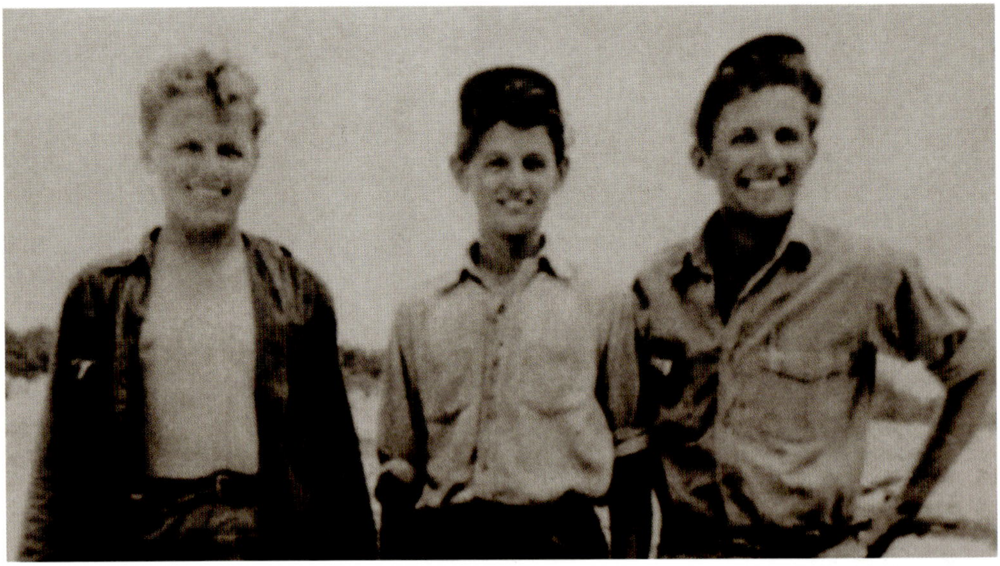

Alfred Garside and John Thomas "J.T." Smith

Garside (1934–present) was one of 14 children. He was born in Lowell, but as a teenager, he and two of his brothers went to work at the Fletcher Granite Quarry in Westford. (The brothers, shown working at the Fletcher Quarry in the 1954 photograph above, are, from left to right, Ralph, Andrew, and Alfred.) After working at the quarry for several years, Alfred went to work for Barretto Quarry in Milford, New Hampshire, and, several years later, decided to take the skills he had learned and strike out on his own. He opened Garside Monuments in Westford and has been providing granite monuments and other granite products to Westford and the surrounding communities ever since. Garside's work can be seen in virtually every corner of the town. Garside's grandson Smith (pictured at right; 1985–present) has been working with the family business his entire life. Garside handed the reins of the company to his grandson in 2007, and the two continue to work side-by-side, promoting Garside Monuments in and around Westford. (Above, courtesy of Alfred, Beverly, and Andrew Garside; below, author's collection.)

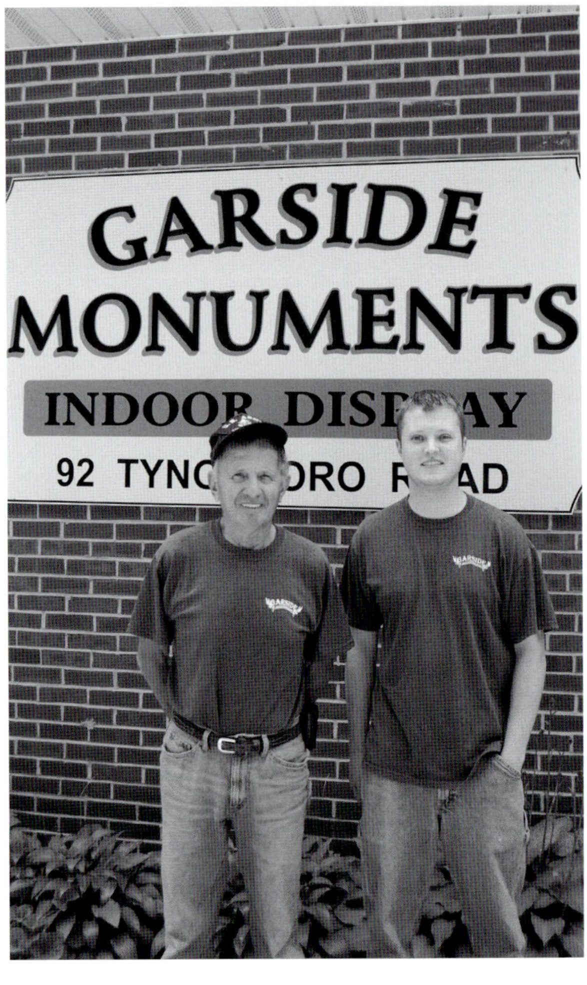

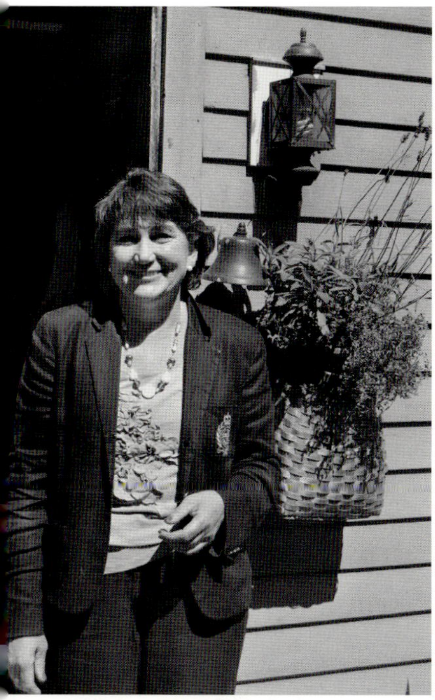

Lynne Romac Smithwood

Smithwood (1958–present) was born in upstate New York and moved to Westford with her family when she was 10 years old. She attended Westford Academy and continued her education at Skidmore College and, eventually, the New England School of Law. She maintains her own law practice in Westford. In 2000, she opened her family home as a bed-and-breakfast. The Samuel Fitch House (below), built in 1711, has a rich agricultural history. The bed-and breakfast features three guest suites, each unique and in keeping with the Colonial charm of the home. The home offers Sunday Teas and Tours and prides itself on "Discovery Weekends," when guests are given several options for experiencing New England. (Author's collection.)

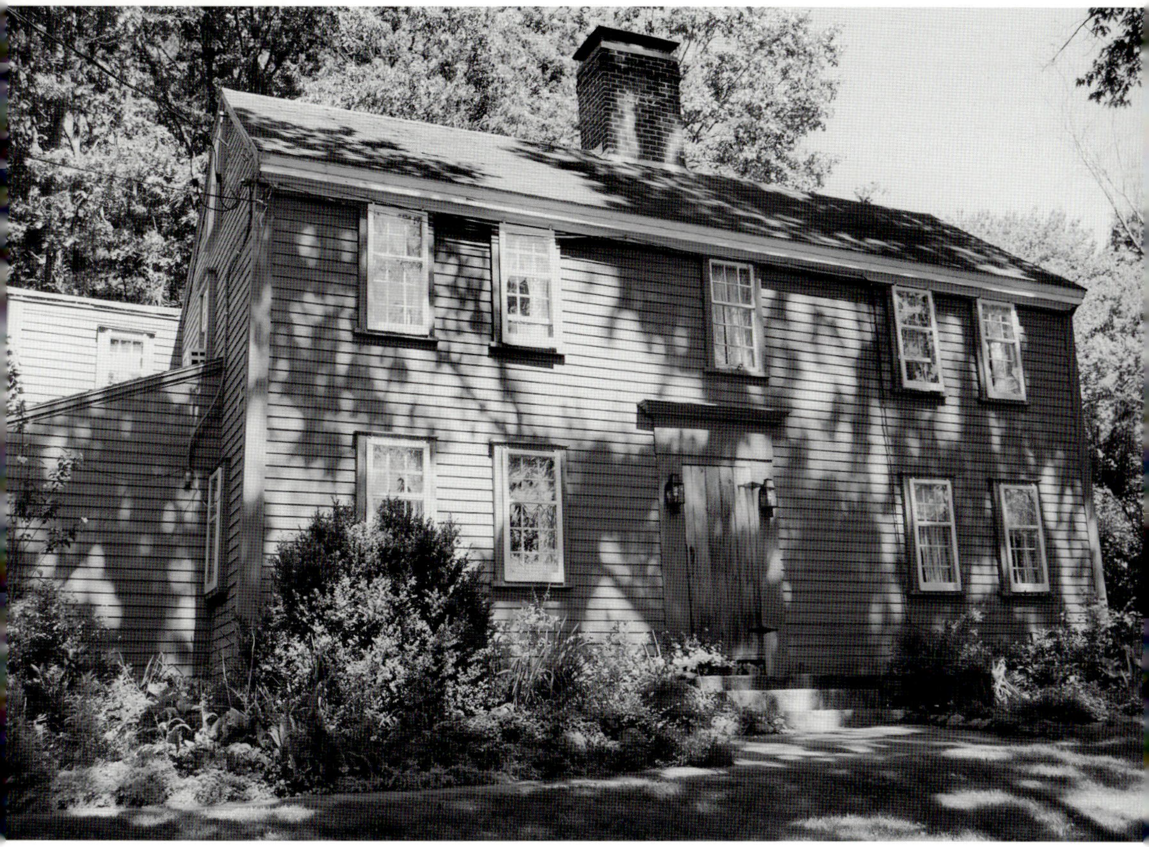

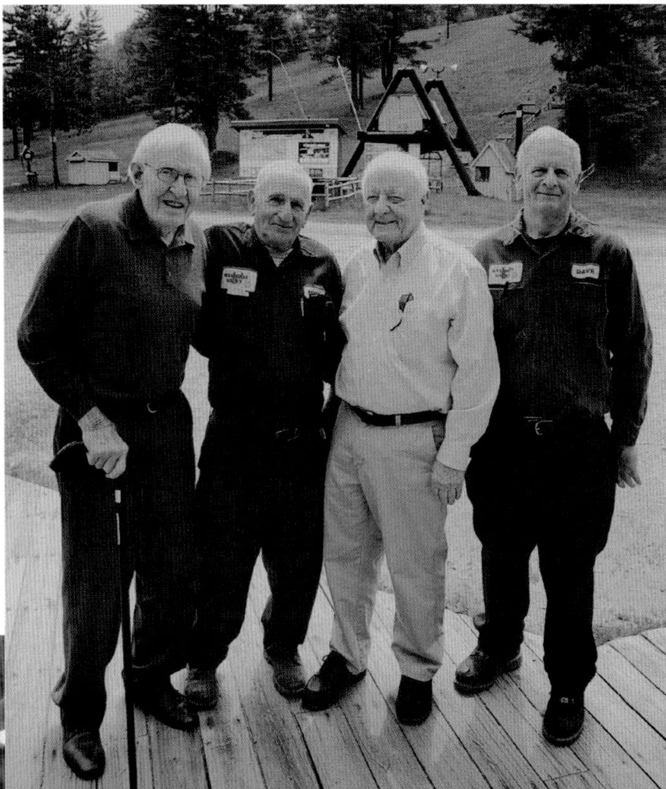
DAVE

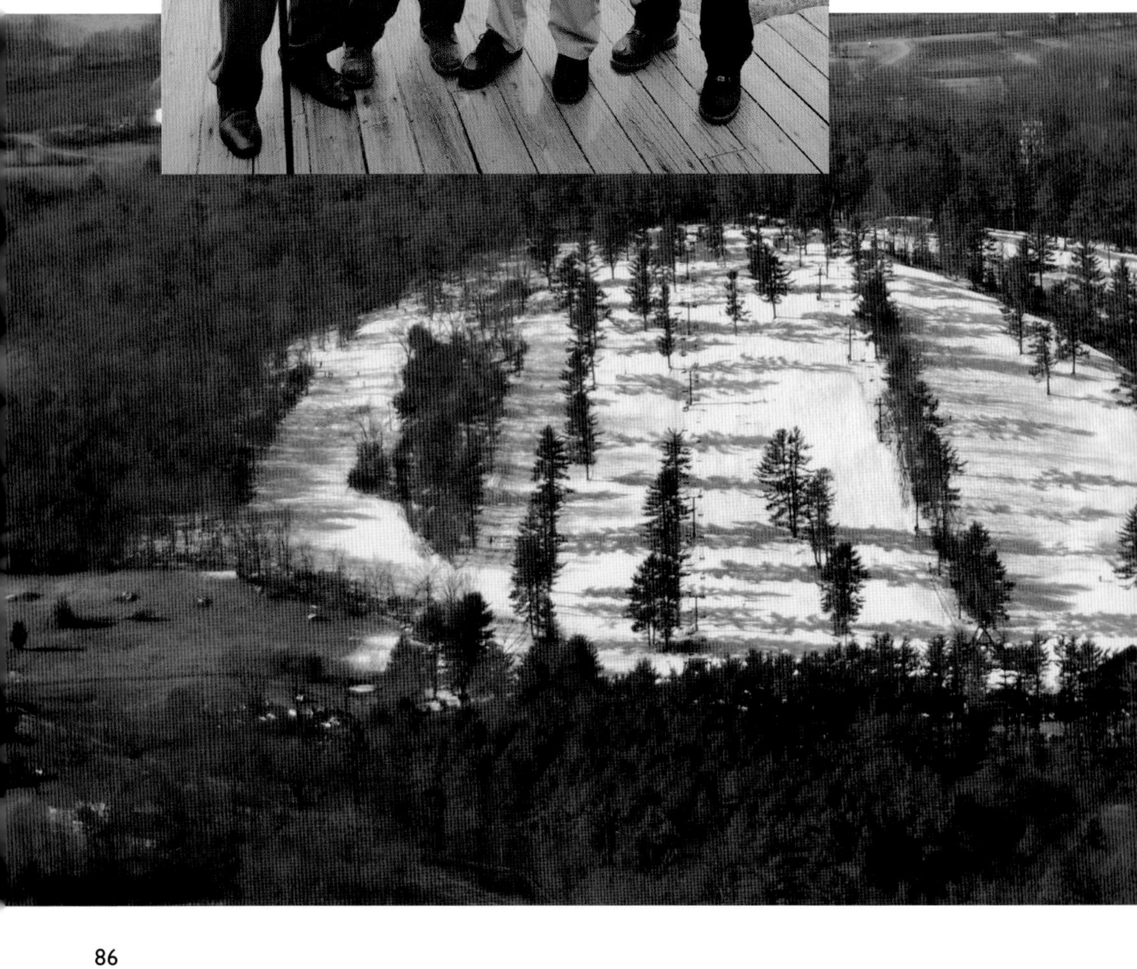

The Men of Nashoba Valley Ski Area

Shown in the photograph to the left are, from left to right, Peter Whitcomb (1922–present), Mederick "Midge" Zaher (1923–present), Alan Fletcher (1931–present), and David McPhee (1946–present). The men set out to start the Nashoba Valley Ski Area in 1964 in an effort to bring skiing to Westford and the surrounding communities. Fletcher, a graduate of Boston University, embarked on starting the ski area while he was still working in the information technology field. Upon purchasing the property that is now the ski area, Fletcher went to inspect the land and found Zaher waiting there with a chainsaw. Zaher stated, "If you're going to start a ski area, I'm going to cut the trees for you to clear the land." It has been said since then that Zaher "came with the property." Whitcomb, a local contractor at the time, managed the business and took on the task of building the first ski lodge and rental building, while McPhee went to work on the mechanics of the new venture. Nashoba saw its first chairlift in 1977 and has been growing ever since, having long since established itself as a fixture of the Westford community. (Author's collection.)

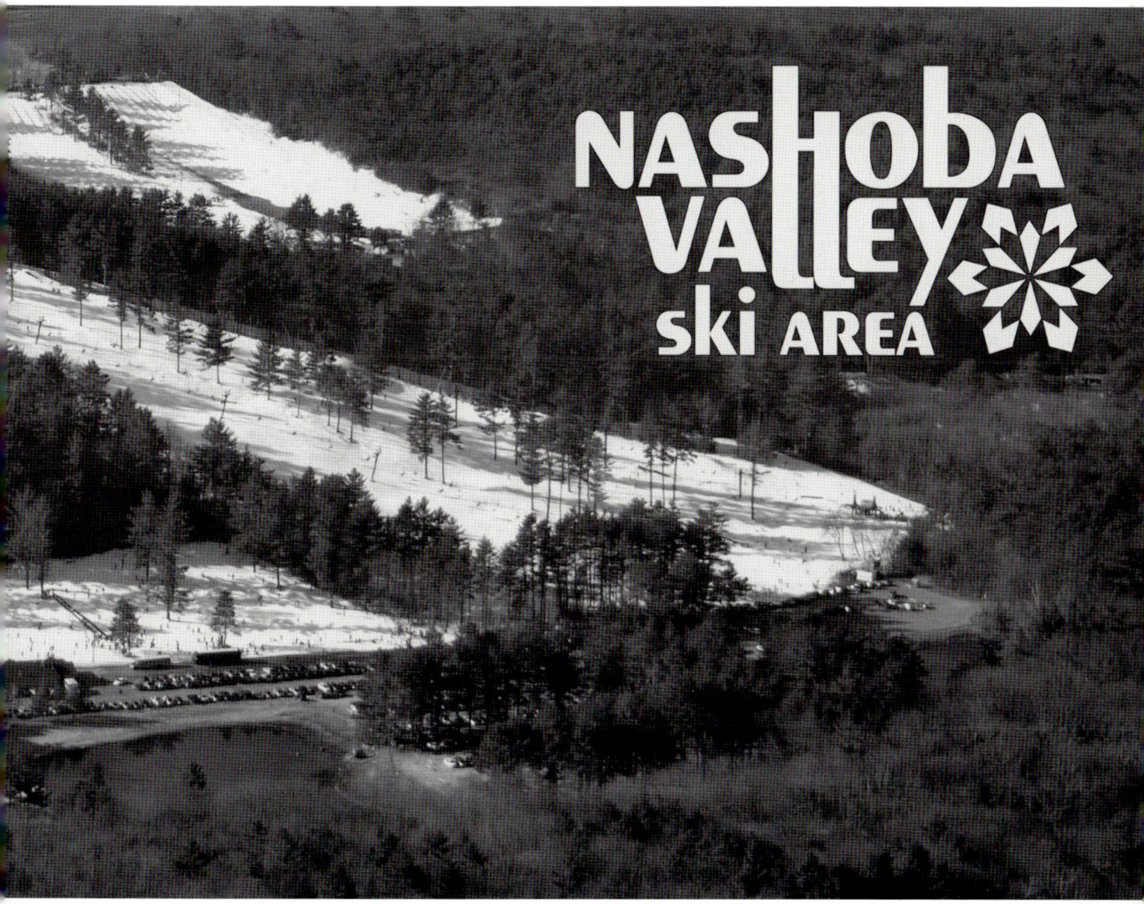

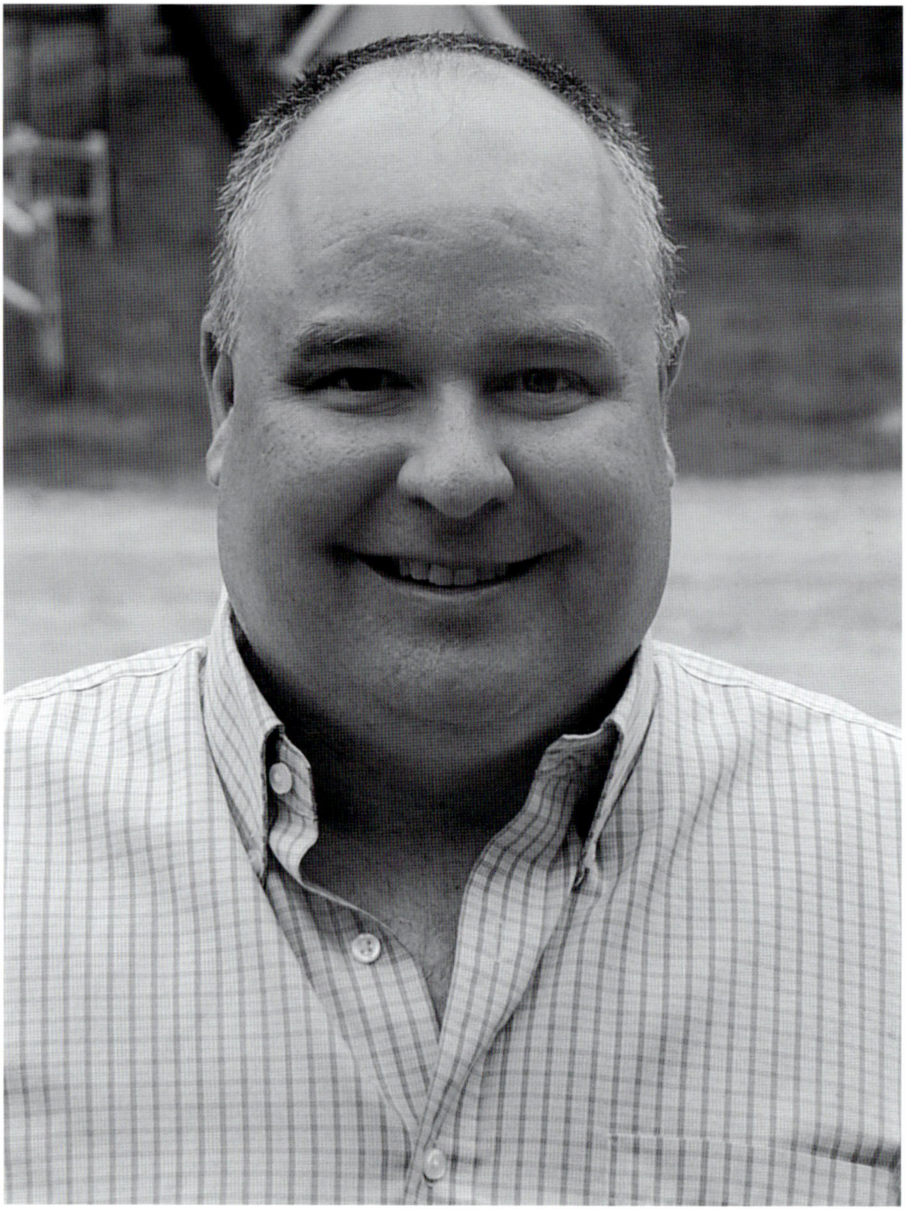

Alan Fletcher Jr.

Fletcher (1971–present), from Acton, Massachusetts, has been an active member of the Westford community his entire life. The son of Nashoba Valley Ski Area founder Alan Fletcher Sr., he grew up on the slopes. He graduated from the University of Massachusetts with a degree in business management, and in 1998 he went to work full time for the family business. Assuming the reigns of the company as president in 2010, Fletcher has continued his father's work of transforming a seasonal business into a year-round destination. Complementing the already successful ski area, in recent years the company has added the Sunset Tiki Bar and Grill, which offers an island getaway feel for outdoor events; the extremely popular Witches Woods, a haunted hayride and Halloween Scream Park; and a spectacular snow-tubing park. (Author's collection.)

Perry E. Shupe

Shupe (1873–1974) is pictured here in 1924 with his 1913 Buick loaded with apple boxes marked "Standard Box, Farm Produce." Shupe emigrated from Canada in 1899 and lived at 23 Boston Road. This photograph was taken by his neighbor Charles L. Hildreth.

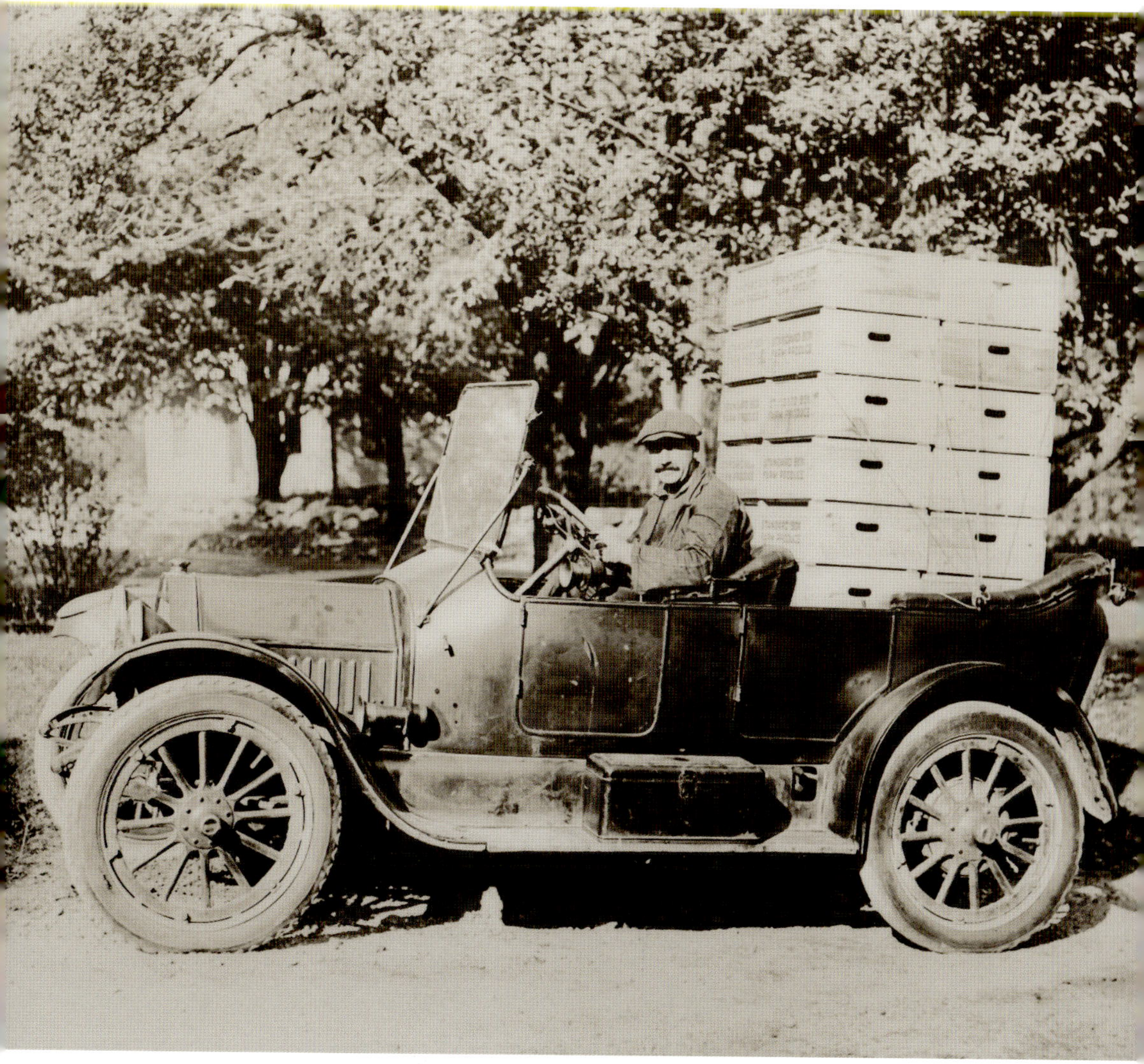

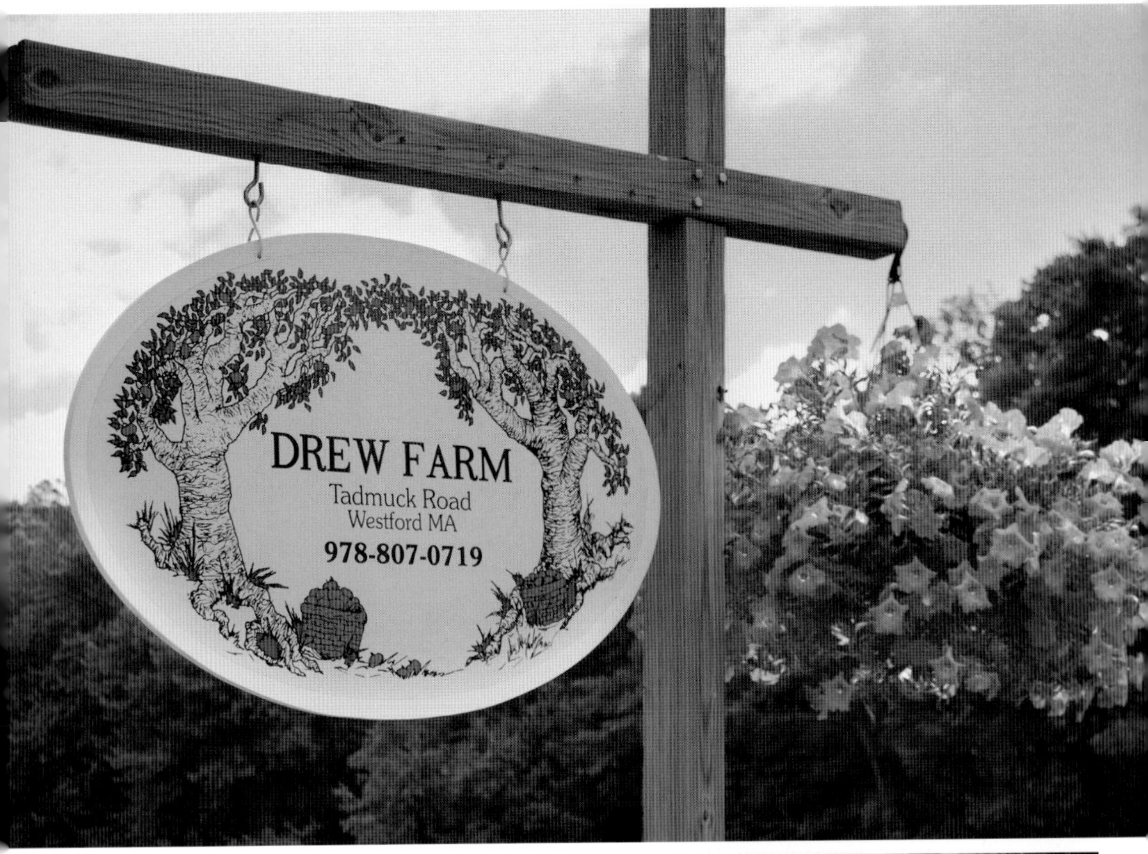

Keith Bohne

Bohne (1944–present) was born in Springfield, Vermont, and received his degree in botany from the University of Vermont. In 1971, a year after meeting Benjamin Drew, Bohne moved to Westford to manage Drew Farms, which Drew had been operating since 1925; a 150-acre apple operation that included orchards, two roadside stands, a cider mill, and apple storage for 30,000 boxes of apples. Bohne purchased the Boston Road stand from Drew in 1976 and grew it into a regional destination, selling everything from apples to specialty foods. He sold the Boston Road stand in 2001 and continued his business in its current Tadmuck Road location, where he runs a "pick your own apple" site and sells plants and flowers. The 30-acre operation draws people from all over the region, continuing the nearly 100-year-old legacy of Drew Farms in Westford. (Author's collection.)

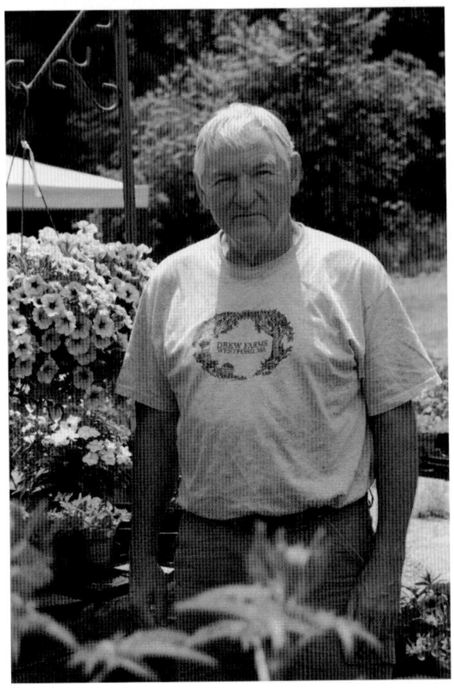

CHAPTER SEVEN

The Everyday Lives

While the people of Westford have done many extraordinary things in the areas of business, public service, art, and literature, what registers with most people are the day-to-day lives of those who call Westford home. Regardless of profession, there are common threads of daily activities that have linked all residents in a common bond of everyday life. From the mail carriers, to recruits during the draft, to children at play, the following images depict residents and their common activities during the early part of the 20th century. The images provide a glimpse into the everyday lives of people, the activities they participated in, and the implements of the period. They also show the architecture of the day that has in most cases endured the centuries and survived to this day. Many of these photographs are from the collections of Charles L. Hildreth (1879–1968) and Quincy Warren Day (1867–1933). Both gentlemen photographed Westford in great detail in the early part of the 20th century. Their collections are now housed in the Westford Museum and provide a window into life during that time.

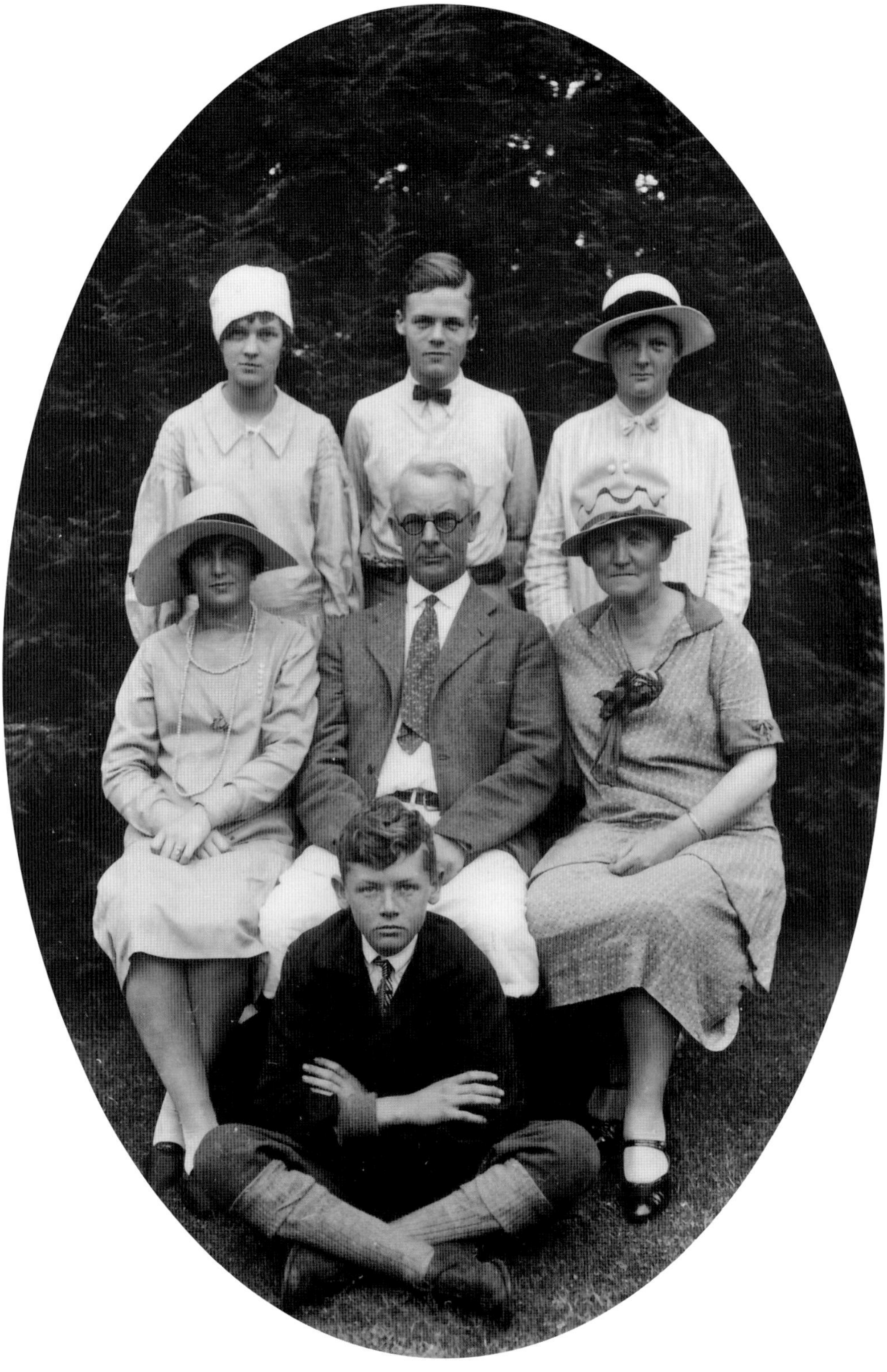

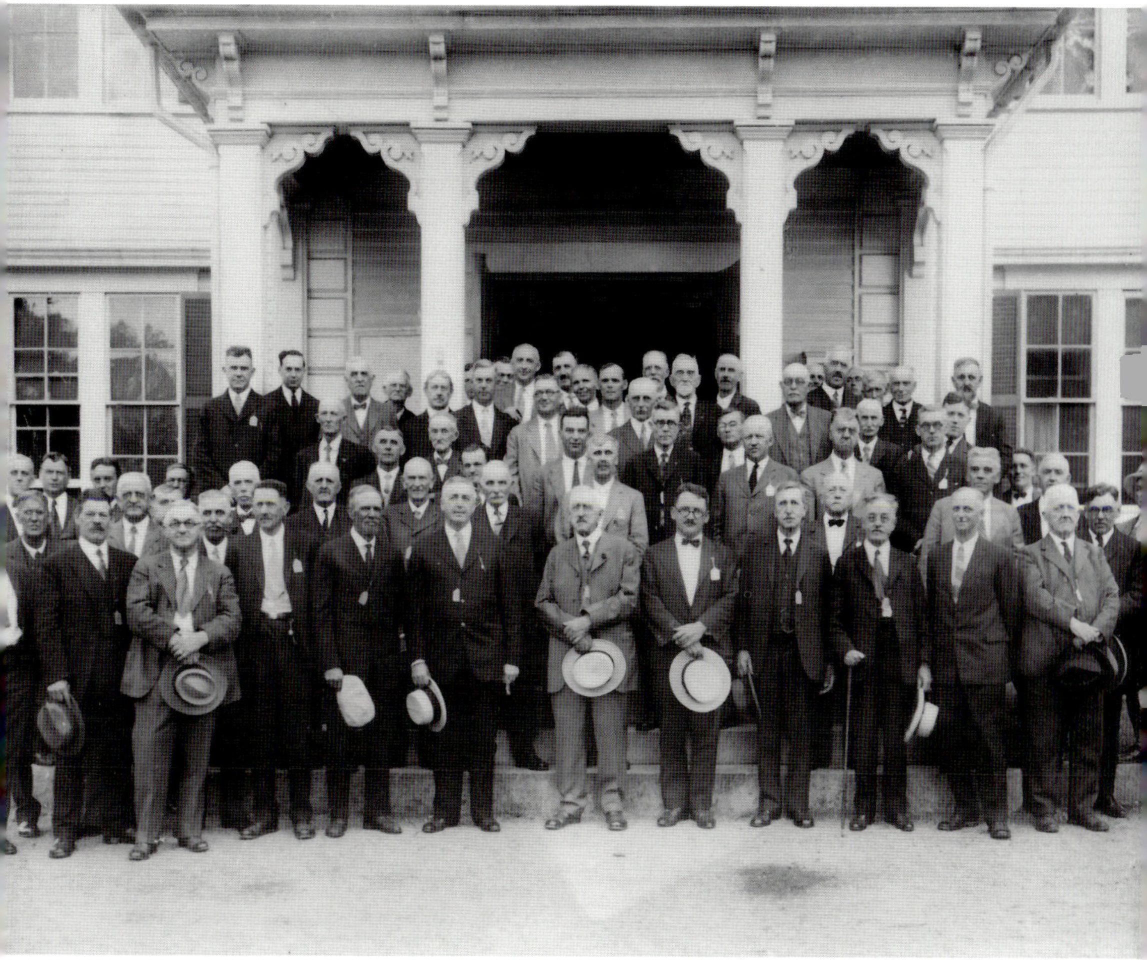

Spaulding Light Cavalry Association

Taken in August 1912, this group photograph shows the Spaulding Light Cavalry Association posing in front of the Westford Town Hall. The organization began as Troop F, 1st Brigade of the Massachusetts Volunteer Militia in 1864 and was known as the "Spaulding Light Cavalry." Its existence was short-lived. The members remained a fraternal organization after the need for the militia ceased. They were tasked with escorting 18 Massachusetts governors and four US presidents and took part in many ceremonies in and around Massachusetts over a 42-year period. As a result of low membership, the adjutant general's office in Massachusetts ordered the organization disbanded in 1907. A veterans association was formed that same year for all honorably discharged members of Company F. In 1908, they were incorporated as the Spaulding Light Cavalry Association, whose purpose was to "foster, develop and perpetuate the bond of friendship and encourage the spirit of good citizenship."

McMaster Family (OPPOSITE PAGE)

This photograph of the McMaster family, taken on September 11, 1927, by Charles Hildreth, is a good illustration of the clothing and formality of the day. This photograph is one of many in the Hildreth Collection taken in the first three decades of the 20th century.

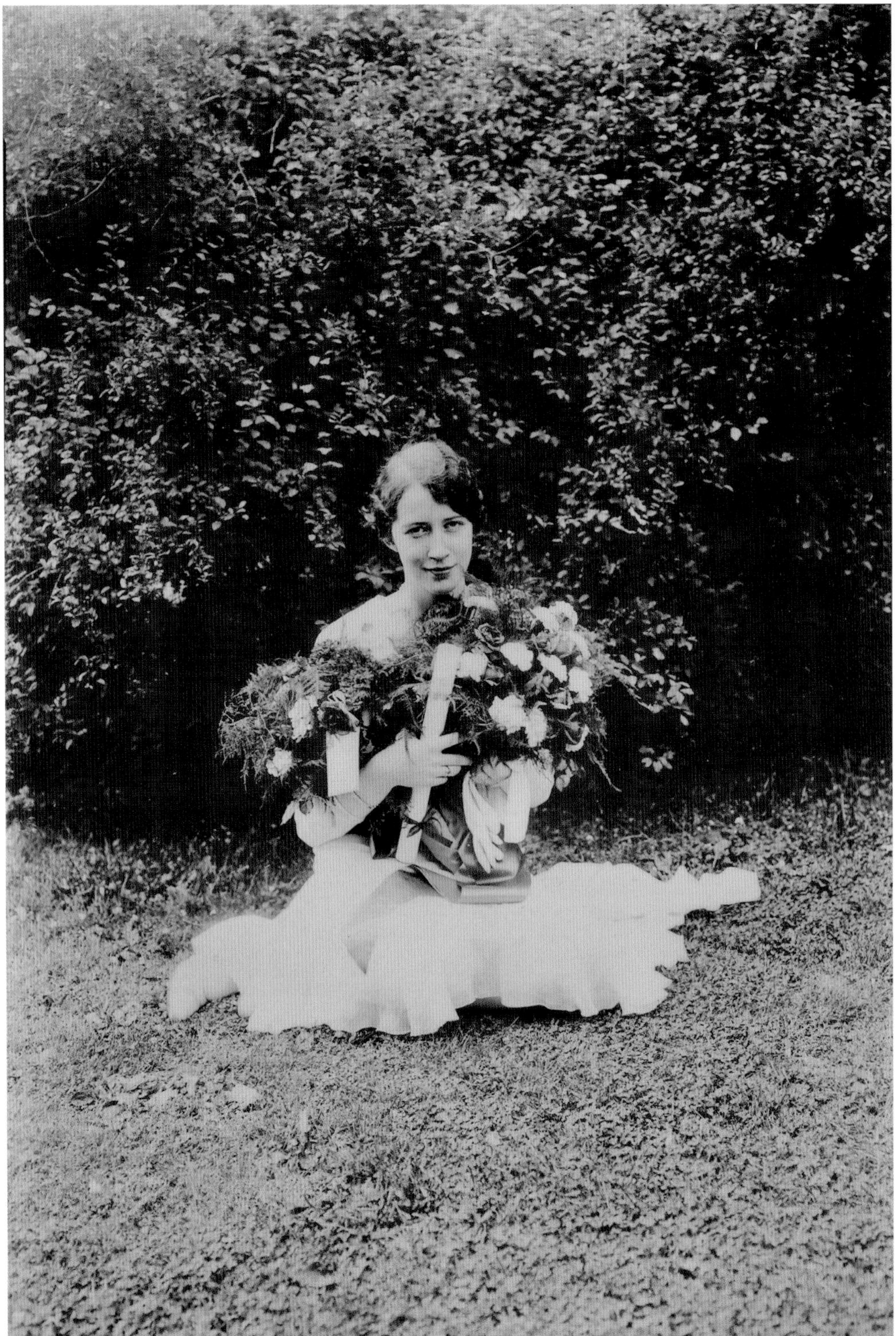

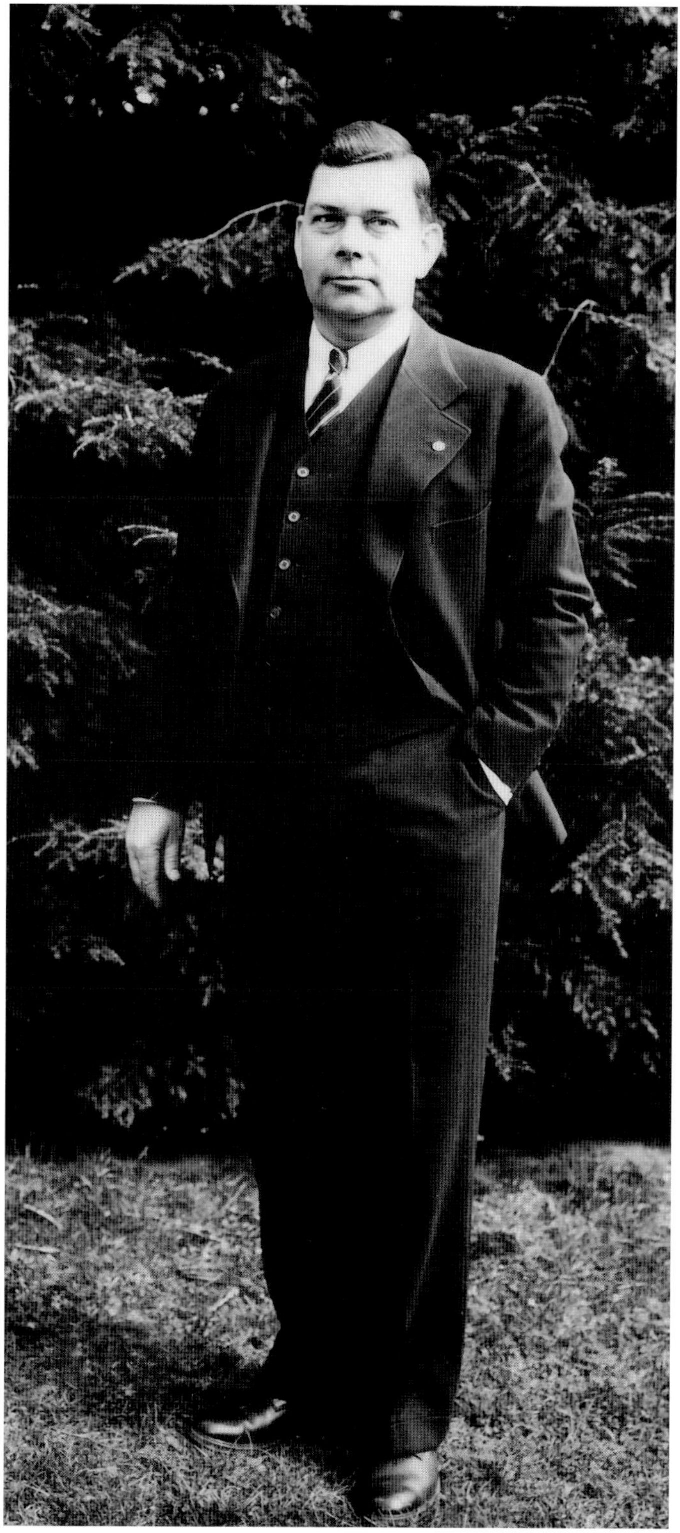

Arthur Perrins
This photograph, taken on April 22, 1936, shows Arthur Perrins during the second-annual Apple Blossom Festival. Perrins, instrumental in the formation of the Apple Blossom Festival, poses proudly here as his daughter had just been crowned the Apple Blossom queen.

Marian Day
(OPPOSITE PAGE)
This photograph of Marian Day, taken by Charles Hildreth in 1929, is an excellent example of the formality of the day. Hildreth took many photographs of family and friends, using the shrubs at the family home as a backdrop.

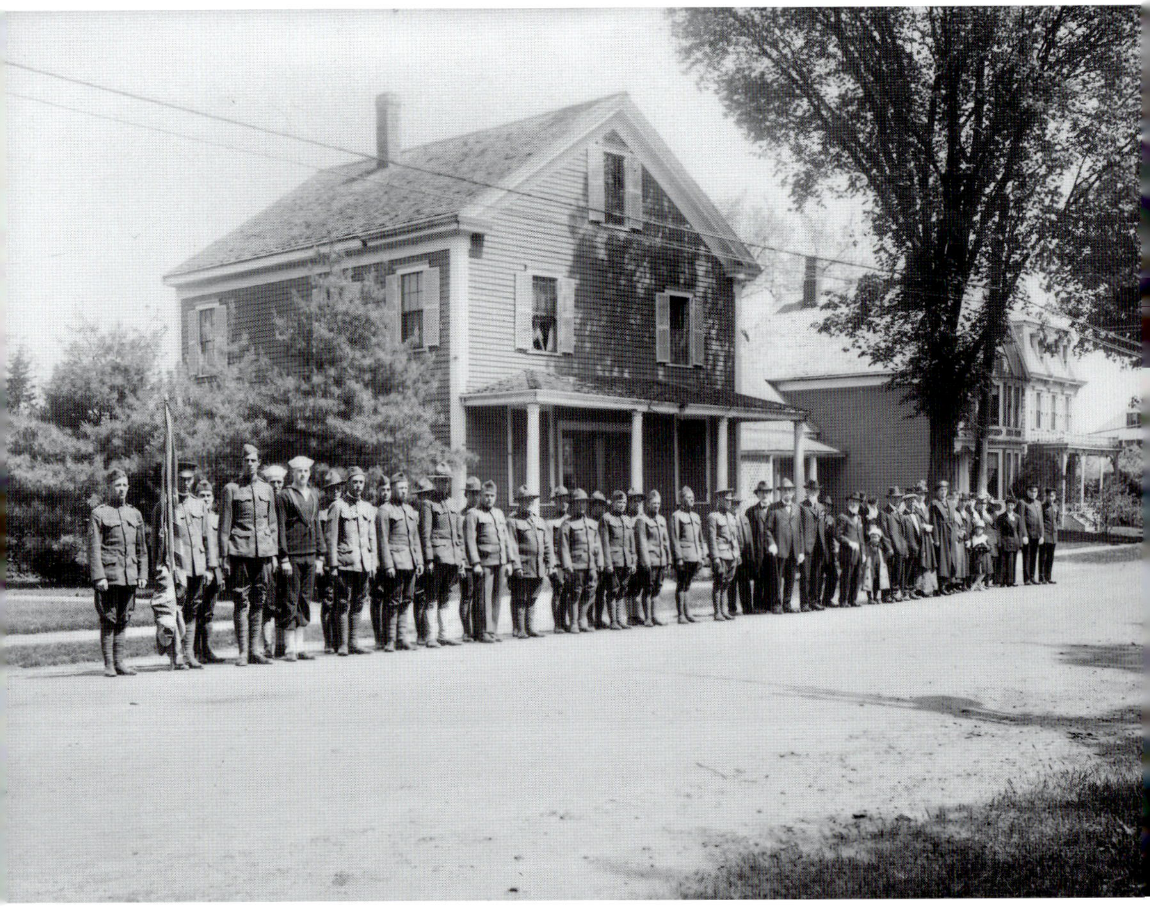

Servicemen
This photograph, believed to have been taken in 1909, shows several generations of servicemen posing in formation on Main Street, across from town hall. Present in the group are the last remaining Civil War veterans at the time. They are dressed in dark suits to the right of the uniformed servicemen.

Marjorie and Alice (OPPOSITE PAGE)
This photograph, taken by Charles Hildreth in 1940, provides an excellent look at the clothing styles of the day. Dressed in vibrant floral prints and with matching handbags, gloves, and shoes, these two ladies posed for this photograph at the Hildreth home.

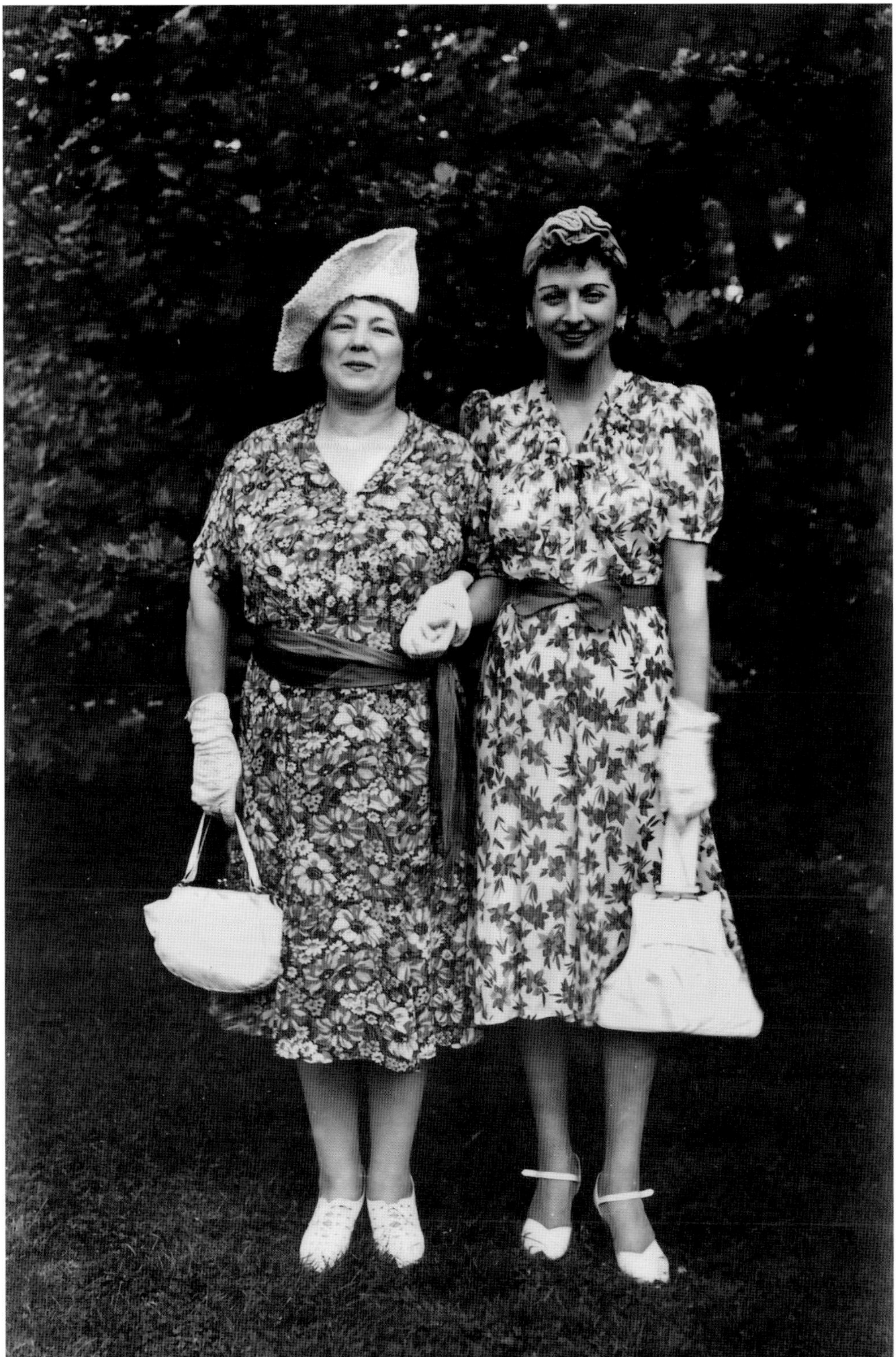

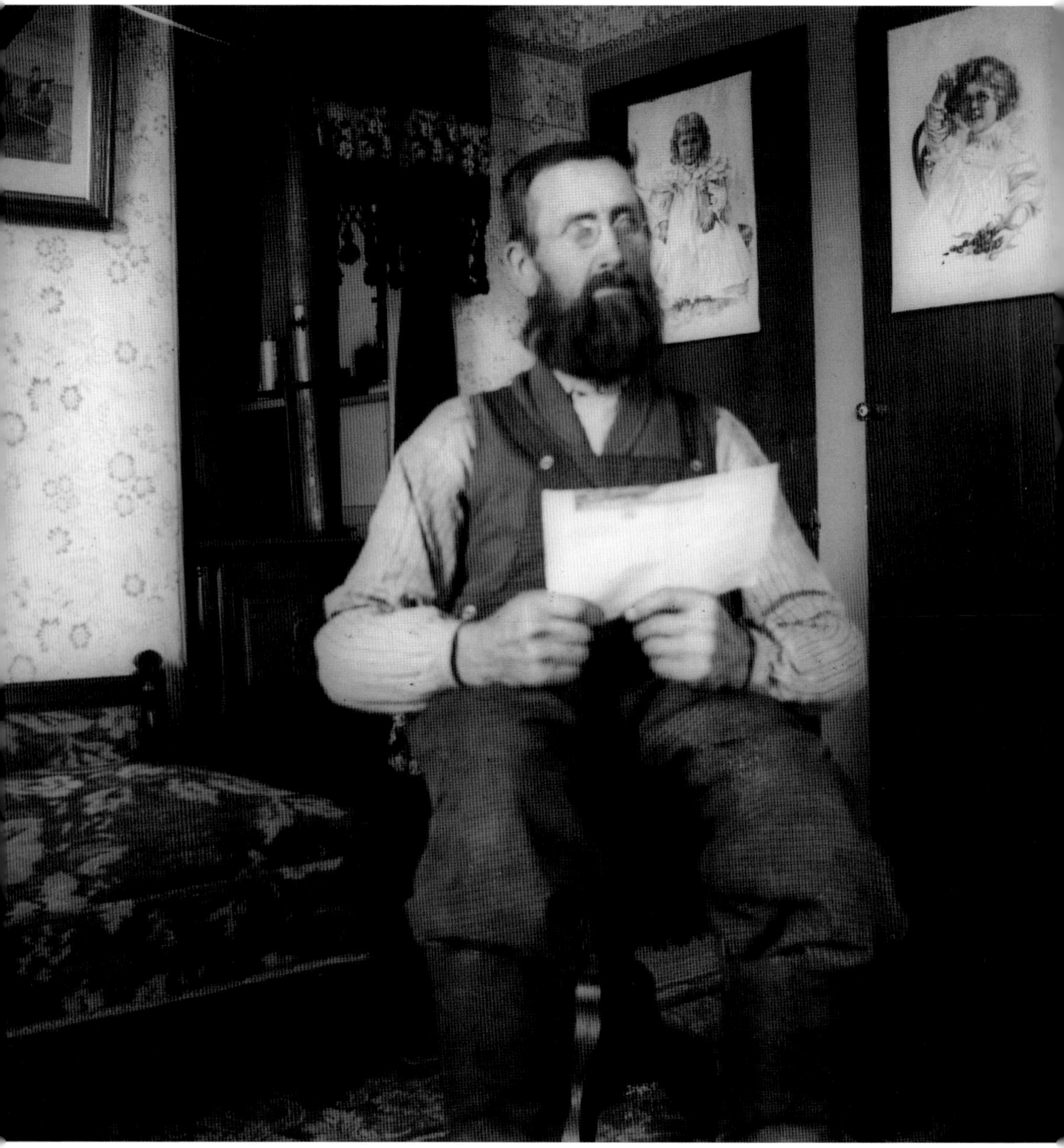

John Warren Day

Day (1837–1900), seen here in his home at 47 Graniteville Road, was married to Emma Meriam (Sprague) Day (1842–1920) and was the father of Quincy Warren Day (1867–1933). Quincy Day took a large number of photographs that do a wonderful job of cataloguing the life of the Day family and of various Westford sites. These photographs are now part of the Quincy Day Collection at the Westford Museum.

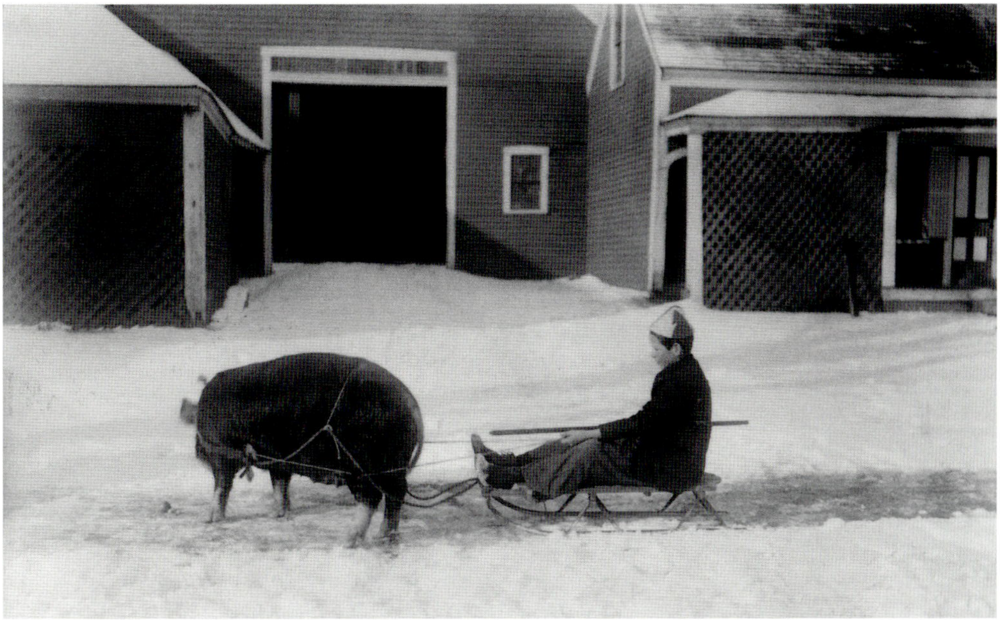

Evolution of Transportation

These photographs from the Charles L. Hildreth collection offer a fun look at the early part of the 20th century. The above image is titled "Gordon & Pig." Gordon Seavey (1905–1996), having harnessed the family pig, seems be enjoying himself as his transportation burden is eased just a bit. The bottom photograph is a great glimpse at one of the automobiles of the day. Here, the Donald Cameron family poses in their automobile on August 19, 1908.

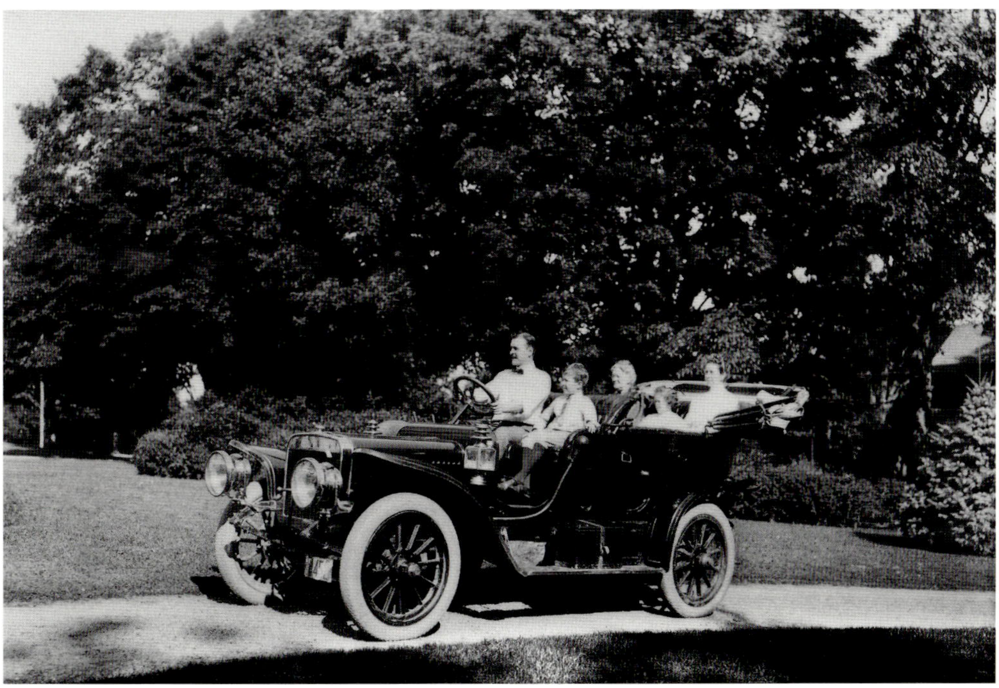

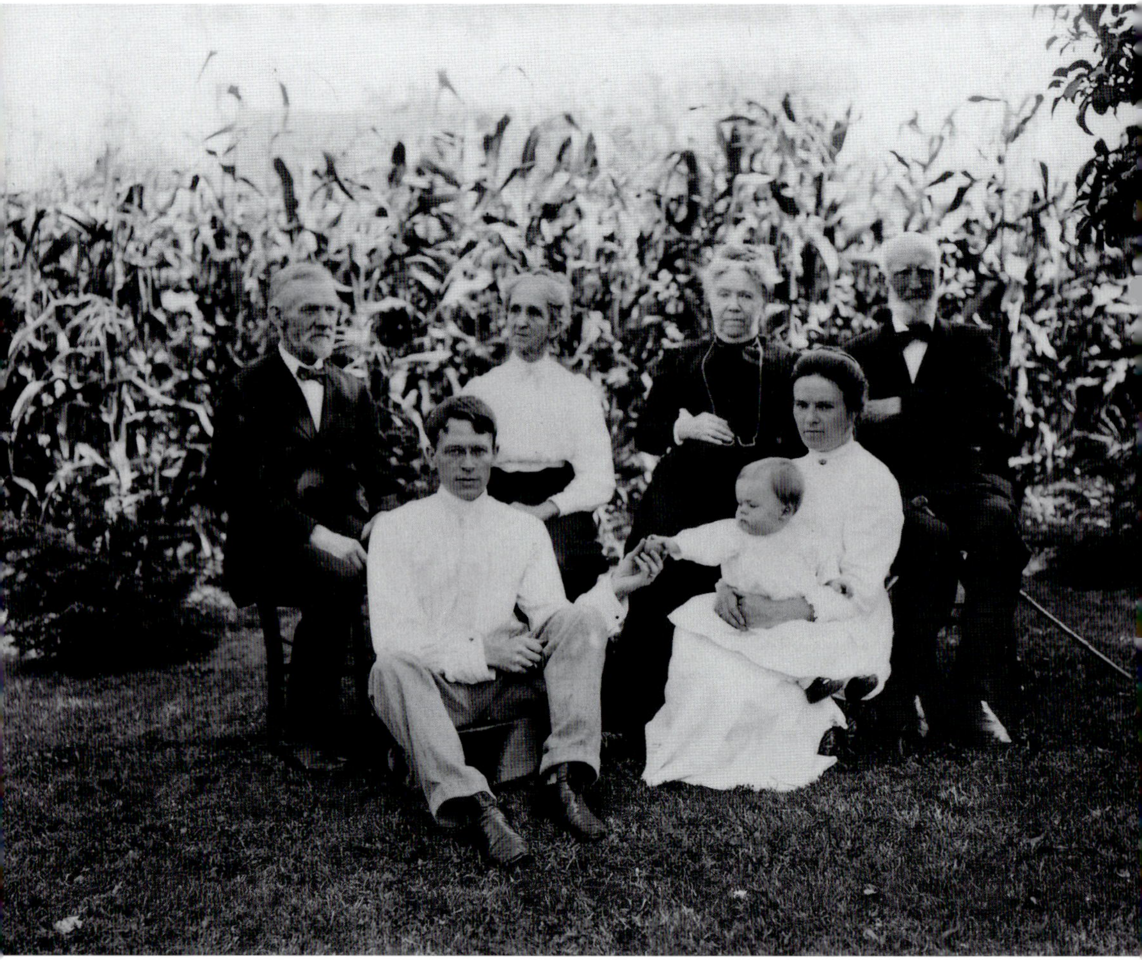

Hildreth Family

From the Charles Hildreth Collection, this photograph, showing three generations of the Hildreth family, is a spectacular illustration of the formality of the time. Taken on August 28, 1910, presumably on the Hildreth property, this photograph reveals corn stalks standing in the background. Charles Hildreth, behind the camera in most photographs, can be seen sitting in front, holding a ball for the baby. Pictured are, from left to right, (first row) Charles Lewis Hildreth (1879–1968), Elizabeth Cushing (Heywood) Hildreth (1879–1925), and Roger Heywood Hildreth (b. 1909); (second row) Charles Willis Hildreth (1847–1934), Lucy Marie (Colburn) Hildreth (1845–1931), Mary E. (Mellen) Heywood (1846–1916), and George Washington Heywood (1829–1914).

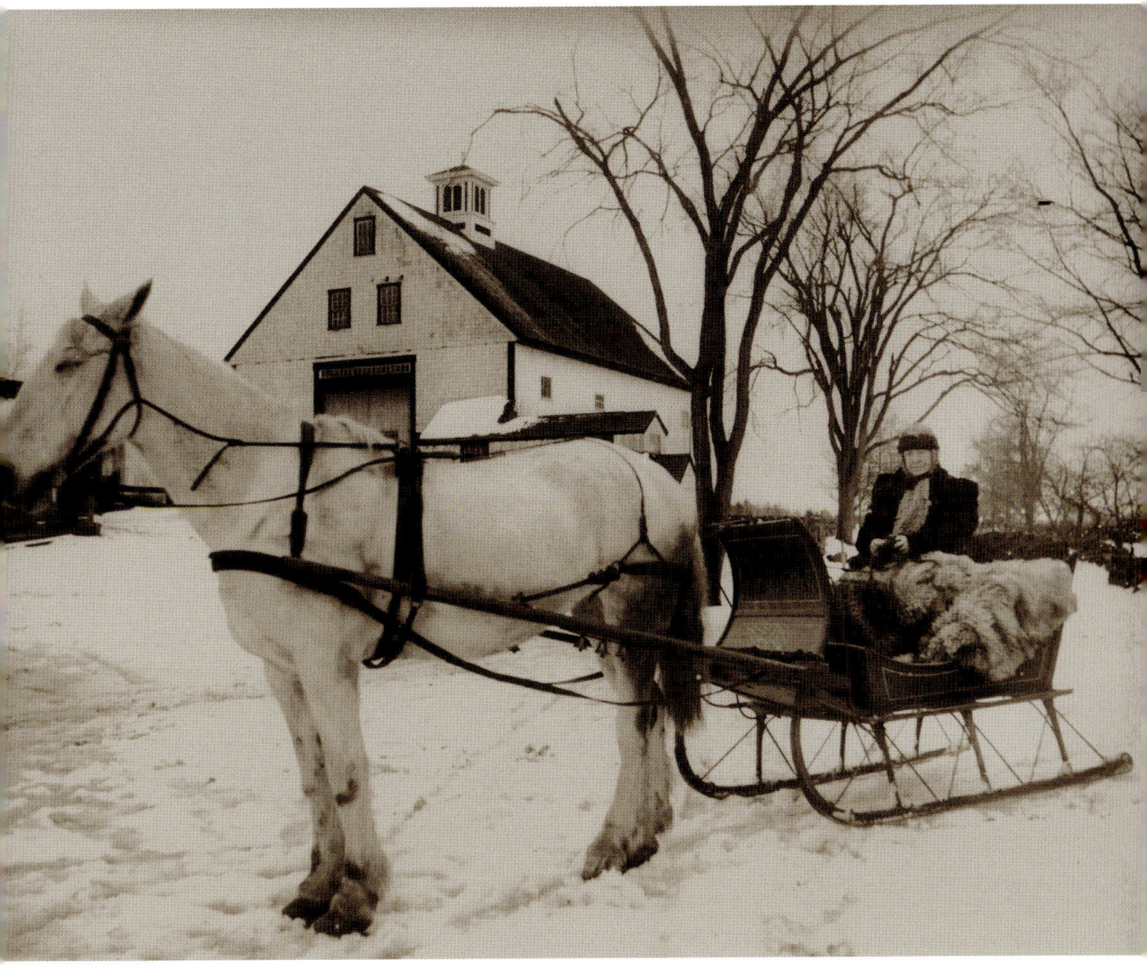

Horse and Sleigh

This photograph from the Quincy Day Collection at the Westford Museum shows an example of the transportation available in Westford around the turn of the 20th century. The horse in this photograph was a popular subject in several of Quincy Day's photographs.

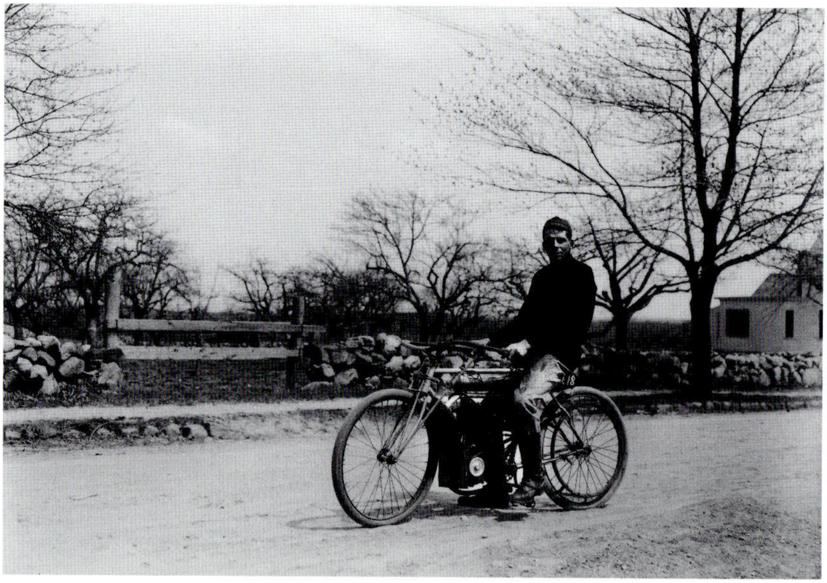

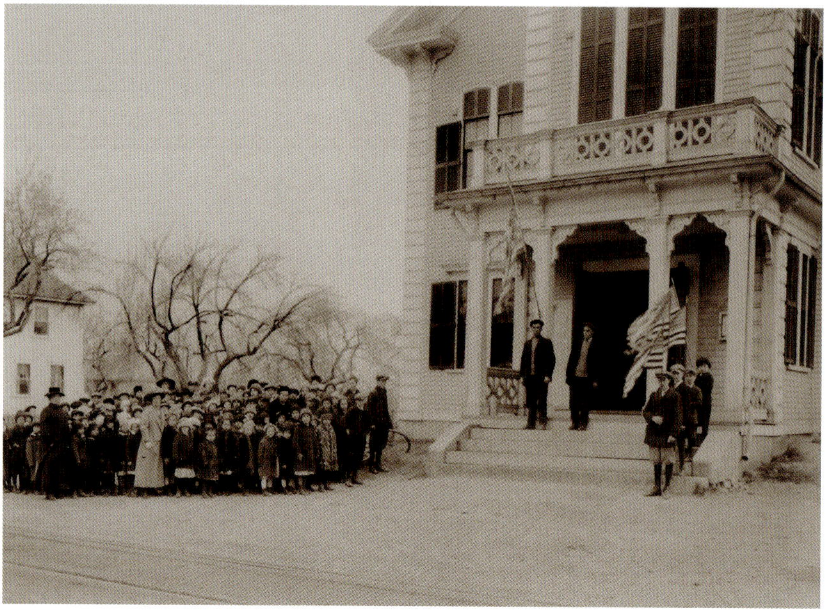

Frederick W. Clement

Taken on May 27, 1911, the top photograph of Frederick W. Clement (b. 1891) posing on an early motorcycle was taken by Charles Hildreth. The photograph provides a great look into early motorcycle development. Motorcycles of the day, with their thin tires, were nothing more than a heavy bicycle with a small motor mounted to the frame.

Schoolchildren

Taken on November 17, 1917, the bottom photograph shows Westford School children waiting for the raising of the flag. Three years into World War I, and with the first draft behind them, the residents of Westford were keenly aware of the dangers of the war that was being waged. As a consequence, patriotism was part of day-to-day life.

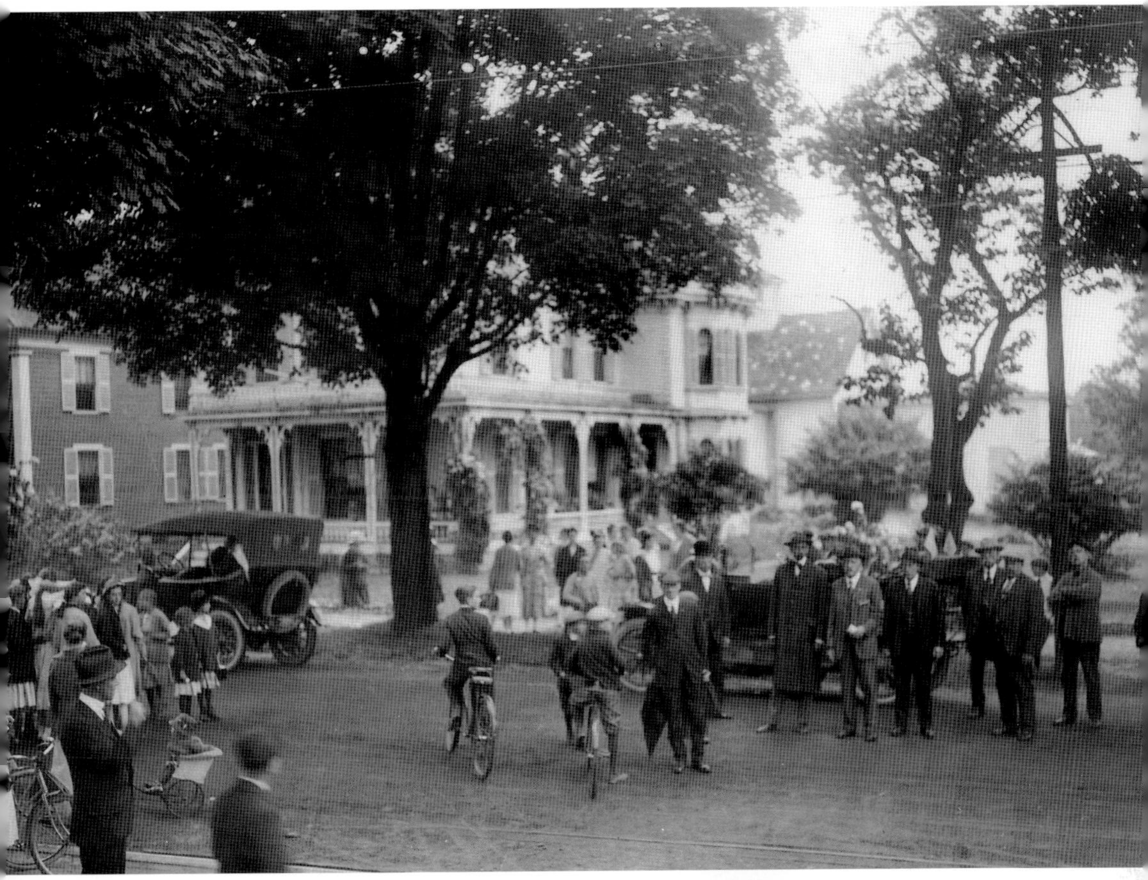

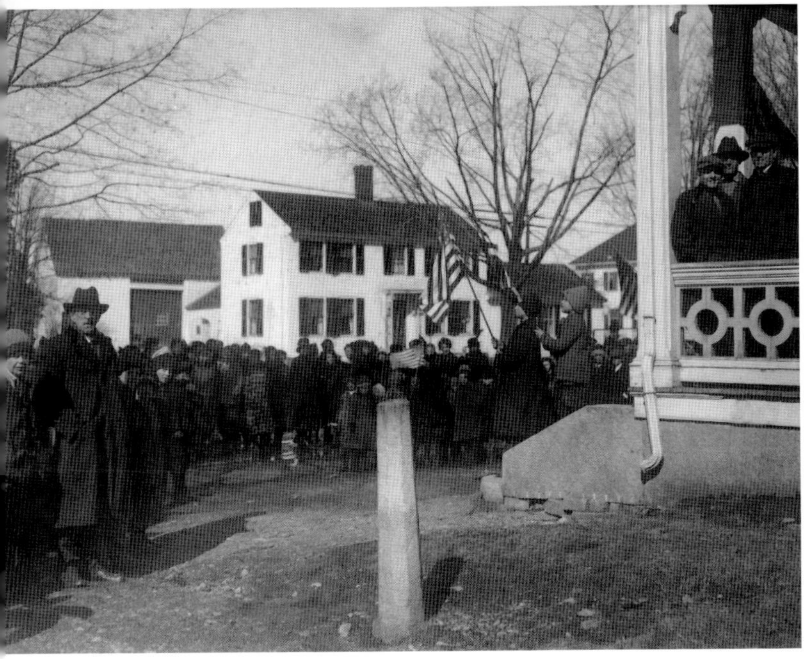

Townspeople
These photographs by Charles Hildreth illustrate the deep interest of town matters in the early part of the 20th century. Taken on September 21, 1917, the photographs capture the townspeople gathering to hear the results of the first military draft.

Abbot Baseball Team

This 1920 photograph by Charles Hildreth shows a local baseball team. The Abbot Worsted Company name ("A W Co" on the jerseys) can be plainly seen. The Abbot Company was a significant sponsor of local athletics.

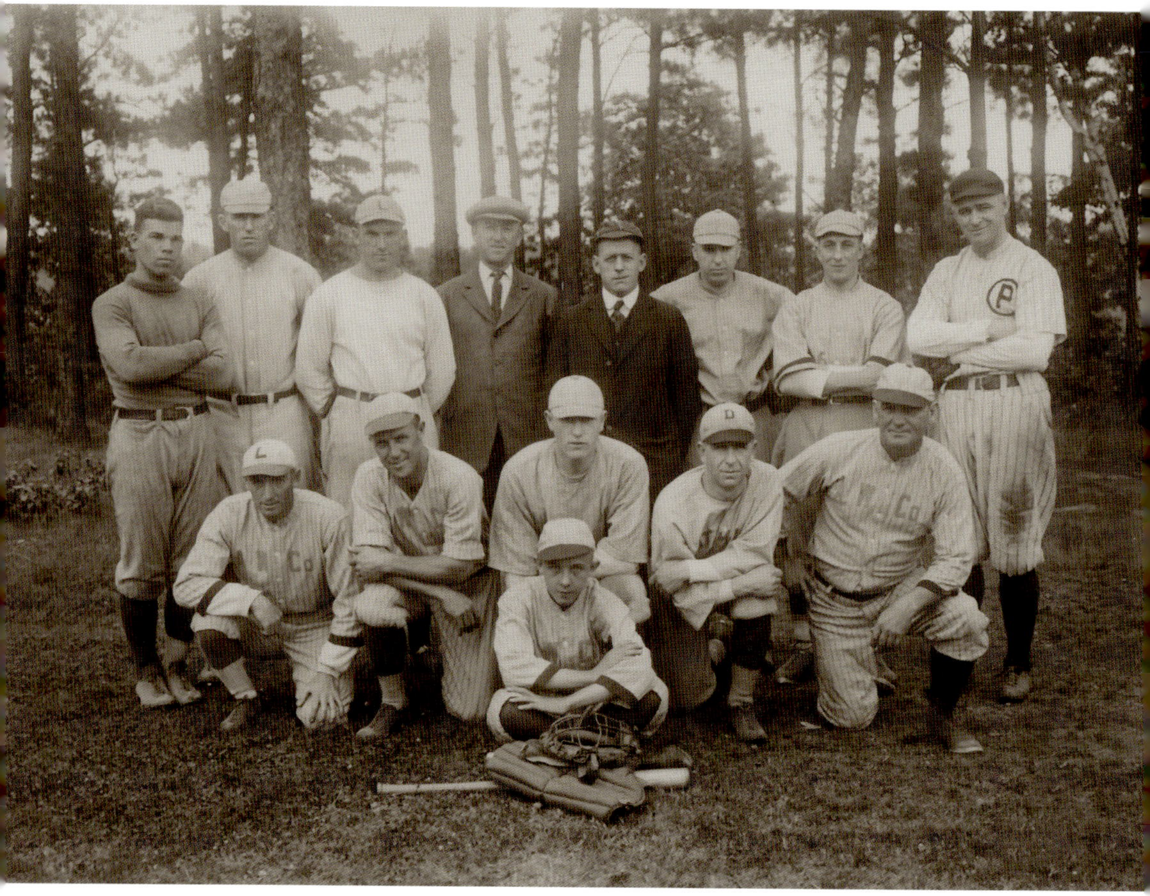

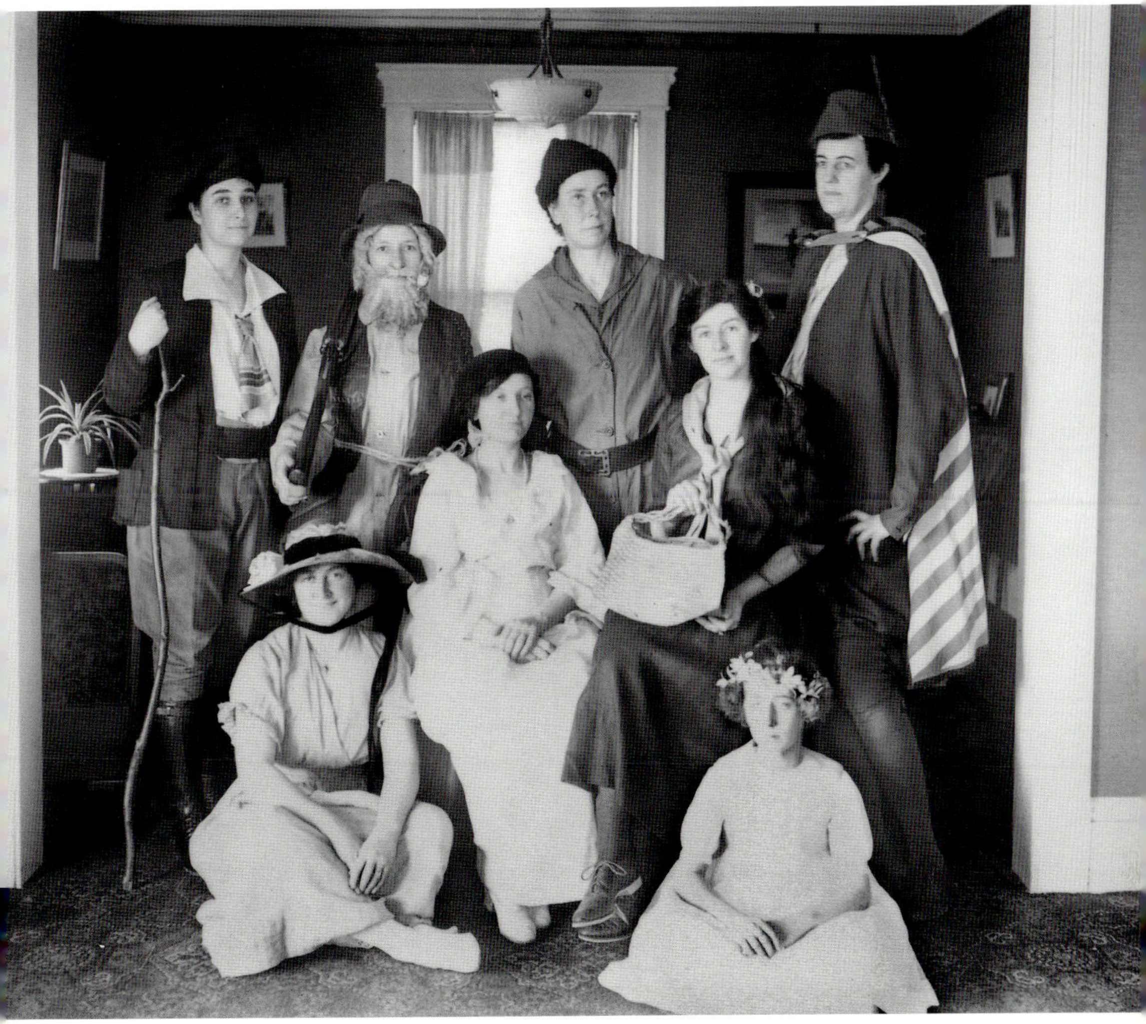

Dramatic Cast

This photograph, taken in a local home by Charles Hildreth, shows a theater group. The photograph, titled "Dramatic Cast," was taken in 1921. Participation in live theater was a popular pastime in the days before movies were readily available to all communities.

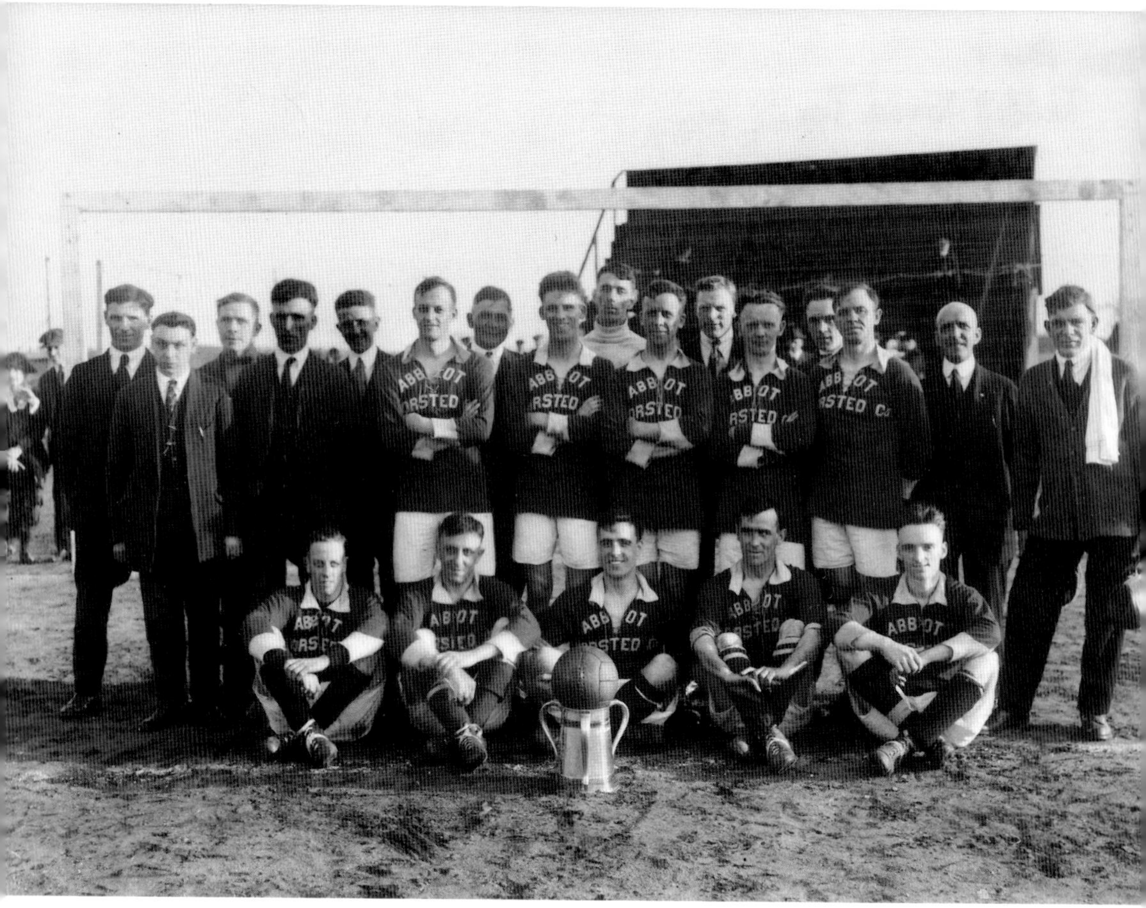

Abbot Soccer Team
This formal photograph of an award-winning Abbot soccer team was taken in 1921. The team, sponsored by the Abbot Worsted Company, was outfitted with what were cutting-edge uniforms of the day, and it is said that the Abbot Company recruited from as far away as Europe to bring top players to the team.

Hildreths (OPPOSITE PAGE)
This formal photograph of Charles Willis Hildreth and his wife, Lucy Marie (Colburn) Hildreth, was taken in the parlor of the Hildreth home on April 6, 1921. It offers a fascinating look into the formality of the day. Gentlemen, especially elders, commonly wore three-piece suits. Note the commemorative pillows on the sofa.

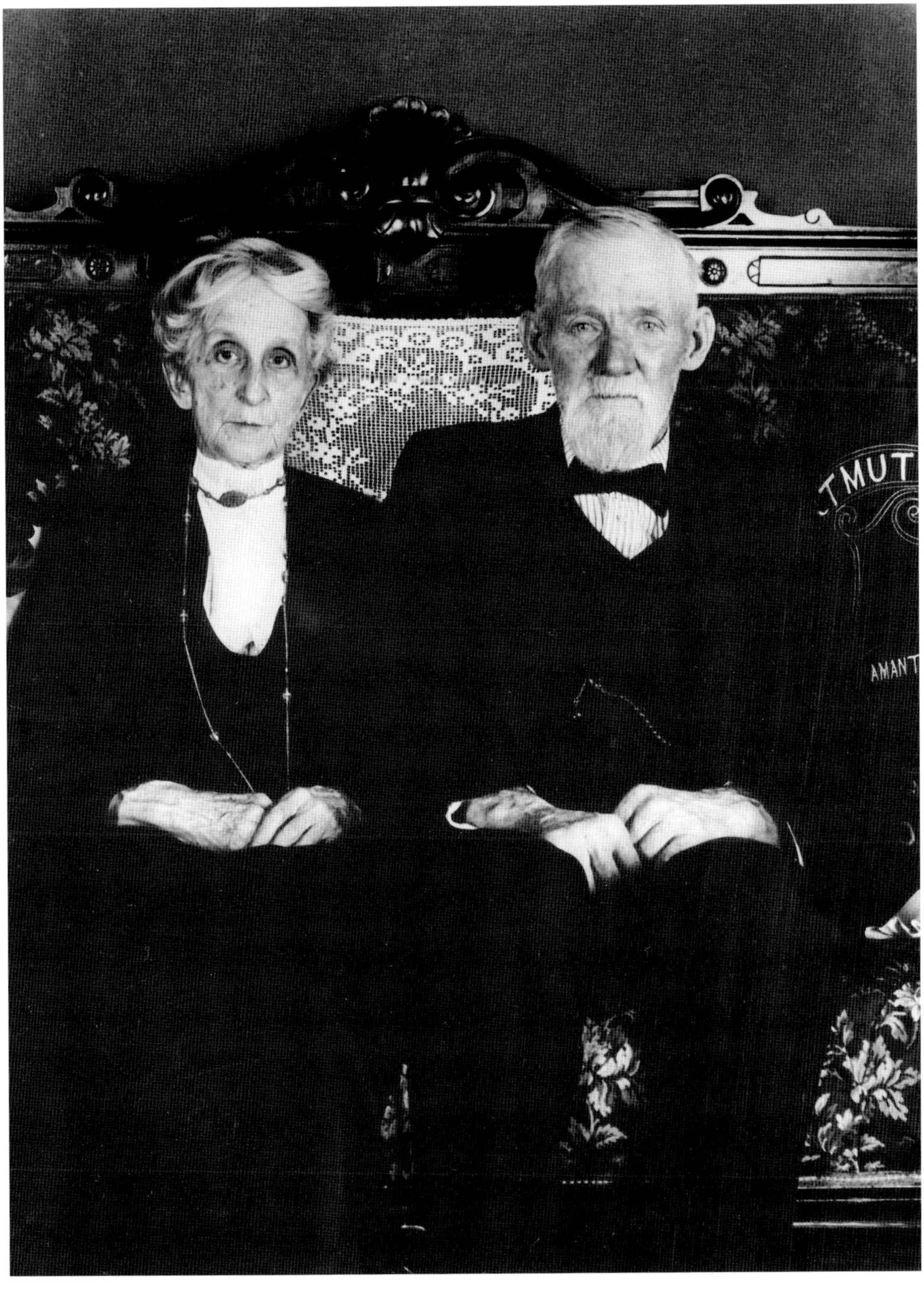

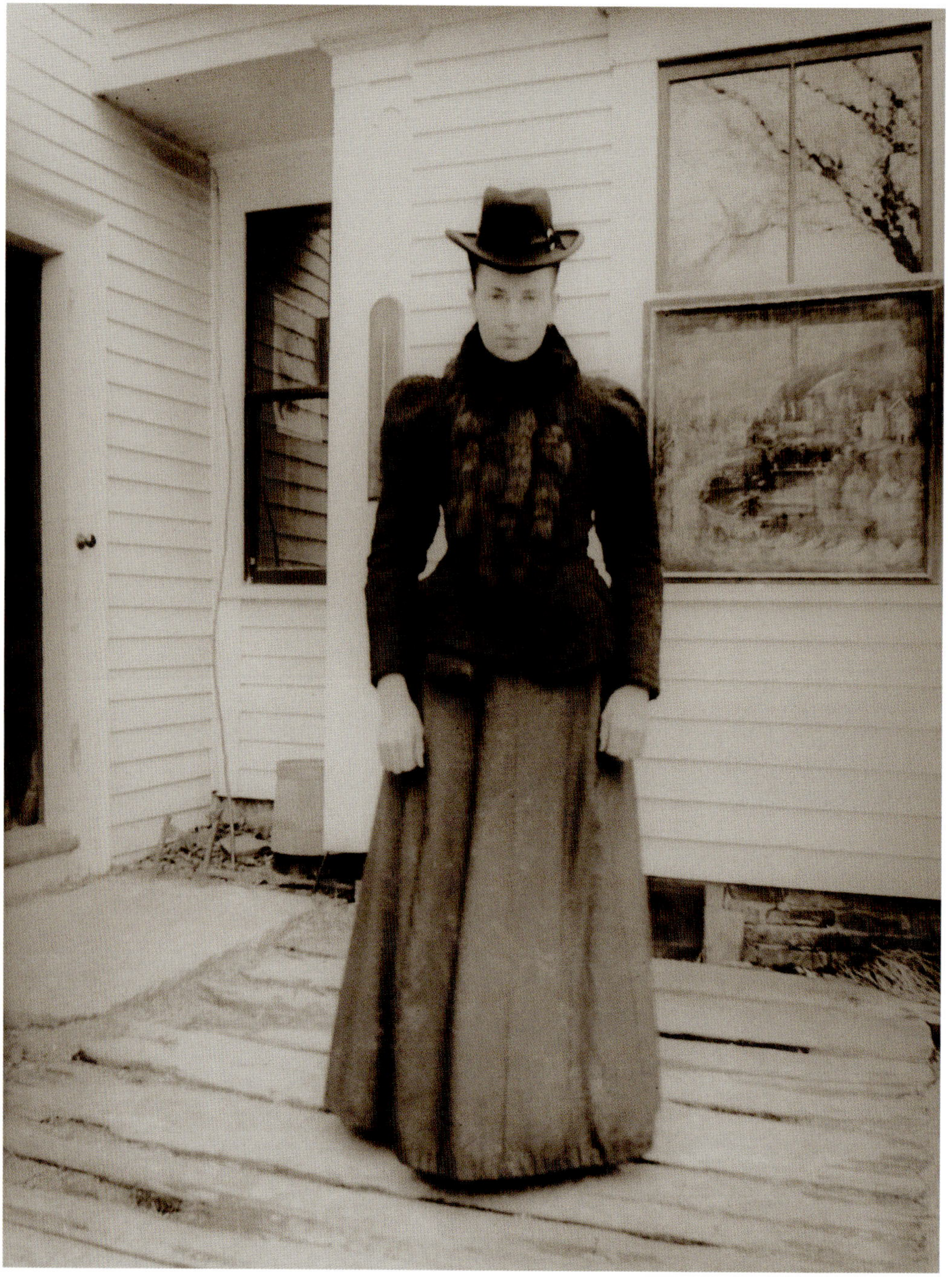

Ada Sharp Day

Day (1864–1964) was married to Quincy Warren Day (1867–1933), who took this photograph, which is now part of the Quincy Day Collection at the Westford Museum. This photograph was taken on the steps of the Day home at 47 Graniteville Road in 1900 (most likely in winter, based on the clothing). The home still stands, and the alcove behind Ada in the photograph is still visible, although the structure has seen many improvements over the years.

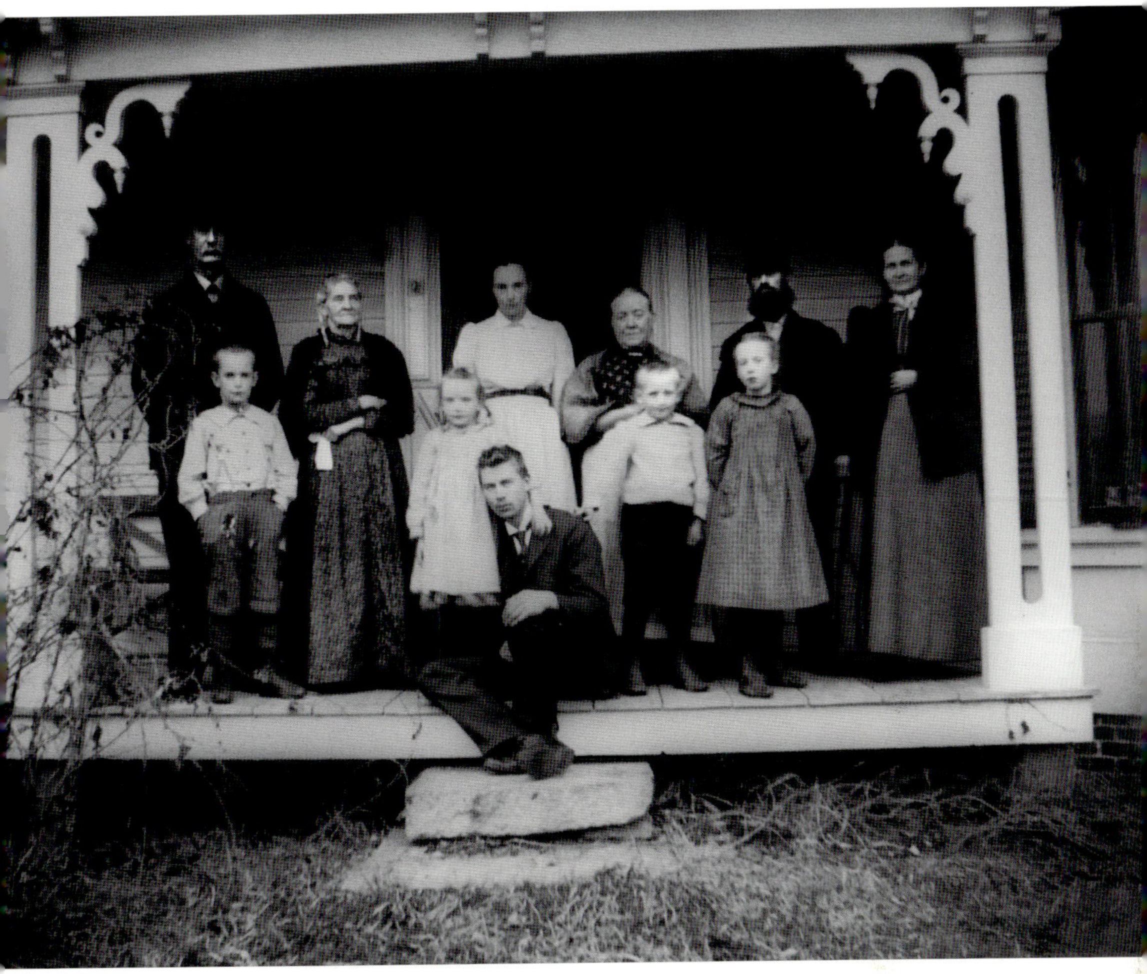

The Day Family

Taken on November 30, 1899, Thanksgiving Day, this photograph is a wonderful portrait of the Day family. Gathered on the "piazza," the members of the family shown here are, from left to right, (first row) Otis Day, Ada Day, Arthur Day (seated), Albert Day, and May Day; (second row) Warren Jones, Susan Rand, Ada Day, Emma Day, John W. Day, and Sara Day Jones.

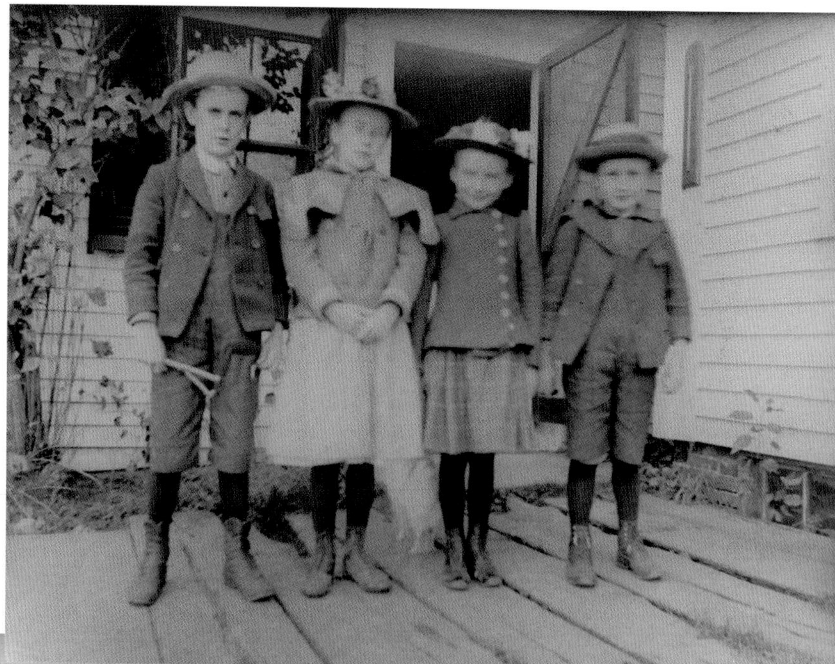

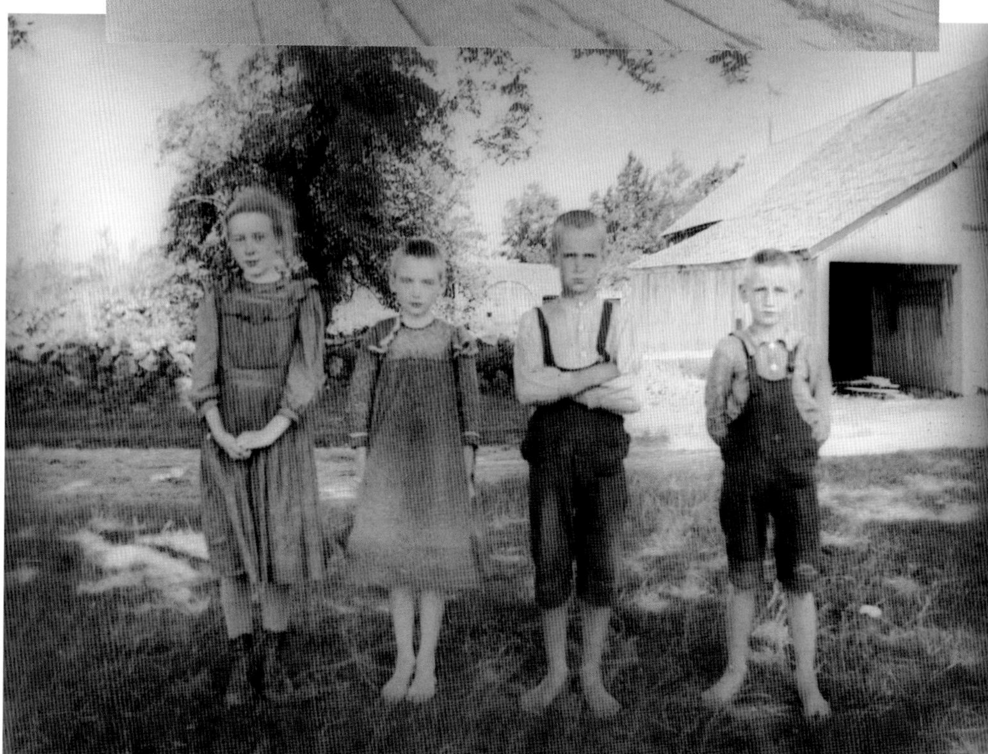

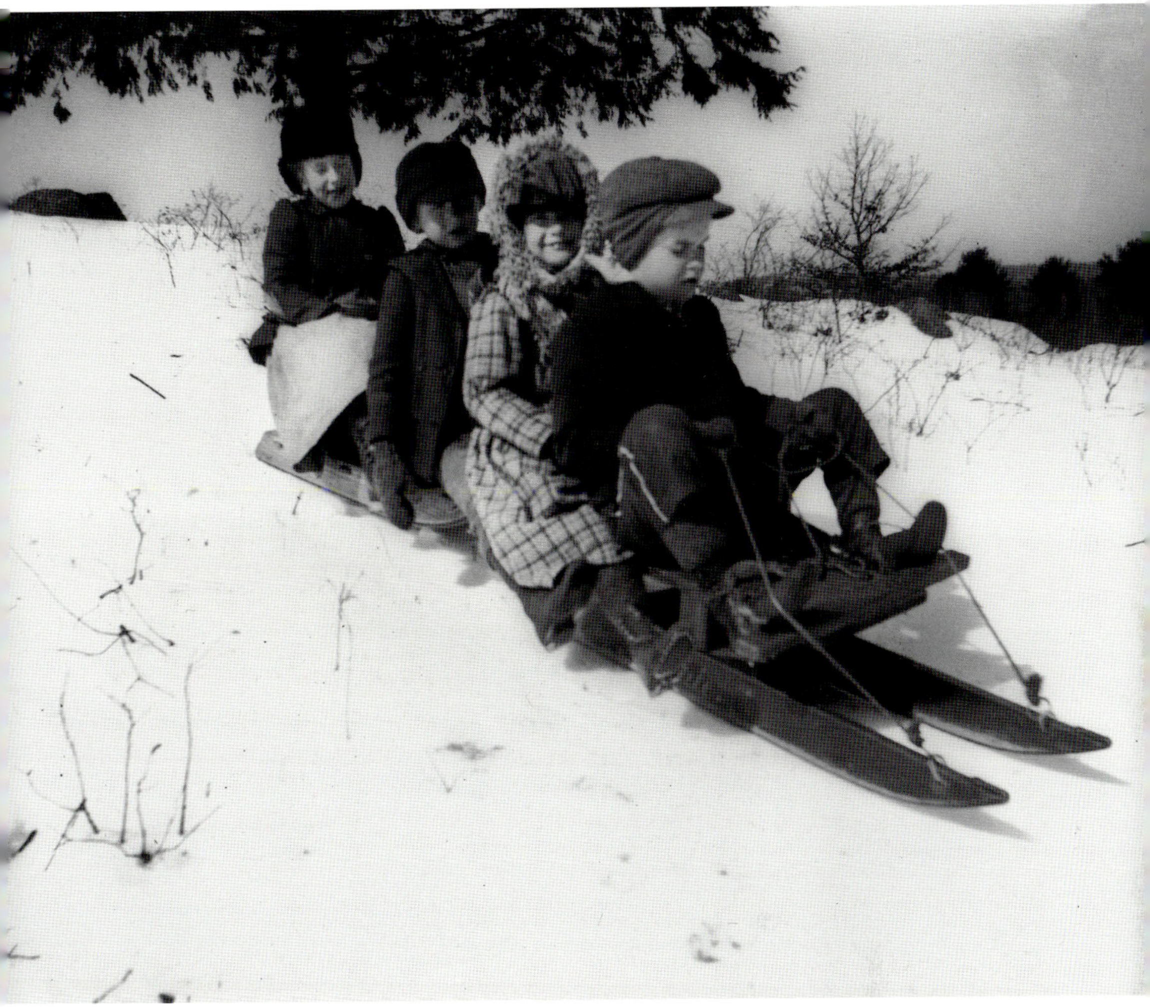

The Day Children
In this photograph, taken on March 16, 1900, the Day children (from left to right, May, Albert, Addie, and Otis) are coasting behind their family barn at 47 Graniteville Road. The barn no longer stands on the property, but the granite that formed the foundation is still visible, and one can imagine them sledding down the adjacent hill.

The Day Children in 1902 (OPPOSITE PAGE)
These two photographs, part of the Quincy Day Collection, show the Day children dressed in both their everyday play clothes and in their more formal school attire. In the top photograph, taken on October 18, 1900, in school attire, are, from left to right, Otis, May, Addie, and Albert. Addie and Albert Day were twins. In the bottom photograph, taken on August 9, 1902, in play clothes, are, from left to right, May (1890–1973), Addie (b. 1893), Otis (1891–1994), and Albert (1893–1987) Day.

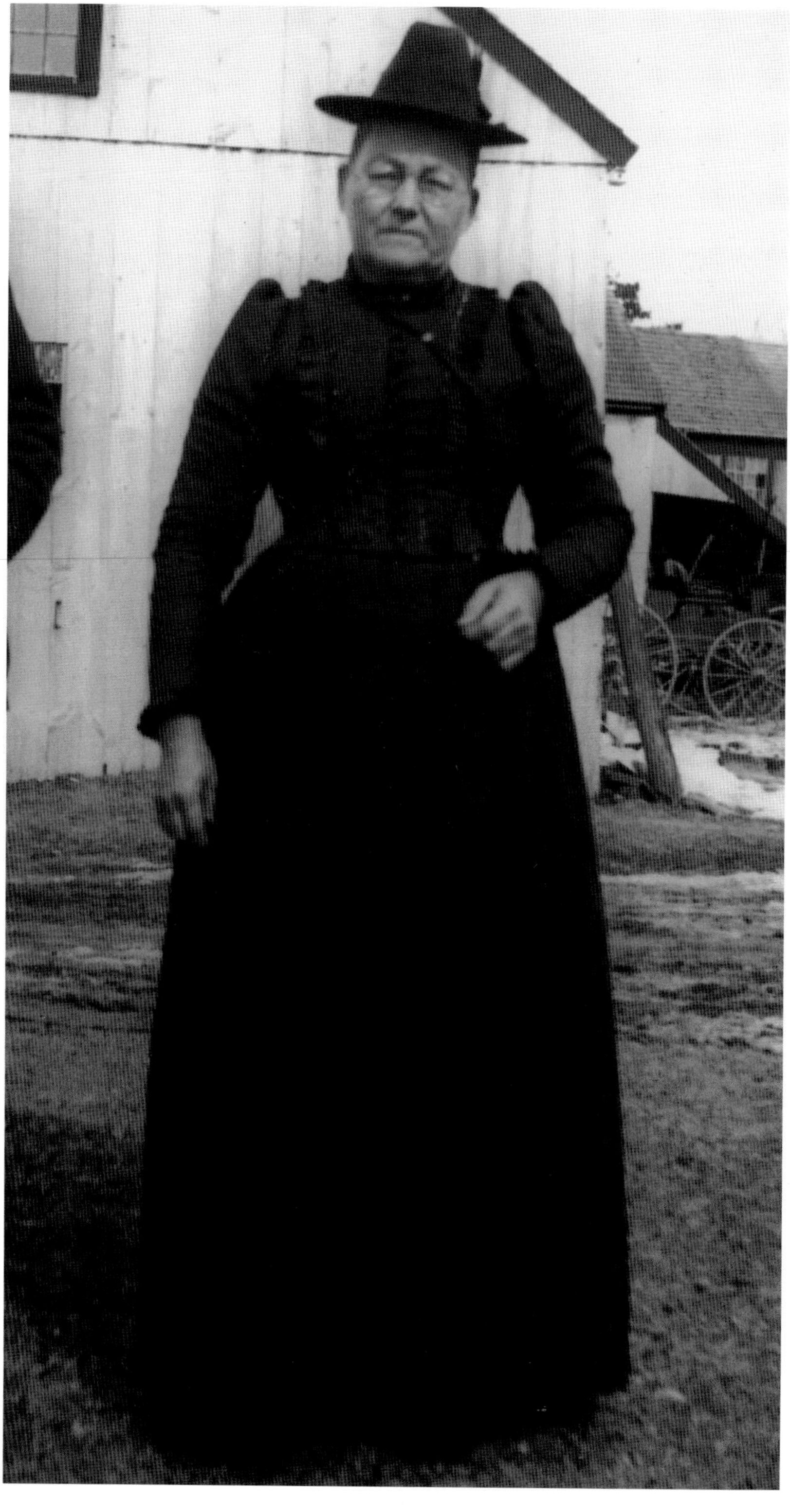

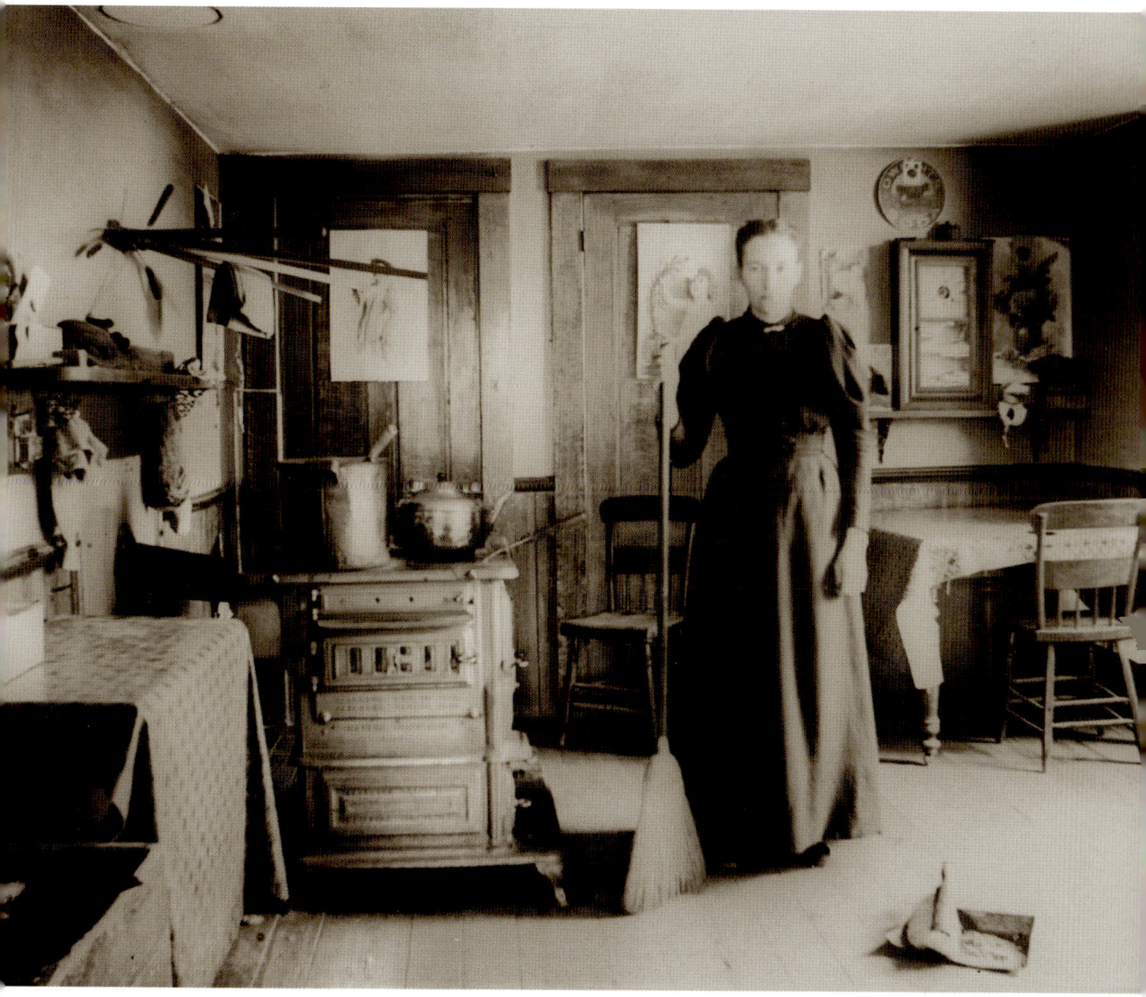

Ada Sharp Day
This photograph of Ada Day, taken by her husband, Quincy Day, shows her cleaning inside the Day home at 47 Graniteville Road around the turn of the 20th century. Even when performing basic household tasks, the people of the era wore what is today considered formal clothing.

Sarah Allen Sharp (OPPOSITE PAGE)
Sharp, mother of Ada Day Sharp, mother-in-law of Quincy Warren Day, is seen here in the yard of the Day house at 47 Graniteville Road, during a visit with her husband, John Sharp, from New Brunswick, Canada, during the later part of the 19th century.

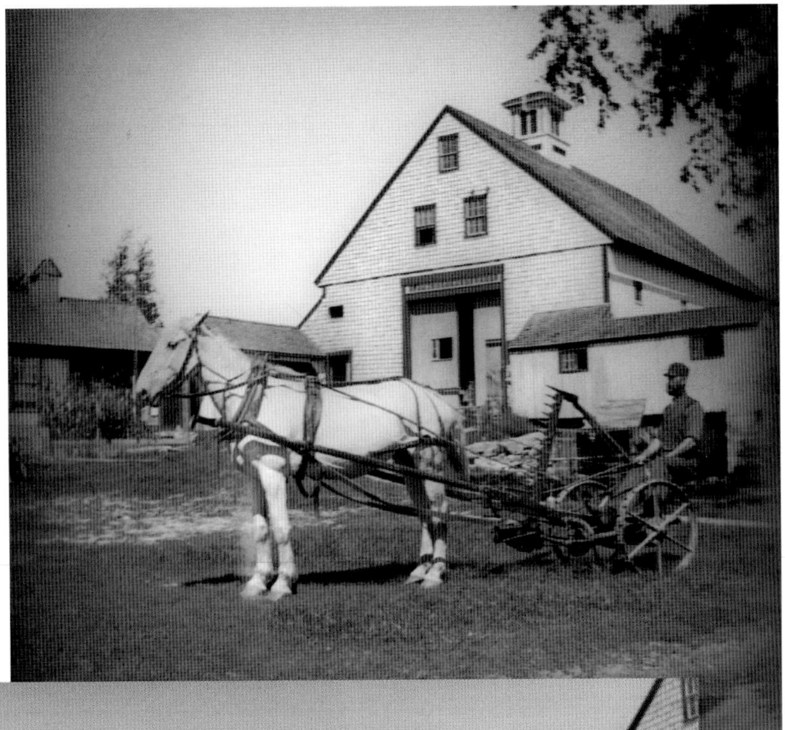

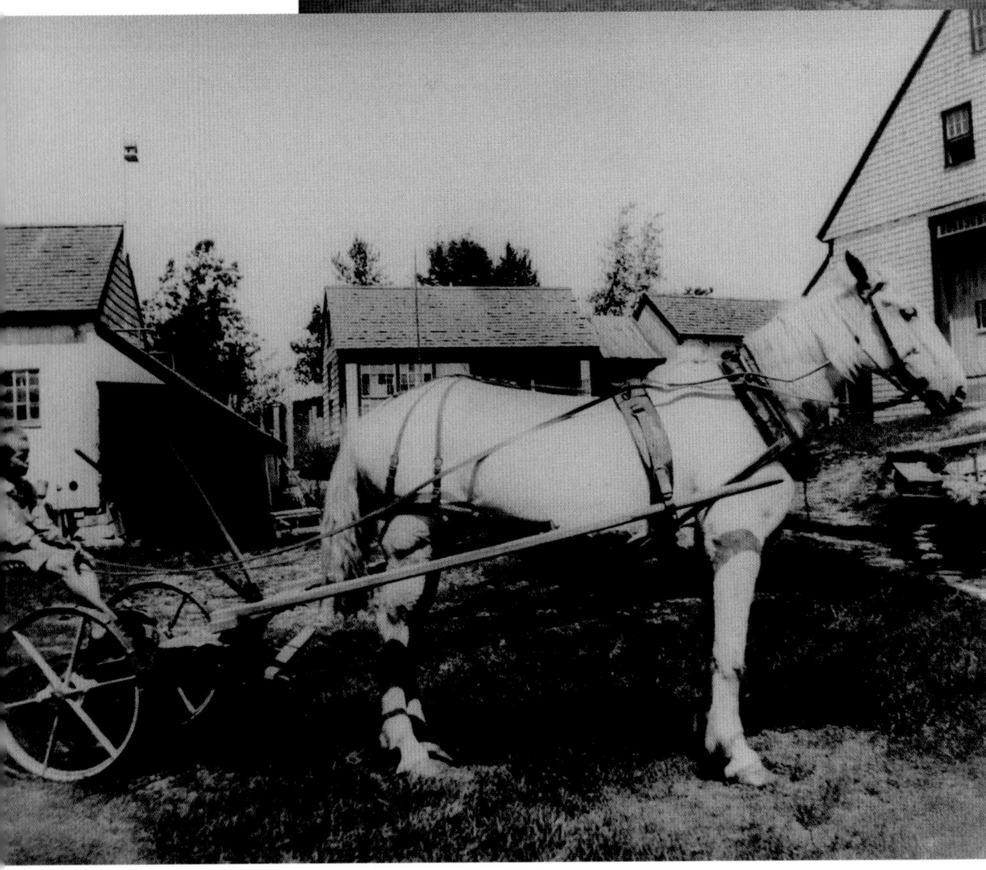

The Day Family Horse (OPPOSITE PAGE)
This horse (name unknown), belonging to the Day family, was a popular subject of Quincy Warren Day's photographs. It is seen above pulling a farm implement with John W. Day and below with one of the Day children. These photographs were taken at the Day home at 47 Graniteville Road.

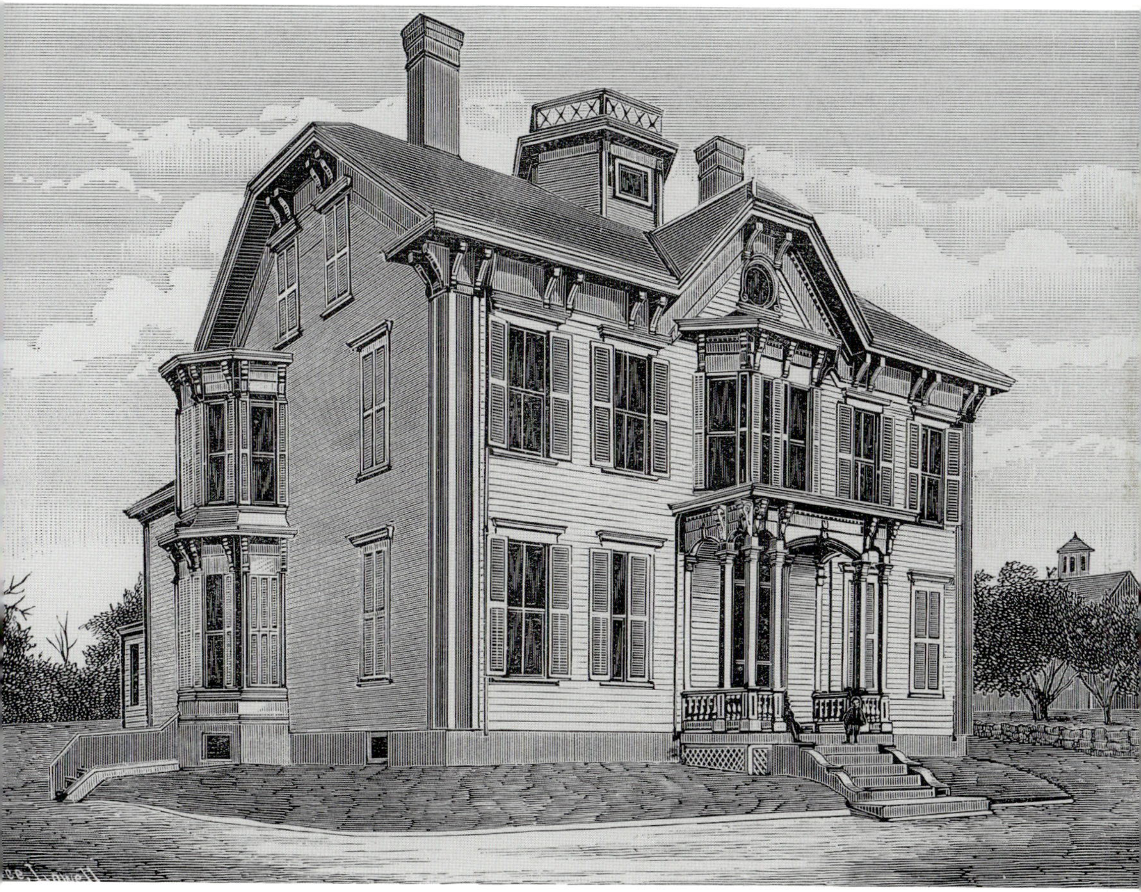

Residence of Allan Cameron
This ink drawing of the residence of Allan Cameron at 39 Main Street was featured in the commemorative pamphlet for the 1896 opening of the J.V. Fletcher Library. Cameron was a trustee of Westford Academy and served as a school committeeman. The home served as the Westford Nursing Home from 1945 to 1993.

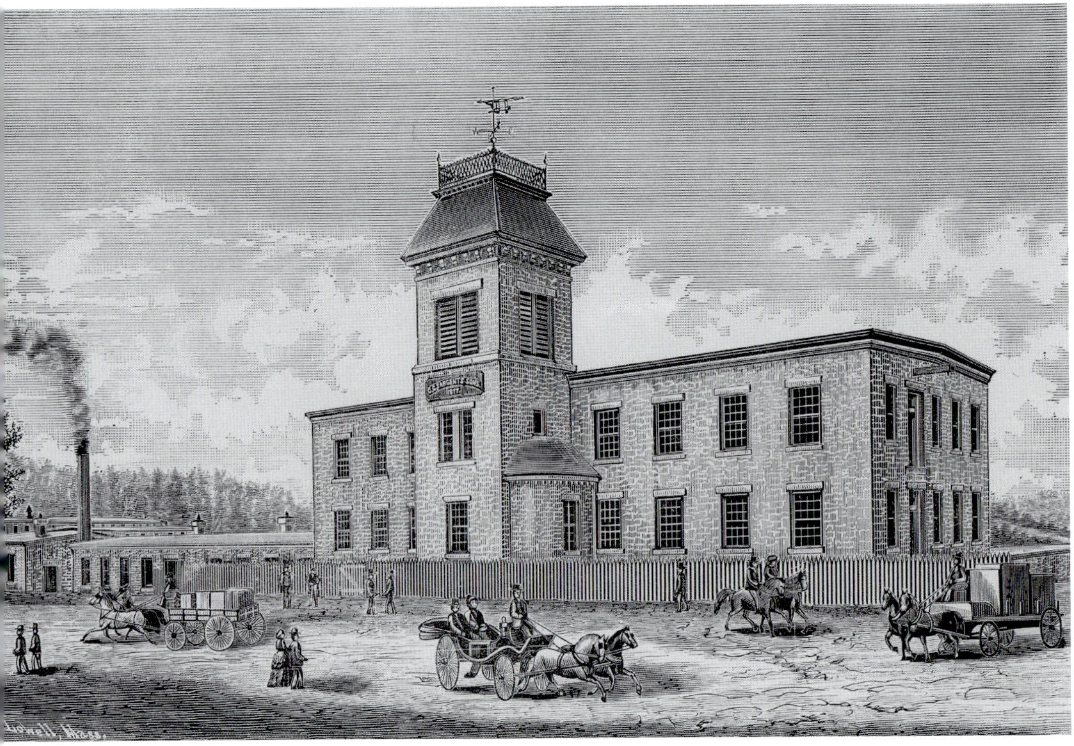

C.G. Sargent & Sons

This ink drawing of C.G. Sargent & Sons machine shop in Graniteville was featured in the commemorative pamphlet for the 1896 opening of the J.V. Fletcher Library. C.G. Sargent & Sons was formed in 1862, when Charles G. Sargent purchased Francis A Calvert's share of the machine shop that they had started together. This wonderful example of granite construction is still standing today.

Residence of Mrs. William Reed

This ink drawing of the residence of Mrs. William Reed of Graniteville was featured in the commemorative pamphlet for the 1896 opening of the J.V. Fletcher Library.

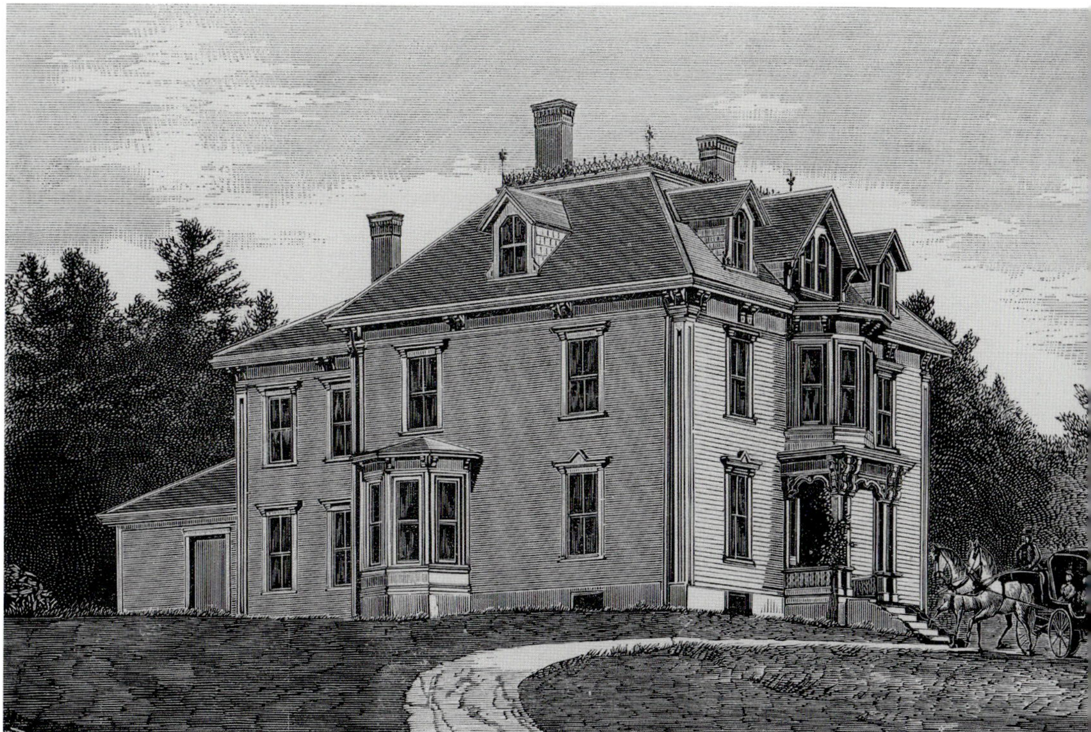

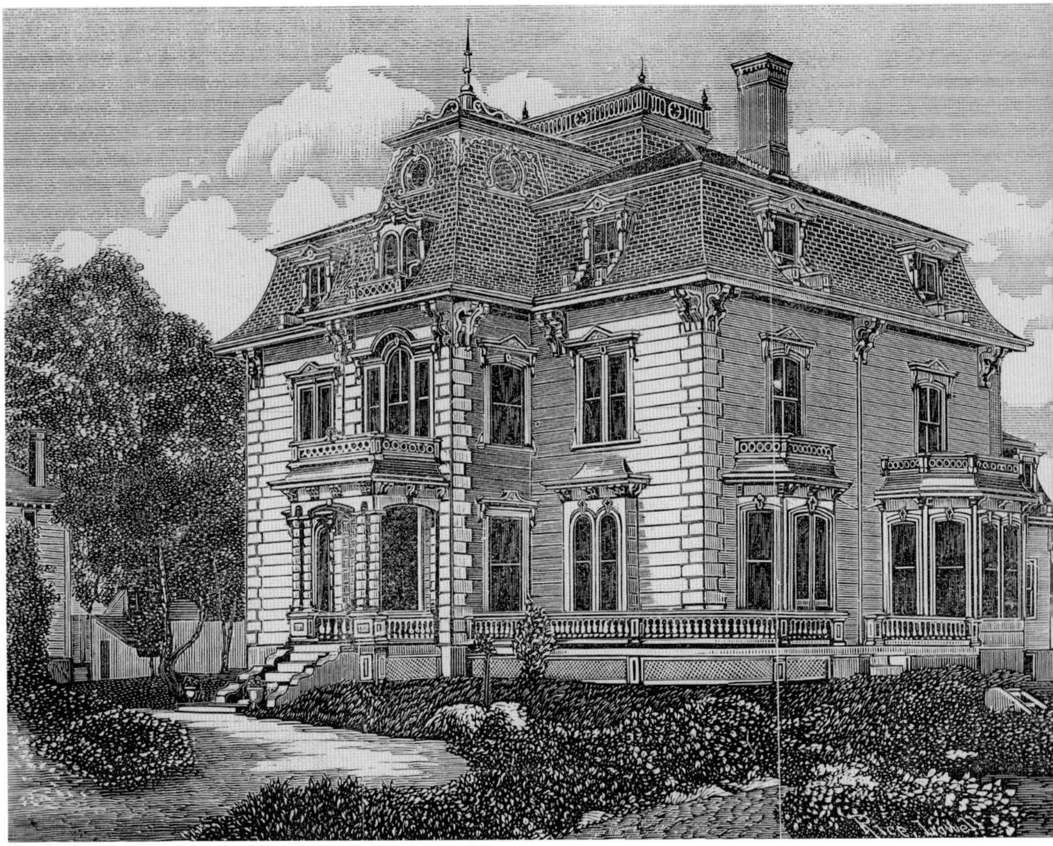

Residence of John W. Abbot
This ink drawing of the residence of John William Abbot (1834–1897) was featured in the commemorative pamphlet for the 1896 opening of the J.V. Fletcher Library. Abbot, son of John W.P. Abbot, was cofounder of the Abbot Worsted Company, the primary employer in Westford in its day.

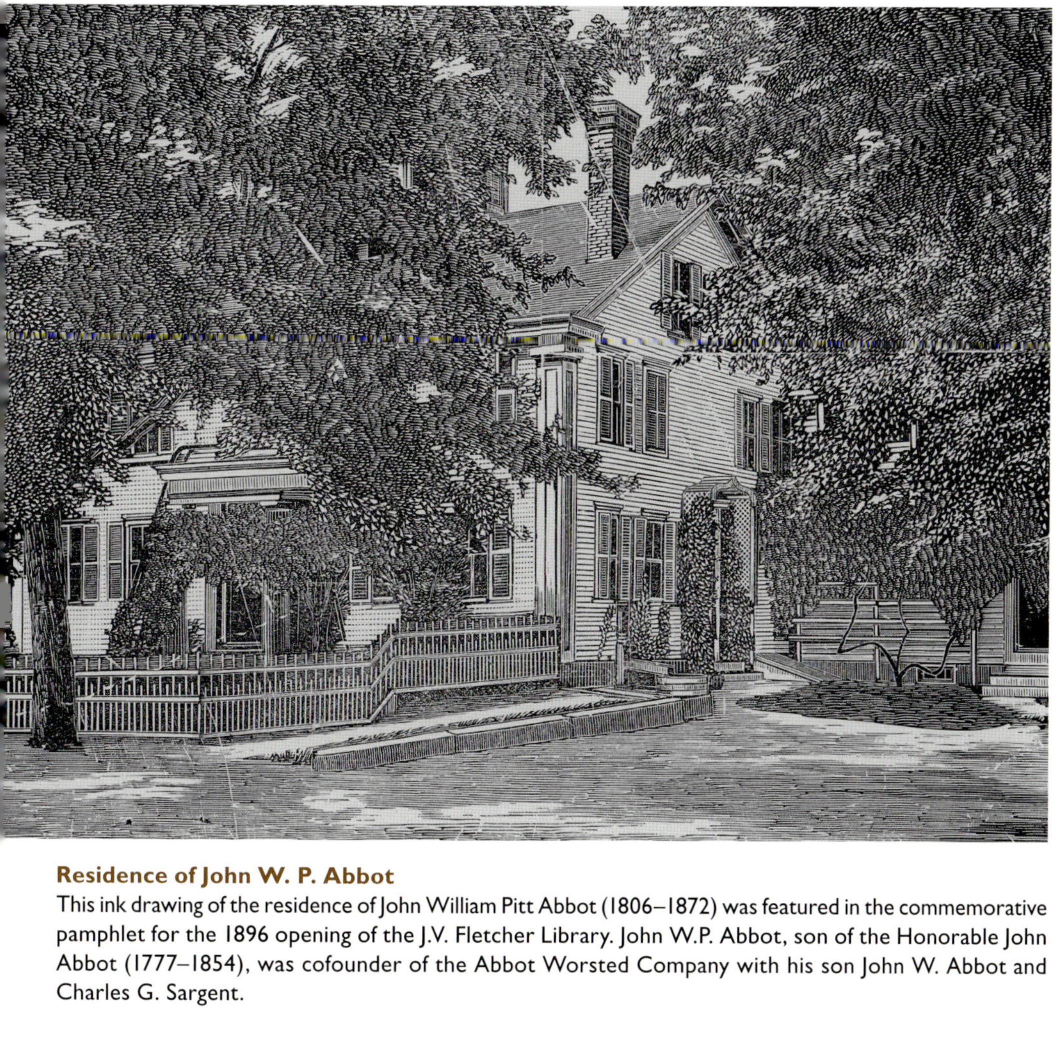

Residence of John W. P. Abbot

This ink drawing of the residence of John William Pitt Abbot (1806–1872) was featured in the commemorative pamphlet for the 1896 opening of the J.V. Fletcher Library. John W.P. Abbot, son of the Honorable John Abbot (1777–1854), was cofounder of the Abbot Worsted Company with his son John W. Abbot and Charles G. Sargent.

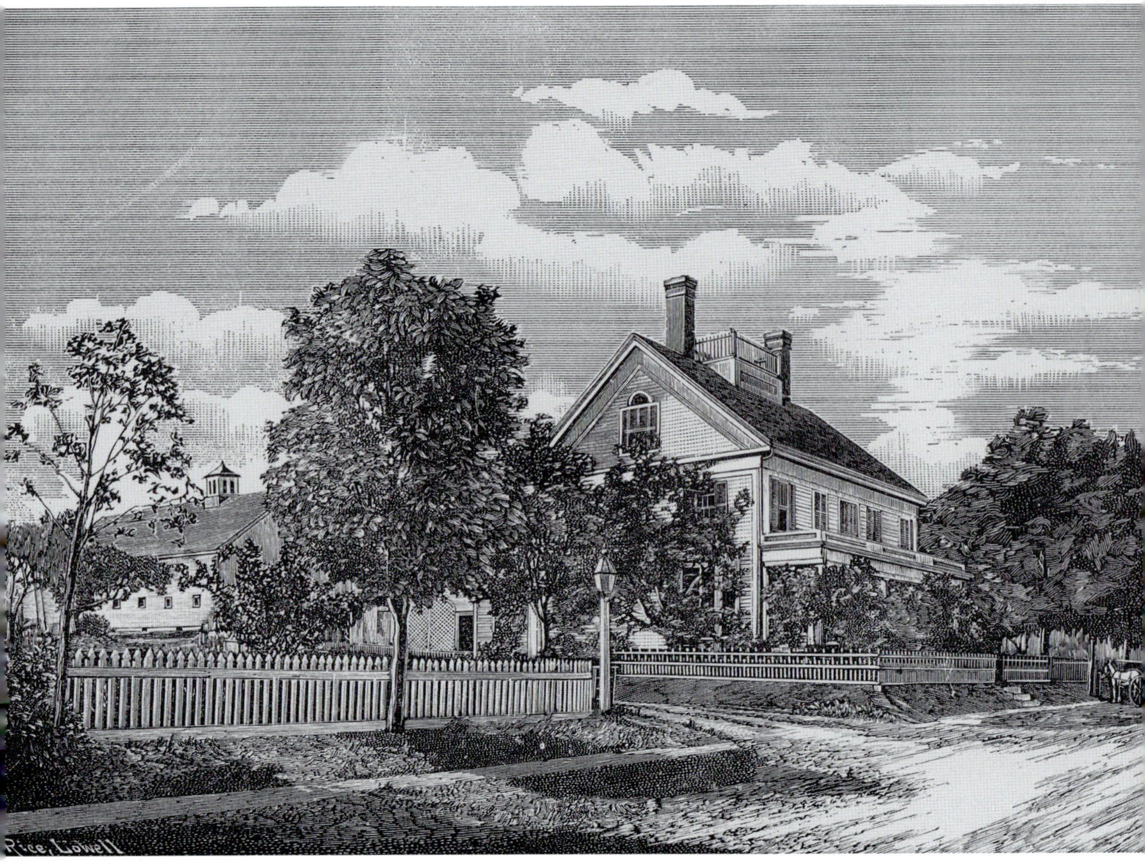

Residence of Sherman Dewey Fletcher

This ink drawing of the residence of Sherman Dewey Fletcher (1810–1886) was featured in the commemorative pamphlet for the 1896 opening of the J.V. Fletcher Library. Fletcher served as town treasurer from 1853 to 1886.

Col. John Robinson Marker

This ink drawing of the marker commemorating Col. John Robinson's service during the Revolutionary War was featured in the commemorative pamphlet for the 1896 opening of the J.V. Fletcher Library. Colonel Robinson was present at the battles of Concord and Bunker Hill. The actual marker can be seen at the site of his home on Robinson Road.

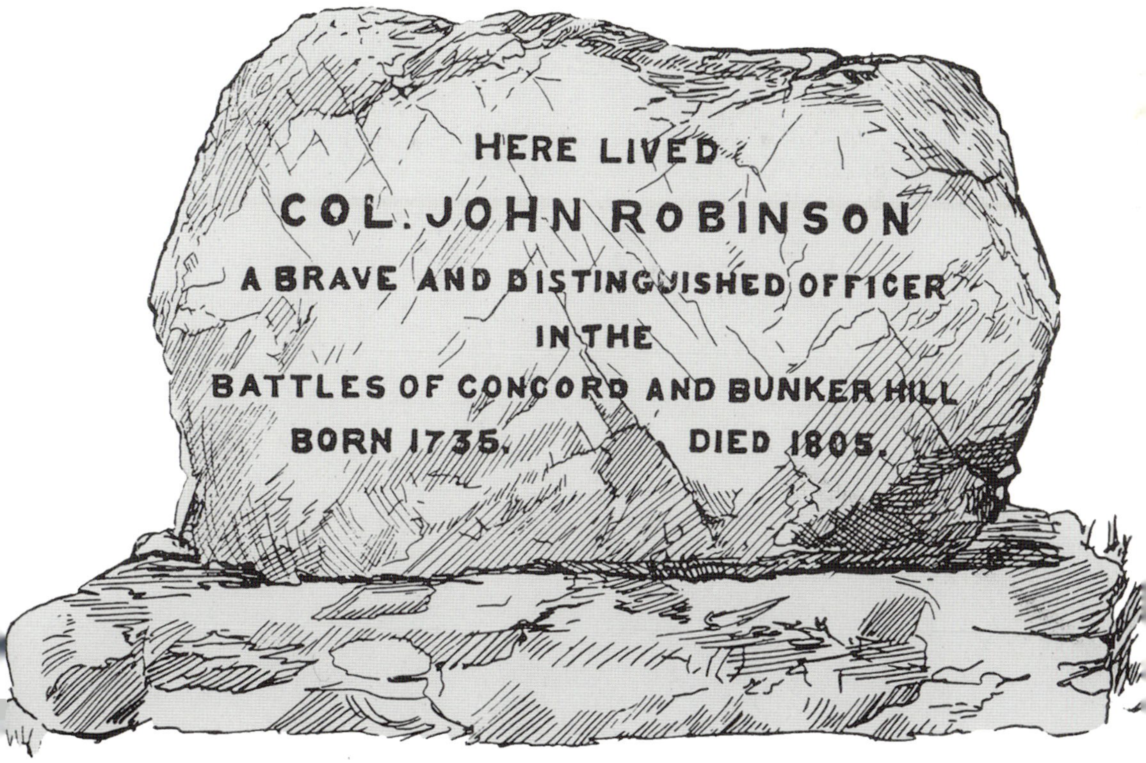

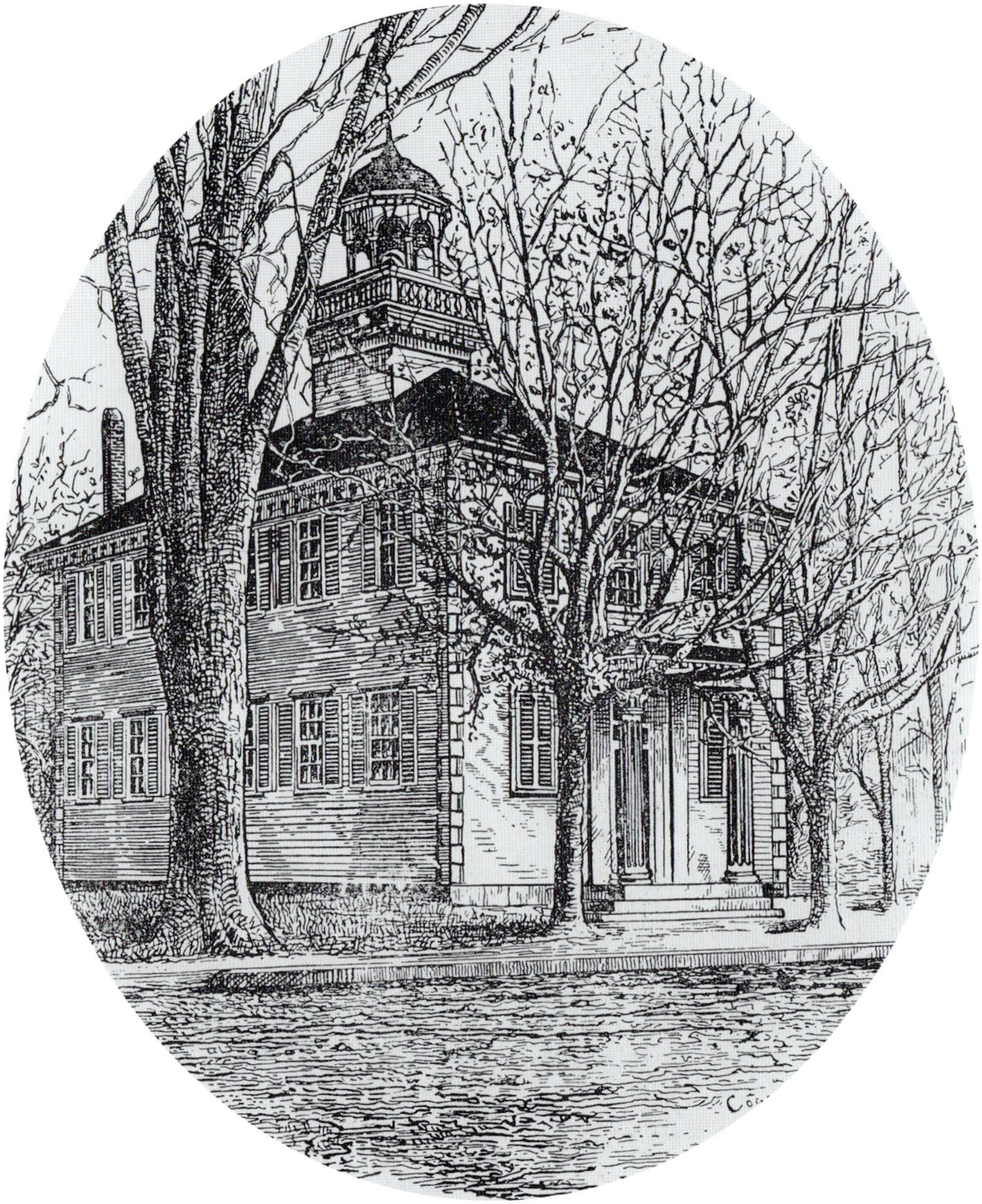

Westford Academy

This ink drawing of the original Westford Academy, built in 1794 (now the Westford Museum), was featured in the commemorative pamphlet for the 1896 opening of the J.V. Fletcher Library. Photographs of all four Westford Academy buildings can be seen on pages 14–16.

Samuel H. Balch

Balch (1854–1939), seen here around the beginning of the 20th century with his horse-drawn mail carriage, held many positions in Westford. According to the annual town report, in addition to being a postman, as shown in this image, his positions included serving on the board of the overseers of the poor, the measurers of wood and bark, and surveyors of lumber, as well as serving as the inspector of meat, agent of the board of health, janitor of the town hall, and workmen's compensation agent. Balch was the last living Civil War soldier from Westford, prior to his death in 1939.

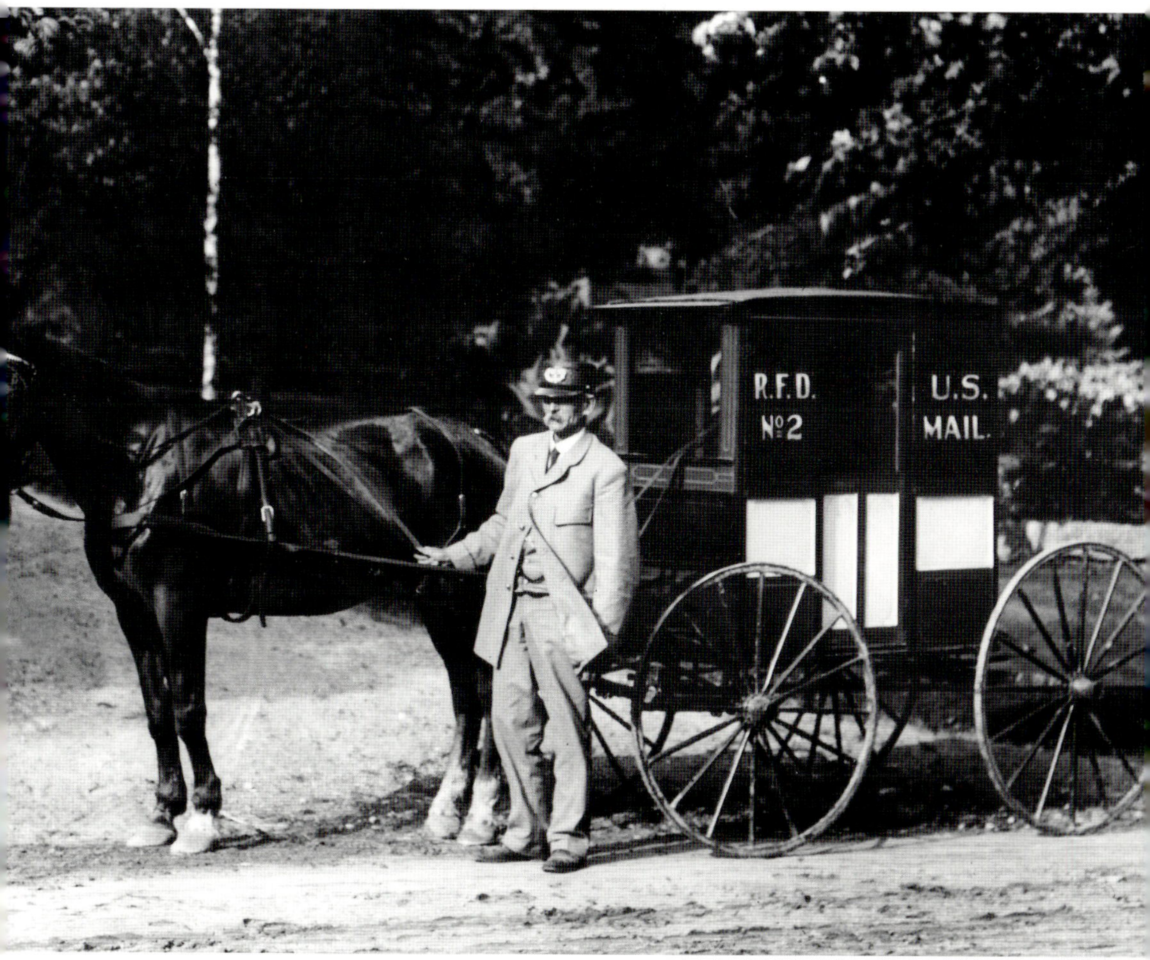

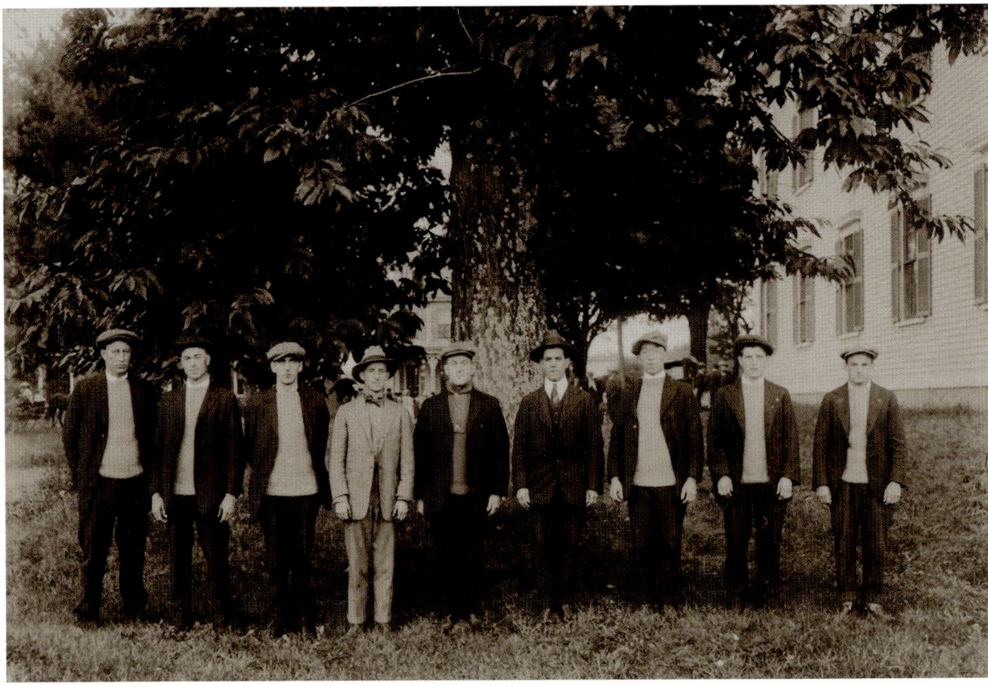

First Draft Recruits

The above image is of the men selected during the first draft on September 21, 1917. The photograph was taken in the town center. Shown here are, from left to right, Gustave Eliason, Joseph Perkins Jr., John Hobson, Frank C. Johnson, Clarence E. Hildreth, Frank Charlton, Rober Orr, Herbert Smith, and Leon F. Hildreth. While this was a difficult time, Westford was proud to be doing its part to defend the nation and came out in support of these new young recruits.

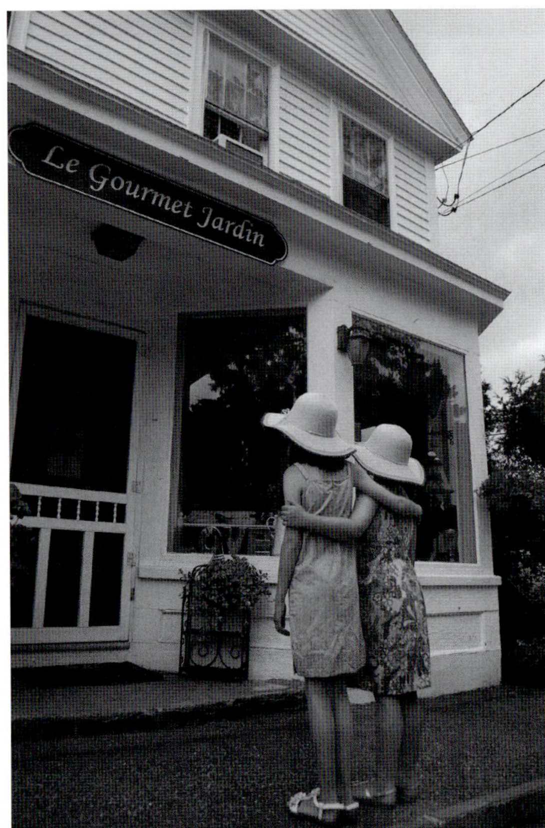

Isabel and Maryellen Sweeney

The Sweeney sisters are seen to the right in front of the original Wright & Fletcher store. As their father did as a child, the sisters, of Lowell, Massachusetts, frequently visit Westford to enjoy the safe play environment that the town common offers residents and visitors alike. For nearly 300 years, Westford, with its rich history and picturesque New England charm, has been a popular place in which to settle and to visit. (Author's collection.)

ABOUT THE WESTFORD HISTORICAL SOCIETY AND MUSEUM

Founded to "study Westford history" and "stimulate the collection and preservation" of related manuscripts and artifacts and to "encourage research and disseminate historical information," the Westford Historical Society—an initial group of about 35 members—first met in the Fletcher Library on November 20, 1958.

Five years later, the society was incorporated under Chapter 30, Section 3 of the Massachusetts General Laws, with Walter Whidden Fletcher as chairman. By 1965, the society had become largely inactive but pulled together in 1968 to hold the first annual Antique Sale on the Common. Seeking a permanent home, it began the process of acquiring the original Westford Academy building. In 1975, care and custody of the building were officially transferred to the historical commission. Through a combination of grants and donations from families and businesses, the building was restored to its original configuration.

In the 1990s, the museum and the historical society merged to become the Westford Historical Society and Museum and, ultimately, the Westford Historical Society, Inc.

The value of the Westford Historical Society and Museum can not be measured. All of the individuals who have had the vision to preserve and promote Westford's rich history will forever be legendary in the town of Westford, Massachusetts.

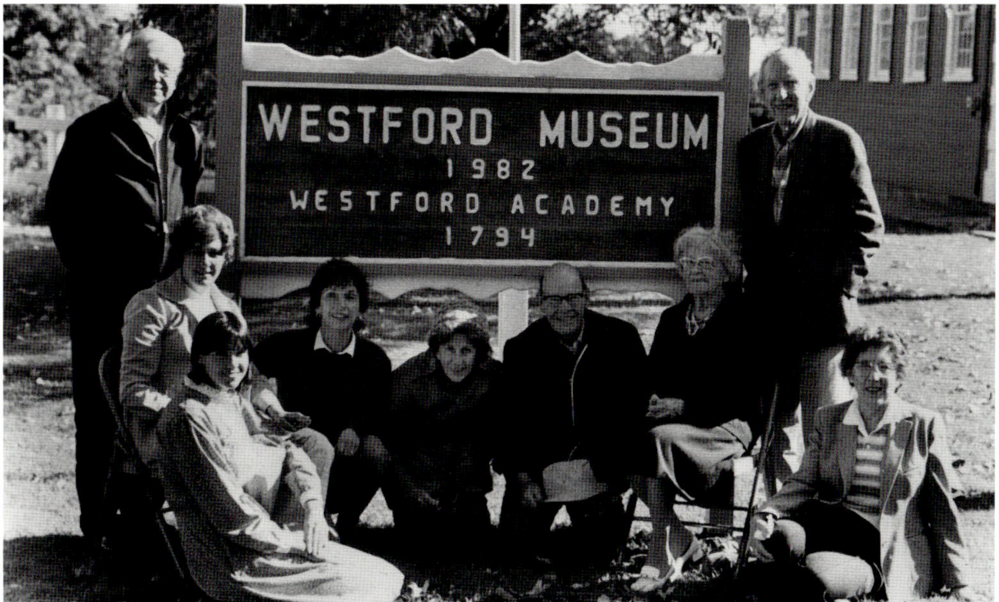

The Westford Museum Founders

Founders of the museum shown here are, from left to right, (first row) Kristin Szylvian and Fran Cooper; (second row) June Kennedy, Beth Shaw, Eva DeForge, Lloyd Blanchard, and Edna MacDougall; (third row) Alex Belida and Allister MacDougall. Not pictured: Dr. David Watson, John Crisafulli.

BIBLIOGRAPHY

Brody, David S. *The Westford Knight, Templars at the Newport Tower.* Groton, MA: Martin and Lawrence Press, 2009.

Harde, Ellen. *The True Story of Cinder the Westford Fire Dog.* Westford, MA: self-published, 2009.

Hodgman, Rev. Edwin R. *History of the Town of Westford in the County of Middlesex Massachusetts, 1659–1883.* Lowell, MA: Morning Mail Company Printers, 1883.

Kennedy, June W. *Westford Recollections of Days Gone By.* Bloomington, IN: Authorhouse, 2006.

Oliphant, Robert W. *Westford Gazetteer, A History of Westford, Massachusetts in Its Place Names.* Westford, MA: Robert W. Oliphant, 2010.

———. *A Brief History of Westford.* Westford, MA: The Westford Museum and Historical Society, 2000.

Prescott, Olive Ann. *Colonel John Robinson, 1735–1805.* Forge Village, MA: The Murray Printing Company, 1967.

Westford League of Women Voters. *Westford* (Images of America). Charleston, SC: Arcadia Publishing, 1996.

INDEX